YOUTH, RISK AND RUSSIAN MODERNITY

This timely and original book offers a new perspective on Russia as a risk society. It considers a variety of theories of risk and applies them to young people in different risk societies.

The volume refers to recent social and cultural theory, in particular the works of Douglas, Beck and Giddens, to examine the challenges facing young people and shows how they have adapted to cope with risk. It tackles a range of aspects of youth transition including individualisation, the impact of the transition to modernity, the pressure of globalisation, trends in youth identity, the role of young people in the process of social reproduction, and changes in the status and position of youth in the world of education and work. The authors analyse similarities and differences of growing up in various stable and unstable risk societies and assess the degree of conflict between youth and society. *Youth, Risk and Russian Modernity* is the most comprehensive and authoritative analysis of Russia's risk society to date.

Youth, Risk and Russian Modernity

CHRISTOPHER WILLIAMS
Department of Historical and Critical Studies
University of Central Lancashire, UK

VLADIMIR CHUPROV
Head of the Sociology of Youth Centre
Institute of Socio-Political Research
Russian Academy of Sciences, Moscow

JULIA ZUBOK
Senior Research Fellow,
Sociology of Youth Centre
Institute of Socio-Political Research
Russian Academy of Sciences, Moscow

Routledge
Taylor & Francis Group
LONDON AND NEW YORK

First published 2003 by Ashgate Publishing

Reissued 2018 by Routledge
2 Park Square, Milton Park, Abingdon, Oxon OX14 4RN
711 Third Avenue, New York, NY 10017, USA

Routledge is an imprint of the Taylor & Francis Group, an informa business

Copyright © **Christopher Williams, Vladimir Chuprov and Julia Zubok** 2003

All rights reserved. No part of this book may be reprinted or reproduced or utilised in any form or by any electronic, mechanical, or other means, now known or hereafter invented, including photocopying and recording, or in any information storage or retrieval system, without permission in writing from the publishers.

Notice:
Product or corporate names may be trademarks or registered trademarks, and are used only for identification and explanation without intent to infringe.

Publisher's Note
The publisher has gone to great lengths to ensure the quality of this reprint but points out that some imperfections in the original copies may be apparent.

Disclaimer
The publisher has made every effort to trace copyright holders and welcomes correspondence from those they have been unable to contact.

A Library of Congress record exists under LC control number: 2002036108

ISBN 13: 978-1-138-70862-4 (hbk)
ISBN 13: 978-1-138-70859-4 (pbk)
ISBN 13: 978-1-315-19855-2 (ebk)

Contents

List of Figures and Tables	*vii*
Notes on Authors	*xi*
Preface and Acknowledgements	*xiii*
List of Abbreviations	*xv*
Introduction	1
1 Risk and Modernity: Theories and Concepts	7
2 Russia's Risk Society	43
3 Coming of Age in Different Risk Societies	67
4 Youth Conflict in a Risk Society	93
5 Resolving Youth Conflict: The Localisation and Globalisation of Risk	109
6 Risk Trends in the Life Situation of Young People	127
7 Conclusion: Reflections on Youth at the Start of the Twenty-first Century	201
Bibliography	*207*
Index	*225*

List of Figures and Tables

Figures

5.1	Models of youth conflict resolution under conditions of the reproduction of risk	110

Tables

1.1	Typology of risk, according to Waldavsky and Dake	19
1.2	Classical versus reflexive modernisation	25
1.3	Shift from pre and simple to reflexive modernity	34
1.4	Aspects of Russian modernity	35
2.1	Economic trends in Russia, 1991–2001	49
2.2	Russian population in 1998 according to income levels	50
2.3	Health status in the Russian Federation, 1991–2000	52
2.4	Comparative measures of 'freedom' in various countries in the New Europe, 2000	54
2.5	Results of the December 1999 Russian Duma elections	57
2.6	Outcome of March 2000 Presidential election in Russia	58
3.1	Youth in different risk societies, 2000	68
3.2	Young people's chances of improving their qualifications and wages in Russia (on a 7 point scale), 1990–1999	81
3.3	Work orientation of Russian youth (as percent of sample), 1990–1999	83
3.4	Young people's monthly wages in Russia (in roubles), 1999	84
3.5	Changes in the level of income and expenditure amongst Russian youth (as percent of sample), 1997–1999	85
3.6	Degree of inter-generational mobility in Russia (as percent of group), 1997–1999	87
3.7	Ranking of different types of leisure activity amongst Russian youth (on a 7 point scale), 1990–1999	88
3.8	Personal evaluation of degree of self-realisation among Russian youth (on a 7 point scale), 1999	89
4.1	Types of risk experienced by young people living in various risk societies	105

5.1	Comparison of youth integration characteristics in different types of societies	113
6.1	Population trends in Russia, 1990–2001	128
6.2	Marriage and divorce trends in the Russian Federation, 1991–2000	129
6.3	Changes in the size of the youth cohort in Russia according to age (in percent), 1989–2000	130
6.4	Morbidity trends among Russian teenagers (cases per 100,000), 1991–1996	131
6.5	Mortality trends among Russian youth by age-group (in percent), 1990–1996	132
6.6	Learning to work in various OECD countries, 1996	136
6.7	Proportion of youth giving up school, 1996	138
6.8	Level of education of young people in Russia aged 15–18 years according to gender (as percent of gender group), 1999	140
6.9	Type of activity undertaken by young people in Russia aged 15–18 years according to gender (as percent of group), 1999	141
6.10	Type of activity undertaken by young people in Russia aged 15–18 years according to gender (as percent of group), 1990	141
6.11	Young people in Europe living alone (in percent), 1995	144
6.12	Changes in interests of young people in Russia (as percent of group aged 15–18 years), 1990–1999	146
6.13	Correlation between the main indicators of youth life start and social differences (by rank), Russia, 1990–1999	148
6.14	Impact of mother and father's education, material well-being and area of residence on young people's activity (as percent of group)	149
6.15	Risk coping strategies among youth	151
6.16	Youth unemployment among 15–24 year olds according to country (in percent), 1979–1997	155
6.17	Youth unemployment coverage in Europe, 1998	157
6.18	Youth unemployment in Russia (in percent), 1992–1999	158
6.19	Changes in the educational level of young people in different occupational groups in Russia (as percent of each group), 1997–1999	161
6.20	Socio-occupational status of youth according to job in different branches of the Russian economy (according to individually specified scales and by average weighting), 1997–1999	162
6.21	Changes in the degree of prestige attached to their work amongst different youth occupational groups in Russia (as percent of each group), 1994–1997	163
6.22	Comparison of young people's possibility to improve their salary, qualification and promotion prospects according to occupation (Mean on 7 point scale), Russia, 1994–1999	164
6.23	Correlation between youth life situations and their estimations of the opportunities for self-realisation (Mean on 7 point scale), Russia, 1999	165

List of Figures and Tables

6.24	Correlation between youth orientations towards stability/risk and their estimations of the opportunities for self-realisation (Mean on 7 point scale), Russia, 1999	166
6.25	Voting by Russian youth in the December 1999 parliamentary elections (in percent)	168
6.26	Level of trust and distrust in different institutions and organisations among Russian youth (as percent of sample), 1997–1999	169
6.27	Youth opportunities for self-realisation depending upon social and economic backgrounds, Russia, 1999	170
6.28	Comparison of youth opportunities for self-realisation depending upon ethnic status (Mean on 7 point scale), Russia, 1999	171
6.29	Youth views of the situation in Russia and their place in it (answers as percent of sample), 1997–1999	174
6.30	Young people's value orientations according to the degree of stability or uncertainty in Russia (as percent of group), 1999	174
6.31	Comparison of the cultural values of young people in Russia at times of stability or uncertainty (average weighting on 7 point scale), 1999	176
6.32	Changes in the cultural values of young people in Russia at times of stability or uncertainty (average weighting on 7 point scale), 1999	177
6.33	Self-estimations of personal characteristics of young people in Russia at times of stability or uncertainty (average weighting on a 7 point scale), 1999	178
6.34	Comparison of the proportion of young people preferring reliability and calm to change and risk in Russia (as percent of sample), 1990–1999	179
6.35	Attitude of Russian youth towards those making money at any price (answers as percent of sample), 1997	183
6.36	Attitude of Russian youth towards those breaking the law (answers as percent of sample), 1997	184
6.37	Correlation between identity indicators and young people's perceptions of their own life situation (Mean on 7 point scale), Russia, 1999	185
6.38	Young people's attitudes towards the 're-writing' of history (answers in percent), Russia, 1999	185
6.39	Correlation between identity indicators and key values in different spheres of young people's lives, Russia, 1999	186
6.40	Comparison of youth civic relations and identity and its correlation with their life situations (Mean on 7 point scale), Russia, 1999	187
6.41	Characteristics of two different models of civic identity among Russian youth, 1999	188
6.42	Correlation between identity indicators and youth orientation towards stability and risk, Russia, 1999	188
6.43	Correlation between civic identity indicators and level of ethnic tension among youth (as percent of group), Russia, 1999	189

6.44	Level of young people's knowledge of their ethnic traditions and ceremonies, depending upon conditions of stability and risk (in percent), Russia, 1999	191
6.45	Correlation between civic and ethnic identities among youth (in percent of different groups), Russia, 1999	192
6.46	Crimes committed in Russia, 1998	193
6.47	Juvenile crimes known to the police according to age group, Russia, 1994–1998	193
6.48	Category of juvenile crimes in Russia (in percent), 1994–1998	194
6.49	Correlation between youth civic identity models and socio-demographic characteristics in Russia (Contingency coefficient), 1999	195
7.1	The reproductive basis of risk among youth	204

Notes on Authors

Christopher Williams is Professor of Contemporary History, Department of Historical and Critical Studies, University of Central Lancashire, Preston, UK. He has published numerous books, chapters and articles on Russia including *AIDS in post-communist Russia and its successor states* (1995), *Young people in post-Communist Russia and Eastern Europe* (co-edited 1995), *Russian Society in Transition* (co-edited 1996), *Ethnicity and Nationalism in Russia, the C.I.S. and the Baltic States* (co-edited 1999), *Ethnicity and Nationalism in East Central Europe and the Balkans* (edited 1999) and of *New Europe in Transition* (co-edited 2000). Professor Williams has been a visiting Professor at the Institute of Socio-Political Research, Moscow, Russia since 1993, was Secretary of the British Association for Slavonic and East European Studies, 1998–2001 and in July 2000 he was elected a member of the Russian Academy of Political Science.

Professor Vladimir Chuprov, Doctor of Sociology, is Head of the Sociology of Youth Division of the Institute of Socio-Political Research, Moscow, Russian Federation. He has co-ordinated a 12 region study on Russian youth since 1982 and is the author of over a 100 works for prominent Russian journals, such as *Sociological Research, Soviet Education* and *Socio-Political Science*. His published works include *Student movements in capitalist countries* (Moscow 1972) and *The Social development of the Soviet scientific intelligentsia* (Moscow 1988). Professor Chuprov is the author of a major multi-volume study on the occupational, educational and material position of Russian youth (Moscow 1992–1993). His most recent works include: *The position of Russian youth in the new power structures* (Moscow 1993); *Migration patterns among youth: Trends and motivations* (with Mikhail Chernysh, Moscow 1993); *The social development of youth: Theoretical and applied aspects* (Moscow 1994); *Russian Society in Transition* (co-edited 1996), and *Youth in the process of social reproduction: Problems and perspectives* (Moscow 2000).

Dr. Julia Zubok is a Senior Research Fellow of the Sociology of Youth Division of the Institute of Socio-Political Research, Moscow. She holds a Kandidate Sociological Science (Russian PhD) from the ISPR, RAN. Dr. Zubok has published two books, *The social integration of youth in an unstable society* (Moscow 1998) and *Youth in the process of social reproduction: Problems and perspectives* (Moscow 2000) together with numerous articles and book chapters including 'Iskliuchenie v issledovanii problem molodezhi', *Sotsiologicheskie Issledovaniiia* 1998, No. 8; 'Exclusion in Study of the Problems of Young People', *Russian Education and Society: A Journal of Translations*, September, 1999, pp. 39–53; 'Social Integration and the Exclusion of the Youth in an Unstable Society', in

V. Puuronen (ed.) *Youth in Everyday Life Contexts*, Joensuu, University of Joensuu, 1999, pp. 297–304; 'Social Integration of Russian Youth – Trends in the Risk Society', in V. Puuronen (ed.), *Youth on the Threshold of 3rd Millennium*, Joensuu, University of Joensuu, 2001, pp. 103–117 and 'Integration versus exclusion: youth and the labour market', *International Social Science Journal*, June, Vol. LII, No. 2, June 2000, pp. 171–183.

The three authors have recently published *Youth in a Risk Society* (Moscow, Nauka 2001) which was voted the best book on Russian youth in the last decade in Moscow in July 2002.

Preface and Acknowledgements

This co-authored monograph is the product of a ten year link between the University of Central Lancashire, Preston and the Institute for Socio-Political Research, Moscow, where Christopher Williams has been a regular Visiting Professor.

The authors are all experienced researchers, especially in relation to Russian youth. This book is the result of nine years fieldwork and empirical research in many regions and cities of the Russian Federation. We were all particularly interested in the impact which Ulrich Beck's *Risk Society* and Anthony Giddens' *The Consequences of Modernity* have had on the development of sociological thinking and practice in the West, but at the same time, rather surprised that no one to our knowledge had applied the concepts of 'risk society' and 'modernity' to a country in transition, such as Russia. Intense discussions between the authors of this volume concerning the relevance of Beck and Giddens' work to Russia have taken place since 1995. They were extremely lively, especially given the absence of a Russian translation of Giddens' work and none of Beck's *Risk Society* until the year 2000. We were convinced from the very start that the notions of a 'risk society', 'modernity' and 'globalisation' are particularly meaningful for analysing trends in Russia since the mid-1980s, but especially in the 1990s. We firmly believe that these concepts and theories offer social scientists and historians the opportunity to develop a new, original way of examining and interpreting the lives of young people in Yeltsin's and Putin's Russia.

It is hoped that this book, which is based on sociological and statistical surveys on the social position of youth in stable and unstable risk societies throughout the 1990s, will enable scholars in the West to gain a greater understanding of the impact of Yeltsin's reforms on Russian youth.

Russia is currently undergoing a deep systemic crisis. When the communist state collapsed in 1991, it was greeted with cheers of joy. Over a decade on, many young people in Russia are highly disillusioned with the past and present and extremely pessimistic about the future. Putin's task will be to try and reverse this situation.

Although young people in many countries face similar problems, this book shows that there are marked differences in youth transition between stable and unstable societies.

Youth, Risk and Russian Modernity will be of relevance to scholars and students of history, modern social theory, sociology, politics and Russian Studies. But it will also be of interest to those in the field of youth studies.

Professor Christopher Williams wishes to thank the Nuffield Foundation for a grant in 1995–1996 to carry out fieldwork and to collect empirical data on Russian youth.

All the authors wish to thank the Russian Ministries of Labour, Education and the State Committee on Youth Affairs (in its various guises) for their financial assistance and their staff for helping to locate material and introducing us to various youth contacts throughout Russia.

The authors would like to express their gratitude to Vadim B. Churbanov, Director of the Moscow Publishing House "Chance", for his support.

Particular thanks go to Vladimir Staroverov and his wife Irina N. Staroverova as well as to Rafik Mamedov for their co-operation in collecting some of the data used in this book.

Julia Zubok and Christopher Williams translated the survey data collected by the authors throughout the 1990s from Russian into English.

Thanks are due, finally to Ashgate publishers for invaluable editorial and technical expertise and for their patience during the long gestation of this book.

Christopher Williams, Lancaster
Vladimir Chuprov and Julia Zubok, Moscow

List of Abbreviations

BR	Birth Rate
BSE	Bovine Spongiform Encephalopathy (Mad cow disease)
CIS	Commonwealth of Independent States
CJD	Creutzfeldt–Jakob Disease (The human form of Mad cow disease)
CPD	Congress of People's Deputies
CPRF	Communist Party of the Russian Federation
CPSU	Communist Party of the Soviet Union
DR	Death Rate
Duma	Lower House of Russia's Federal Assembly
EBRD	European Bank for Reconstruction and Development
EU	European Union
FES	Federal Employment Service
FMS	Federal Migration Service
FSB	Federal Security Service (Russia)
FSU	Former Soviet Union
GDP	Gross Domestic Production
GMF	Genetically modified foods
GNP	Gross National Product
Goskomstat	State Statistical Committee
ILO	International Labour Organisation
IMF	International Monetary Fund
IMR	Infant Mortality Rate
ISPR	Institute of Socio-Political Research, Moscow
KGB	Committee for State Security
Komsomol	Young Communist League
LDPR	Liberal Democratic Party of Russia
MPs	Members of Parliament
MVD	Ministry of Internal Affairs (Russia)
NATO	North Atlantic Treaty Organisation
NTV	Russian independent television
OAPs	Old-age Pensioners
OECD	Organisation for Economic Co-operation and Development
ORT	Russian public television
PM	Prime Minister
PTU	Vocational technical college
r	rouble
RAN	Russian Academy of Sciences
RFE/RL	Radio Free Europe/Radio Liberty
RSFSR	Russian Soviet Federal Socialist Republic

RTR	State owned Russian television and radio
$	dollars
TV	Television
UB	Unemployment Benefit
UK	United Kingdom
UN	United Nations
UNESCO	United Nations Educational, Scientific and Cultural Organisation
USA	United States of America
USSR	Union of Soviet Socialist Republics
VCR	Video cassette recorder
VTsIOM	Centre for Public Opinion Research, Moscow
VUZy	Higher education establishments
WHO	World Health Organisation

Introduction

This is a book about youth. *Youth, Risk and Russian Modernity* examines the relationship between youth, state and society in contemporary Russia and compares the situation with that in the West. At this moment in time, the younger generation are faced by a number of global changes and scholars are in a better position to evaluate the impact of the past and present as well as future possibilities. Citizens in all countries of the world are concerned about whether or not the future will be better for their children than it was for the previous generation in the twentieth century, a century that started and ended with wars. When considering this question, we must carefully evaluate past mistakes and their impact on present and future directions, on the one hand, and on the attitude of today's youth, on the other. For many young people, the changes in the last decade of the twentieth century have been highly significant, but for Russians in particular, changes made during the 1990s were of a more fundamental nature.

The primary aim of this volume is to assess the implications of the collapse of communism and the transition to a risk society on youth and youth identity in post-Soviet Russia. It takes as its backdrop the legacy left by the Soviet era, especially the Soviet authority's attempt to construct a particular role for young people. This role focused in particular on young peoples duty to be 'good communists', to help build communism and to provide the social foundations of the new Soviet social order. The place of youth in the process of social reproduction was defined by the Soviet state and youth transition, for instance, from school or university to the world of work was also determined by the dominant ideology of Marxism–Leninism and by the needs of the state, hence the requirement to serve the state for three years after graduation. Young people, like many other social groups in Soviet society, were exploited by the Soviet regime. In return for this loyalty, as shown by membership of the Komsomol, young people were actively encouraged to participate in social, economic and political affairs. Integration into the economy, politics and society was relatively smooth and largely successful.

Of course, this process was not without its faults and contradictions. Thus although young people poured into the labour force after leaving school or university, they rarely became managers or leaders, as this was the preserve of adults. As the tension became apparent, the Party and the state increasingly viewed young people in negative terms talking in terms of *razvrat* (depravity) when levels of youth sex, drug taking and crime soared or in general of an overall problem of *razlozhenie* (decay) if Soviet youth copied their decadent Western counterparts. For most of the Soviet era, though, these acts were restricted to a minority; most young people in Soviet Russia were successfully integrated into the Soviet system and enjoyed the stability it offered in terms of jobs, welfare and so forth. They were aided in the process by their families, friends and by the existence of *blat* (networking).

However, by the late Soviet period, and especially during Gorbachev's glasnost and perestroika, the tendency by successive Soviet regimes not to reward young people for their efforts, gradually had an adverse affect upon morale, motivation and above all influenced their faith in the Soviet state and Communist Party. Able to voice their opinion of the contradictions, young people complained, amongst other things, about low wages, poor prospects of promotion and the lack of opportunities to become leaders.

As this book shows the collapse of the Soviet state at the end of the 1980s–early 1990s has had enormous implications for young people's relations with the state and society in post-Soviet Russia. The state no longer guarantees jobs or successful integration into the economy and society. It also no longer provides any moral guidance. The lack of a clear alternative model to the old ideology has led to further confusion and anxiety regarding the role of young people and their role in the process of social reproduction.

We will analyse the process of social change by using a number of key ideas – social reproduction, social status, position in the labour market, the impact of educational reform and so on and utilise three key concepts – risk society, modernity and globalisation – when seeking to assess youth values and the reasons behind the conflict between youth and society.

In utilising these concepts, we were not just following the current sociological fashion, but instead deliberately searching for concepts that would facilitate comparisons of the position and status of young people in various societies, East and West. Risk, in our view, was a particularly fruitful concept that would enable us to compare what young people had in common with each other and also to assess how their position varied according to which risk society they lived in.

Although this book relies on a number of social science disciplines – history, economics, political theory, government, philosophy – its underlying base is that of sociology, in particular what might be called the sociology of risk. We will outline Western and Russian theories of 'risk' and 'risk society' but in doing so, it is necessary to anchor modern social theory, including our own, in the real world. We will therefore be offering concrete, not merely, abstract definitions of risk, risk society, modernity and globalisation.

The second noticeable feature of this book is its tendency not to separate European youth from Russian youth. Although we will focus primarily on the latter, as it is largely neglected in current literature, the notable exceptions being Roberts et al[1] and Wallace and Kovatcheva,[2] a deliberate decision was made not to artificially separate the two groups for several reasons: firstly to facilitate comparison; secondly to show the extent to which young people in the 1990s faced diverse situations but similar issues; thirdly to put Russian youth in its global context and finally, and most importantly, this volume hopes to assess the position of youth in different risk societies – the more 'stable' West European and American ones in comparison to the more 'unstable' societies in transition.[3] We will use Russia as a case study of youth in one particular twenty-first century risk society.

The third, and final distinctive feature of this book is that it views Russia as a risk society, one which has some things in common with other Western risk societies, but because of the nature of its transition since the collapse of Communism, Russia also has many unique features of its own. In this way, this volume hopes to advance modern social and sociological theory by offering a different depiction of Russia and by drawing a careful, more nuanced distinction between different categories of risk society. As a result, on the one hand, we will demonstrate the usefulness of modern social theory in analysing trends in transition countries, and on the other, increase awareness of the youth transition in various risk societies.

Today, the current younger generation faces different challenges, problems and risks to those of previous generations, but the differences do not end there. The risks faced by young people vary according to the degree of stability in their country. We will argue in *Youth, Risk and Russian Modernity* that although young people in many countries face similar risks, these and other risks are more pronounced in unstable societies, such as Russia, the former USSR and many East-Central European countries,[4] where a larger proportion of young people are poor, face ecological catastrophe and are confronted by seemingly out of control science and technology. Furthermore in these unstable societies in transition, the economic and political crisis, which varies in its intensity, has been extremely prolonged and shows no signs of ending. On top of this, terrorist acts are widespread, especially in Russia, and the gap between rich and poor is growing daily. Children[5] and young people in these countries risk receiving no education, having no jobs and often do not wish to start a family. In fact, the very basis of many of these transition societies is threatened by uncertainty and risk. Young people in Russia in the present modernisation phase face severe risks and using youth as a case study, this volume examines the nature of Russia's risk society, by comparing it to Western Europe and the United States, and also assesses what impact transition to a risk society has had on the younger generation throughout the 1990s and at the start of this century.

There are two possibilities, in our opinion, with regards to risk, either it can be overcome or else the risks increase. Young people are probably amongst the most progressive groups in any society, Russia included, as they have very little to lose. They are willing to try new things, to take chances, to carefully consider how best to resolve key issues and finally they are frequently ready to take a gamble in order to solve any risks.

In order to assess the impact of the tremendous changes that occurred during the 1990s on young people, *Youth, Risk and Russian Modernity* will examine the role of young people in the process of social reproduction. We will use comparative data covering many global risk societies, including the major EU member states and the United States as well as specialist longitudinal sociological data which we have collected in 12 regions of the Russian Federation since 1990.

As noted earlier 'risk' can be examined through the spectrum of a number of social science disciplines, but we will rely on a sociological framework for our analysis. Soviet, post-Soviet and Western scholars have all studied 'risk' and highlighted different aspects and features of it. Risk as we see it, is not just an abstract concept, it also refers to activity and hence is a set of conditions which characterise individuals, groups and societies as a whole. Therefore, we will not simply limit our conceptualisation of risk to something which is vague and hard to define, instead we will utilise the idea of risk as a concrete theoretical framework largely associated with the works of Anthony Giddens and Ulrich Beck, who use the term 'risk society'. They link the crisis of society in the late twentieth and early twenty-first centuries to an overall crisis of modernity.

This book is therefore concerned not with the distribution of wealth but with the reproduction of risk in different societies, including Russia, and its impact on the younger generation. Our theoretical framework is outlined in chapter 1, where debates concerning the nature of 'risk' and the development of a 'risk society' are outlined. The conclusion drawn is that although many West European countries, as well as so-called countries in transition, can be described as 'risk societies', each of these societies has its own specific characteristics, problems and paths to modernity.

Without doubt Russia's economic, financial and technological position makes it a different risk society, perhaps even a somewhat unique one, in comparison to its relatively stable Western European and US counterparts. This book shows that the way in which Russia's latest modernisation phase and transition from communism to the market has been handled since 1985, especially during the 1990s, has led to the reproduction of risk at an accelerated pace and on a larger scale. This has had dire consequences for Russia's economy and its road to democracy, which has been far from smooth. It is clear that Russia has gone from one risk situation to the next.

In this context, it is important to distinguish between risk in stable and unstable societies, as the possible solutions to risk and the nature of risk vary significantly between them. Although we will make reference to more stable Western (European and US) risk societies, particular attention is devoted to risk in unstable societies in transition. As scholars from different countries – two native Russian sociologists and one English born Russian specialist – we were particularly interested to see whether 'risk society' theory would throw any new light on Russia's process of modernisation and reform since Gorbachev, but especially under Yeltsin. The argument advanced in this volume is that Russia is best viewed as a 'risk society'.

It is impossible in a single, relatively small monograph, to analyse the impact of a transition to a risk society on all social groups in Russia. For the sake of simplicity and drawing upon a common interest in one group in particular, we decided to narrow our focus on youth in post-communist Russia. Using young people as a case study, this book proceeds in as follows.

Chapter 1 sets the scene by examining the evolution and development of the idea of 'risk' from early insurance-driven probability approaches through to Mary Douglas' ground breaking research on socio-cultural aspects of risk before outlining the theories of Giddens concerning modernity and Beck on the emergence of a 'risk society'. Russian theories, previously unknown to Western scholars, will also be outlined. The inter-relationship between risk, certainty and uncertainty will be explored, an assessment of the pros and cons of Western and Russian risk theory will be given and a working definition of risk for the purpose of this volume offered.

The next chapter then outlines the major changes in Russia since the collapse of communism. The nature of Russia's risk society is outlined and particular emphasis is placed upon the peculiarities of Russian modernisation in the late Soviet period and beyond and the adverse consequences of Russia's reforms on the economy, politics and society. Three types of risk factors and environments are highlighted: socio-economic, socio-legal and socio-political. The general and unique features of risk in Russian society are emphasised.

Chapter 3 then turns our attention towards youth. It examines the role of young people in the process of social reproduction and assesses the degree to which young people in Western Europe, the US and Russia are able to achieve their goals and aims and reach their full potential. The problems encountered in 'coming of age' are outlined and particular attention is given to the material well-being of youth, their work values, leisure patterns, living standards and attitudes towards education in various risk societies, East and West.

The following chapter explores the nature of the conflicts between youth and society focusing in particular on the notion of social status, conflicts with socialisation agencies, and on the issue of an identity crisis (i.e. the socio-cultural basis of conflict). Finally a typology of risk amongst young people, based on the situation in Russia, is developed.

Chapter 5 looks at ways in which youth conflict might be resolved. Two alternative models are discussed: integration and differentiation. A complex conceptualisation and model for the resolution of youth conflict is outlined. Particular emphasis is placed upon the contradictions of the social integration of youth in Russia's risk society, the social determinations of risk and on a clear distinction between the localisation and globalisation of risk.

This book, even though it relies on modern social theory, and especially on the sociology of risk, is also firmly grounded in quantitative and empirical analysis. Our findings based on over a decade of research on Russian youth are presented in Chapter 6 which assesses risk trends in the life situation of youth in several senses. A detailed examination of the socio-demographic position of young people, the impact of life start, the opportunities, or not, for self-realisation, the desperate search for moral support and a firm foothold and the problem of Russia's social identity crisis and its impact on different sections of the younger generation is presented.

Throughout these six chapters the goal is to identify the main lines of conflict and sources of uncertainty facing youth in post-communist Russia. By introducing a new framework, that of Russia as a risk society, *Youth, Risk and Russian Modernity* will analyse changes in the social position of youth in Russia in comparison to their counterparts in the West and look at the difficulties of growing up and coming of age in various risk societies. Particular emphasis will be placed on the implications of the collapse of communism for youth employment and education, health and welfare, youth policy; and for youth identity. We will explore, for instance, what the transition to the market and the retreat of the state means for young people's entry into the labour market and other spheres of society. Do young people face social exclusion, discrimination and marginalisation? If so, what can be done to resolve these conflicts? We also assess whether or not these elements of risk are the consequence or cause of the localisation and globalisation of risk. Can these risks be avoided? Is risk just a negative phenomenon? As a means towards resolving various youth conflicts with society, especially in the education system and labour market, this book suggests ways in which social integration theory, when applied to Russia and its younger generation, can be a useful tool for resolving youth conflict.

For all these reasons we believe this book will make a major contribution to the youth studies field in relation to Russia, show how modern social theory can increase our understanding of societies in transition and finally, we hope it will lead to the re-conceptualisation of Russia as a risk society.

Notes

1. K. Roberts, S.C. Clark, C. Fagan and J. Tholen, *Surviving Post-Communism: Young People in the Former Soviet Union*, Edward Elgar, Cheltenham, 2000.
2. C. Wallace and S. Kovatcheva, *Youth in Society: The Construction and Deconstruction of Youth in East and West Europe*, Macmillan, London 1998.
3. On American youth see N.J. Davis, *Youth Crisis: Growing up in the high-risk society*, Praeger, Westport, Conneticut, 1999.
4. On the situation of youth in former East Germany see K. Evans, M. Behrens and J. Kaluza, *Learning and Work in the Risk Society: Lessons for the Labour Markets of Europe from Eastern Germany*, Macmillan, London, 2000.
5. On the plight of children see A. Zouev (ed.), *Generation in Jeopardy: Children in Central and Eastern Europe and the Former Soviet Union*, UNICEF/ M.E. Sharpe, Armonk New York, London 1999 and I.V. Zhuravleva, *Zdorov'e podrostkov: Sotsiologicheskii analiz*, Moscow, Nauka 2002.

Chapter 1
Risk and Modernity: Theories and Concepts

The concept of risk is fundamental to any notion of modernity. The process of modernisation involves a multiplication of risk for both individuals and social groups.[1]

In examining the position of youth in various risk societies, it is necessary to define the four key concepts used throughout this book: 'youth', 'risk', 'risk society' and 'modernity'.

The key questions which this chapter explores are: what are the grounds for an assessment of risk in Russia and among Russian youth? How relevant are the ideas of Giddens and Beck and other Russian scholars to our understanding of trends in Russia and the problems facing countries in transition? Can current theories regarding Russia and sociological theories concerning youth be challenged using risk theory? What does risk discourse consist of? What role should the individual have in terms of managing risk? What role, if any, should the state have in this process? What are the flaws in Giddens and Beck's theory? and finally, how might risk theory be developed further to take account of the specifics of Russian modernity and the position of youth in particular?

The first of these concepts, youth, is relatively easy to define as there is a broad consensus. Scholars tend to agree that young people wherever they live, East or West, are generally aged between 15–25 years, with the age group extended up to 29 years in the case of Russia. Whilst the concept 'youth' is relatively unproblematical, the same is not true of either 'risk', 'risk society' or 'modernity'. This chapter focuses on the different schools of thought concerning 'risk' and 'modernity'. Whilst this book is sociological in emphasis, and hence will rely largely upon social and sociological theory, in the case of 'risk' a range of diverse disciplines will be used (statistical, cultural, sociological and political) in order to demonstrate how the meaning of 'risk' has changed over time and also to examine the inter-relationship between 'risk', 'risk society' and 'modernity'.

The theoretical and conceptual approaches to risk outlined here must be viewed in their wider social context. The key terms – 'risk', 'risk society' and 'modernity' – are all closely linked to one another. As Deborah Lupton writes: 'Changes in the meanings and use of risk are associated with the emergence of modernity.'[2] On the related question of 'modernity', Anthony Giddens defines modernity as: 'the institutions and modes of behaviour established first of all in post-feudal Europe, but which in the twentieth century increasingly have become world historical in their impact.'[3] We would now like to focus on the notion of 'risk' and 'risk society'.

The origins of risk: Probability approaches

> [Risk is] the product of the probability and consequences (magnitude and severity) of an averse event (i.e. a hazard).[4]

What is risk? What types of risk exist? What different theories exist to explain risk? Can risk be distinguished from danger/hazard? Is risk the opposite of security? Does risk involve negative and positive aspects? Finally, can risk be prevented and avoided (i.e. what policies can be introduced to combat it)?

In order to answer these questions, it is important that the nature of 'risk' is clear and that the determining factors of 'risk' are evident. One major problem in trying to define 'risk' in the English language is that the terms 'risk', 'hazard' or 'danger' are often used synonymously. In pre-modern times, no real distinction was drawn between these notions, but in late modernity, much more was made of the difference between risk and danger. One was not seen as the same as the other. Thus 'danger' in this case might refer to anything from a danger to morals to the dangers posed by technology. In the Russian language the idea of 'risk' comes from the Spanish for 'cliff' or 'reef' and is associated with the dangers posed by the sea.[5] So in Russian too, risk, hazard or danger are often used inter-changeably.

Risk has always existed and probably always will. But what constitutes 'risk' is a subject of great debate. According to the German sociologist, Niklas Luhmann in his book, *Risk: A Sociological Theory* (1993), there are few comprehensive studies on the origins and use of the term 'risk'.[6] Luhmann believes that the widespread use of the notion of 'risk' originated in the sixteenth century when risk was used in maritime insurance in connection with navigation and trade.[7] In the pre-modern period, 'risk' referred to the need for human beings to guard (insure) themselves against the probability of losses due to the dangers posed by 'a natural event, such as a storm, flood or epidemic rather than a human-made one'.[8]

In general, it is possible to argue that there are objective and subjective aspects to risk. Risk was generally associated with nature and it was thought that via the use of scientific methods (the probability techniques developed by science and mathematics) it was possible to identify, evaluate and control risk.[9] These early approaches assumed that we could calculate the degree of 'risk', estimate the 'losses' incurred and merely needed to protect ourselves against it.[10]

Individuals can be characterised as having two attitudes towards risk: risk avoidance or risk-taking.[11] In the first case, people take the safe option and avoid risk; whereas in the second, risks are taken because individuals believe the potential gains far outweigh the potential losses.

Thus up to the eighteenth century, risk was conceived of in economic terms and by and large this insurance perception of 'risk' still exists today. As the anthropologist Mary Douglas points out most people are willing to pay a small premium in order to avoid large losses in the future.[12] For instance, most citizens in Western Europe or the USA, and fewer Russians, are willing to take out house insurance to cover the contents of their homes, to insure themselves against theft and burglary, to sign policies to cover the repairs of consumer goods (microwaves; refrigerators, cookers), central heating or computers and/or even to insure against life and death. This is now a normal part of all our lives.[13]

In earlier approaches to risk, it is evident that risk and security are closely connected. People desire security (protection) against risk. By using these twin concepts of risk, a dichotomy develops in which risk is contrasted to safety. In this case, 'safe' means no losses; with an individual's calculation of 'risk' (too large or worth taking) shaping the entire decision making situation.[14] However, although for some individuals the safe option is to avoid risk, for others 'certain opportunities that could prove advantageous' encourages them to take a risk. In the latter instance, potential losses become the consequences of the 'risk decisions'.[15] Developing this point, Douglas notes that 'the essence of risk-taking lies in the structure of the probabilities [and] their variance. A prudent individual seeks less, the risk-taker prefers more variance'.[16] All of these factors 'influence risk perception and the willingness to take risks'.[17] Thus the possibility of realising goals or taking action becomes the key element in the notion of risk.

According to the probability approach, risk is a 'neutral concept, denoting the probability of something happening, combined with the magnitude of associated losses or gains'.[18] These early definitions of risk, which existed until the late twentieth century, believed that:

> risks are pre-existing in nature and in principle are able to be identified through scientific management and calculated and controlled using this knowledge.[19]

Nowadays, however, insurance companies make assessments based on their risk perception of individuals (i.e. do they constitute a good/bad risk based on past experience).

This combination of a probability and activity approach is now more widely used. In analysing this inter-connection the Russian scholar, Anatoly Al'gin, stresses the importance of awareness of risk and argues that this 'process is a necessary component of the inter-relationship between a risk situation and risk activity'.[20] Understanding the nature of a risk society allows individuals the possibility of overcoming its constraints by making a clearer choice and by realising other alternatives. However this involves taking a risk. There are only a certain number of ways in which we can obtain a reliable evaluation of the degree of risk and this requires walking the tightrope between victory and loss. Nevertheless as awareness of the possible alternatives increase, so does ones chances of resolving risk. This situation is characterised by two responses: if individuals/groups are aware of the risks and choices then they can take a *motivated risk*, but if the possibilities are uncertain and it is difficult to calculate the outcome, then individuals/groups are likely to take *non-motivated risks*. It follows, therefore that risk can be defined as the 'situational characteristics of activity which consist of uncertainty of its outcome and the possibilities of an unfavourable outcome in instances of failure'.[21] But uncertainty of outcome or result does not necessarily mean that there is uncertainty in the risk situation. Instead, it points to the probability that success will depend on the degree of certainty of possibilities. In other words, uncertainty of outcome occurs because of individuals/groups lack of awareness of the possibilities open to them.

This approach, which is widely used in psychology, reflects the individual and/or personal character of the activity and in this sense risk has three possible meanings:

firstly, risk is a measure of the expectation of an unfavourable event as a consequence of previous failure; secondly, risk is a action which more or less results in loss, trauma and/or damage; and finally, risk is a situation of choice between two possible variants of action: the first one, less attractive but more reliable; the second, more attractive but less reliable.[22] There can be no doubt that this view of risk is very useful in so far as it allows scholars the possibility of empirically verifying 'risk' and applying the concept to the real world.

Uncertainty and risk

In developing countries during late modernity, risk has become a permanent and consistent feature. Even allowing for the fact that individual autonomy and freedom is possible under modernity and that this opens up new possibilities for economic growth and for the development of a civil society, it is still nevertheless evident that social relations in the modern world tend to be more abstract, formal, rational and uncertain. Modernisation is therefore a highly contradictory process in which both the advanced and less advanced nations are in constant crisis, in varying degrees, and often threatened by catastrophe.[23]

From the 1960s onwards, risk became the object of inter-disciplinary research and the conclusion reached was that risk was closely related to uncertainty, which by and large refers to our imperfect and inexact knowledge of the world. At this time, the category of 'uncertainty' was investigated by natural scientists (specialists in physics and cybernetics) as well as by philosophers. Philosophers' interest in the inter-relationship between certainty and uncertainty stemmed from the legacy left by Hegel's *Science of Logic* (1812–1816) and this tradition strongly influenced Soviet and post-Soviet thinking on this topic as shown in the works of V. Gott, P. Vizir and A. Ursul.[24] These scholars argued that certainty was characterised by a strong uni-directional link whereas uncertainty refers to a multi-directional process. Under conditions of certainty, once individuals/groups make a choice this quickly turns into action but for uncertainty to be transformed into certainty necessitates realising one of many possibilities. In making a choice, we gauge the uncertainties associated with various alternatives and after examining them all we take the appropriate action. Uncertainty should therefore be understood as a category with the following two characteristics: firstly, the transformation of many possibilities into reality and secondly, the start of links and inter-relationships between attributes and conditions of specific phenomenon.[25]

A state of uncertainty occurs not just in natural but also in social processes. All social groups are influenced by their external environment, which in many cases creates uncertainty. For example, any socio-economic system is directly influenced by the rules governing its function. However, if there is uncertainty, and instability and social disorder occurs, then this can have an impact on social norms. Following Eisenstadt, it can be argued that the degree of certainty and uncertainty is systematically linked to the organisation of social relations (i.e. to the structure of collective institutions and the macro social order).[26] In the case of this book, we will be analysing the characteristics of youth and their possibilities for achieving various goals and objectives under the conditions of a risk society.

Hence, if there is a high degree of uncertainty and the consequences are great then the risks will be high; but conversely, low uncertainty and fewer consequences brings with it low risks. Either way, when a choice is made under risk society conditions we must be prepared to live with the results (i.e. with the impact on human activity). Thus under conditions of uncertainty, where many elements are unknown, there is not just one possible choice but many. Individuals and groups are therefore forced to make a choice or take a risk to overcome risk. Thus risk can be defined as a way of overcoming uncertainty, via the conversion of possibilities into reality and by the resolution of contradictions in the case of multiple possibilities and escape routes from risk.[27] Although uncertainty is equated with risk and generally regarded as negative and undesirable, as some parts of this book show, *Youth, Risk and Russian Modernity* also argues that risk and uncertainty can have positive aspects in so far as the former gives some individuals and groups the freedom to initiate new social processes. As Immanuel Wallerstein points out:

> uncertainty is wondrous ... If everything is uncertain then the future is open to creativity, not mere human creativity, but the creativity of all nature.[28]

Thus innovation and risk taking are ways of coping with or even resolving uncertainty and this in turn might create greater social stability.

Technological Risk

The transition of most economically advanced countries to the so-called consumer society is one of the most fundamental contradictions of modernisation in the present day world.[29] The proclamation of material well-being and the non-stop satisfaction of our material needs as the main goal of society has not been achieved due to limited resources. The fight for these scarce resources initially led to the redistribution of resources but thereafter produced military conflicts and we are now well on the road towards ecological catastrophe. Qualitative changes in the social sphere and in the environment, which have led to a global threat to human life and the planet itself, have given risk a new meaning in the twenty-first century. Not only external threats, but human beings themselves and their often barbaric attitude towards nature, have become the main factor in the reproduction of risk in the modern world. More than this, risk has become global, planetary in character and has had an impact on humankind and its life goals.

By the mid-1970s, the new scientific problem was human survival under growing pressure from the new wave of technological risks and the need to keep risk under control. The new environmental movements of the 1960s and 1970s, as typified, for instance, by the Rome Club founded in 1968, concluded that if we continued along our present paths of development, then this would lead to severe ecological difficulties in the future. These predictions proved to be accurate as the accidents at Third Mile Island in the USA, Chernobyl' in the former Soviet Union and Bhopal in India all demonstrated. The dangers of the so-called scientific and technical revolution (progress) had showed how close the world had come to global catastrophe.[30] The following are the main forms of technological risk.

Risk of ecological (environmental) catastrophe

This is the product of human interference with the course of nature which has led to the destruction of its balance and of its physical, chemical, geological, biological and climatic conditions, all of which are central to the functioning of the planet. Air and water pollution, the accumulation of industrial refuse, the use of nuclear energy, pesticides, mineral fertilisation, the destruction of forests, the creation of man-made lakes, reservoirs and drainage of marsh land, has produced irreversible changes in nature and is generating a major threat to health and people's way of life today. Public opinion polls across the world, but especially in Western Europe in recent years, demonstrate growing public concern about one scare/risk after another. In the UK alone, examples include 'mad cow' disease (BSE) and its link to CJD in humans, E-coli poisoning and the recent foot and mouth outbreak; but in the world as a whole, global warming and ozone layer depletion is also of serious concern. The fear is one of biodiversity loss and eventual ecosystem destruction.[31]

Scientific and technological development

This has produced other types of risk. In the twenty-first century we no longer automatically think of science and technology as representing the source of progress instead there is great ambivalence towards scientific and technological innovations. As Ulrich Beck points out in his book *Ecological enlightenment*:

> 'Risk society' means an epoch in which the dark sides of progress increasingly come to dominate social debate. What no one saw and no one wanted – self endangerment and the devastation of nature – is becoming a motor force of history.[32]

Thus we are now highly concerned about the health, social and environmental effects of science and technology. Accidents and catastrophes in nuclear power stations, transport (the recent devastating UK rail crashes are just one example among many) and space and gas explosions, all of which have taken the lives of thousands of people, is clear evidence that there has been a proliferation of risks and that the costs of such imperfections of modern science and technology far outweigh the benefits.

Human Factor

In late modernity we now realise, unlike in pre-modern times, that old risks (plagues, floods, famines) are not acts of god or nature going wrong (except in popular opinion) instead risk is the outcome of human action. As Turner points out:

> ... the risks of modern society are the unintended but inevitable consequences of the very *process of modernisation* and in particular they are the product of the *scientific management of society and nature*.[33]

Therefore some risks are the consequence of the human factor. The use of modern technological and scientific methods increases the likelihood of mistakes and having to pay the price for them, especially those relating to management. Negligence of scientific discipline, breaking the rules of technical safety and carelessness are some of the reasons for different types of accidents, many with serious or lethal consequences. This risk factor becomes particularly dangerous as soon as it is connected with managerial mistakes. In such instances, any individual can become a victim. For instance, a car drivers error may cost just a few lives; a pilot or air traffic controllers mistake could cost hundreds of lives, but finally, a serious error in the management of a nuclear power station could cost thousands of lives and even destroy an entire community, and if the problem goes beyond national boundaries, it may even end up as a global catastrophe.

Globalisation of risk

The advent of a 'risk society' has meant that further economic and technological growth is unlikely to engender significant progress and development. It is clear that the ecological, health and other risks mentioned above are not just national but often global in scope. The causes of the above mentioned technological risks are threefold: modernisation itself, technology and globalisation. On the first of these Beck notes that: 'Risk may be defined as a systematic way of dealing with the hazards and insecurities *induced and introduced by modernisation itself.*'[34] An obvious example here would be the side effects of industrial modernisation, such as pollution and environmental degradation. The second factor – technology – is also a cause for concern and instances of anxiety here include fears around the development of genetically modified food. Finally, there is globalisation. The emergence of a 'global market' in the 1990s has led to a situation in which events in remote parts of the world can have a significant impact on other locales. This is particularly true of multinational corporations. Although most theorists equate globalisation with modernity, attitudes towards globalisation vary. Some view globalisation in negative terms, seeing it as 'the Westernisation of the world' and as a 'cover for [the] ascendancy of capitalism' which eventually results in 'the devastating destruction of local traditions, the continued subordination of poorer nations and regions by richer ones, environmental destruction and [in the development of] a homogenization of culture and everyday life';[35] whereas others see globalisation as a positive trend which leads to the development of 'new connections and the integration of economies, [societies] and cultures into the world economy, overcoming previous divisions and distances'.[36] At the start of the 1990s, the globalisation of risk had become so serious that the UN Assembly was debating the issue and stressing that we all needed to learn to live in harmony with, rather than against, nature. Humankind's failure so far to exist in harmony with nature is a major cause of risk. It is possible, unless attitudes change, that the entire population of the planet is gradually losing the fight for survival and this will inevitably affect future generations. Another significant development in the mid-late 1990s was the rise of subcultures of resistance, the so-called anti-globalisation protesters, including many members of the younger generation. These protesters, ranging from peasants in Peru through to students in Britain, Italy and the USA and environmentalists from throughout the world launched a new backlash against globalisation as typified by the World Trade Organisation clashes in Seattle in 1996 and subsequent events in

Genoa and elsewhere in recent years.[37] These protesters view globalisation as a threat and wish to reverse its impact by rejecting what they view as world leaders adherence to a corporate agenda.[38] These trends have led, in Beck's opinion, to the emergence of a World risk society[39] and to the development of new world youth subcultures whose slogan is 'Think locally, act globally'.[40]

Risk in an information society

During the 1970s and 1980s many advanced countries made a transition to the information society in which knowledge became the main source of dynamic growth and innovation as well as the mechanism of political power and the base for social organisation. The availability of large disposable incomes and more leisure time led to new consumption patterns and the subsequent development of computers, VCRs and colour television. This was followed in the 1990s by mobile phones, e-mail and the Internet. This is why knowledge and information and its production (the emergence of an entertainment industry) rather than property are becoming the driving forces and the main reason, on the one hand, for the high economic growth of many industrial societies, especially Japan, the Far East, the USA and other European nations, and on the other for their difficulties in the 1990s.[41] This has led to what McLuhan and Powers call 'The Global Village'.[42] Frank Webster argues that an information society centres upon five key elements: technology, economy, occupation, culture and spatial aspects.[43] Hence changes in information and communication technology, the economic system, the labour force (information sector workers), the process of cultural production and in information networks are all crucial to the emergence of an information or (in Manuel Cassell's view) network society.[44] Thus the global information networks are the organisational and technological basis of the new information age. These trends are much in line with Giddens' view that the consequences of modernity are becoming more universalised.

At the same time, though, as Scott Lash points out, there is the paradox of the information society. Thus the intangibility and remoteness of risks, the uncertainty and unpredictability of risks and the general publics fear, yet also ignorance of risks, has meant that knowledge is becoming more reflective and acts as the basis for the development of a critical analysis. It changes the way in which we organise our lives as individuals or social groups because knowledge informs and defines the shape and content of risk. This paradox, according to Lash, is the consequence of 'the incredible irrationality of information overloads, misinformation, disinformation and out of control information'.[45]

Hence, together with the development of the information and communication sphere, the uncontrolled, uncalculated consequences of the so-called 'third wave', which Ye. A. Toffler refers to as the information society, are now becoming more evident. This process has undermined the reliability of past and present scientific methods and the exchange of knowledge has thereby threatened our faith in science and other transmitters of information (i.e. the mass media). The latter – science and the mass media – have failed in their duty to inform the population about possible risks, of the types referred to earlier. This has engendered greater uncertainty at a societal level and makes the risks more acute. Consequently, this means that science itself acts as a source of risk.

The epoch of knowledge and the formation of a new world order informational space overlap with the continuing process of globalisation in the economy, science and culture. All these processes demand the provision of informative inter-relations between and within different societies. The emergence of the global telecommunication system, the Internet, has facilitated the interconnection between financial and banking structures and has helped in the struggle against international crime and environmental problems. Thus in the last decade we have seen the spreading of information throughout society. The development of the information superhighway has led to a significant reduction of geographical, spatial and other factors as constraints on the development of different societies. As Giddens points out, the advance of information and communication technologies is the central driver of globalisation.[46]

Whilst new developments in the information technology field are an essential part and a key agent of social development, changing the way institutions, individuals and groups communicate, view and shape the world, it is also the case that mankind and its inner world, its motivation, consciousness and behaviour have become the object of a fierce informational struggle.

Unfortunately, as one of the other main functions of the information age is to facilitate trade and increase the profits of the producer and distributor, this has meant that the liberal value of freedom of self-expression, on the one hand, and an open mass media, on the other, hardly exist. They are sacrificed at the alter of profits and the consumer becomes the major target of information, regardless of its reliability or quality. The free for all that follows, meaning that virtually no limits are imposed, results in the media audience (viewers, readers etc.) being subjected to negative socio-cultural influences. This can led to the development of perverted orientations, tastes and priorities, such as the global desire for particular goods and services, such as products by McDonalds, Nike, Reebok and Sony. This has an impact at a macro and micro level. With regard to the former it might mean that we all identify with global brands and as a consequence fail to identify with nationally produced goods and services which leads to declining demand, closures and unemployment. At a micro level, on the other hand, multi-national corporations often create new types of consumer behaviour in so far as demand for McDonalds, Nike, Reebok, Sony and the like tends to be socially or culturally constituted, as we shall see below. Young people are particularly vulnerable to this type of manipulation. It is well known that there is a lack of sustainable patterns of behaviour among youth, hence young people tend to be flexible and open to new types of identification, often fostered onto them by the media. This tendency can have negative consequences and engender problems.[47]

Social information is particularly important to management. It is directed towards internationalisation of certain types of knowledge and ideas and in the process seeks to shape individual and social group norms and values. An extremely powerful tool is the use of information streams, which are particularly effective in manipulating mass public opinion and in getting the corporate message, and interests, across. This not only occurs at an individual level, it also happens at national level and is reflected in something called 'national mentality'. The information age has therefore had a long-term impact not just on individuals but on particular societies and nations.

There are many reasons why sociologists and social philosophers draw links between the globalisation of information and social risk. Russians view the aforementioned trends in terms of their national security and in the light of the growing threat posed by the globalisation of information seek to preserve the cultural and historical uniqueness of Russia. In general, Russian specialists argue that the new information age is a complex issue which involves a delicate balance between providing individuals, society and the state with the information they need whilst at the same time protecting the population from organised or spontaneous information which serves the interest of particular socio-political groups but might eventually engender economic crisis, socio-cultural deformation or increase social tension. The desire for informational security must be therefore set against the informational challenge, insecurity and risk caused by the globalisation of information.[48]

If the information risk includes the possibility of using various methods in order to manage interests, needs, goals and values, then informational insecurity is having a major impact. Informational risks can also be used positively but so far most of the evidence suggests that the producers and distributors of information have used them to manipulate individuals and groups in order to meet their own mercenary aims. We can see, following, the Russian scholar Ye Iu. Mitrokhina, that informational risk can therefore be defined as 'a frontier state in between an informational hazard and the stage at which the latter becomes a reality'.[49]

The Socio-cultural basis of risk

The globalisation of technological risk challenged the new way of thinking that brought to modern risk theory some human, moral and humanistic imperatives. This search for factors of rationalisation and the limits of appropriate risk centralised the discussion of its socio-cultural basis.

One of the major thinkers in the forefront of this theory of risk is the cultural anthropologist, Mary Douglas. Analysing the evolution and development of the notion of risk, Douglas points out that the dangers posed by the globalisation of risk have impacted on the meaning of risk and challenged the old probability approaches. Thus as Lupton notes, Douglas was one of the first thinkers to highlight that:

> traditional risk research ignores the conceptual, ethical and moral difficulties around the definition of equality and justice.[50]

Douglas does not deny the existence of a wide variety of risks in either the pre-modern or modern periods, but she does point out that even though risk becomes increasingly 'politicised' it is not clearly linked to the idea of 'justice' or 'emancipation'.[51] Hence Douglas states:

Risk, danger and sin are used around the world to legitimate politics or discredit it, to protect individuals from predatory individuals or to protect institutions from predatory individuals.[52]

Douglas' conceptual framework is built upon a victim/villain dichotomy in which innocent individuals/groups exposed to 'risk' need to be given compensation, the only question is how much.[53] Developing the socio-cultural approach to risk, the Russian scholar Natalia Smakotina notes that 'risk always concerns a value decision and this is a vital element of any choice made' and she concludes that a moral risk is also part of this process.[54]

Thus, the main premise here is that risks are *socially constructed*, hence risk assessments are not value-free. It is also the case that risk decisions are based on individual perceptions of risk. For Douglas, therefore, we must not forget that 'political, moral and aesthetic judgements' influence risk analysis and management.[55]

Another central thread throughout Douglas' work is the importance attached to cultural and political variables in determining responses to risk. In 1990, Douglas concluded that:

> [it is] futile to study risk perception without systematically taking the cultural bias into account.[56]

This was a central theme in Douglas' later work, *Risk and blame: Essays in cultural theory* (1992) in which she emphasises that risks are culturally biased, meaningful and influenced by socially embedded values and beliefs.

Finally Douglas argues that risks are now increasingly politicised. Here Douglas links risk and blame together. As she points out:

> Whose fault? Is the first question. Then, what action? Which means, what damages? What compensation? What restitution? ... Under the banner of risk reduction, a new blaming system has replaced the former combination of moralistic condemning [of] the victim and the opportunistic condemning [of] the victim's incompetence.[57]

The key issue therefore is making sure that risk is minimised and if possible overcome. If this is not possible, then those responsible must be held accountable. Unfortunately professional experts are used to settle 'risk' disputes, but they cannot be trusted to act in the interests of victims of risk because 'when science is used to arbitrate in these conditions [risk disputes and compensation], it eventually loses its independent status ...'.[58]

In Douglas' view the so-called 'objective' approach to risk taken by experts is false, even though their assessments of risk are 'represented as *neutral* and *unbiased*'; by contrast a 'subjective' approach is favoured by the general public.

Douglas and others have sought to examine how individuals or groups manage and respond to risk. Lupton summarising the findings of these theorists concludes that:

> lay people over-estimate and under-estimate some categories of risk and find it difficult to assess risk using probabilities.[59]

This situation is closely tied to the widely held assumption that risk avoidance is 'rational' whereas risk taking is 'irrational'. But is it as simple as this? Are individuals free-actors or are they constrained by a range of variables (ignorance, the 'risk environment', institutional constraints etc.)? The answer which Douglas gives to these questions is that we must assess the knowledge of anyone involved in risk activity, be it positive or negative. This can be done by investigating how much knowledge individuals/groups have of risk and by assessing whether or not they feel threatened and vulnerable.

In *Risk acceptability according to the Social Sciences* (1986), Douglas argues that in pre-modern times, the main perception of risk focused on famine, economic recession, war, crime, nuclear and environmental problems. Debates also centred on the notion of 'acceptable risks' (which increase as benefits rise and vice versa). These variables in turn were linked to the notion of freedom of the individual and justice.[60] At the same time, one of the main problems is that risk is still seen as objective and not subjective and as a consequence individuals 'underestimate risks which are *supposed to be under their control*'.[61] In this way Douglas shows how socio-cultural factors influence the perception of and reactions to risk and she rightly argues that this needs to be taken into account by scientists and experts.[62] There are two reasons why this occurs: firstly, a 'weak and erratic' (or in more modern times, controlled) memory; and secondly, national education systems consistently fail to increase awareness of the *real* risks.[63] In the light of this it is hardly surprising that few individuals have any sense of injustice, have little desire for retribution and therefore do not demand any accountability when the adverse consequences of risk are known.[64]

In this context, Douglas' former collaborator Aaron Wildavsky and his colleague Karl Dake argue that there are various theories of risk perception. The first theory centres upon knowledge of risk, awareness of the dangers and on the degree to which risk perceptions and knowledge coincide. The second theory points out that attitudes towards risk (avoid or take risks) is determined by personal characteristics. Therefore the relationship between individual personality/dynamics and risk perception/preference is central. The third theory, relying more on political theory, argues that the struggle over interests plays a key role and this is why risk perceptions tend to be gender, age and social class based. Finally, reinforcing Douglas' position, Wildavsky and Dake conclude that risk perceptions correspond to cultural biases, world-views, ideologies and different patterns of social relations.[65]

Socio-cultural factors of risk have had a great impact on social organisations. On the one hand, some members of society have a strong commitment to strengthening and maintaining internal bonds in risk conditions and tend to blame those facing risk for getting themselves in this situation; whilst, on the other hand, there are those individuals who firmly believe in individual enterprise and competition, and so their lives are based upon conflict rather than solidarity. Here exposure to risk is viewed more as a matter of fate/chance rather than as a punishment.[66]

Table 1.1 Typology of risk, according to Waldavsky and Dake

Type of personality	Main characteristics
Hierarchists	respect authority, conform to group norms and expectations regarding risk and trust established organisations;
Egalitarians	strongly identify with their group and tend to blame outsiders for risk, are distrustful of externally exposed norms and believe in participatory approaches to risk resolution;
Individualists	have low group identity, favour self regulation of risk, realise that risk taking has benefits and dangers, resent external constraints;
Fatalists	lack strong group cohesion, tend to leave risk to luck and fate and generally see themselves as having little control over risk.

Source: A. Wildavsky and K. Dake, 'Theories of risk perception: who fears what and why?', *Daedalus* Special issue on *Risk*, Fall 1990, pp. 42–44.

Different people view risk in different ways and also worry about different kinds of risk. The first group possess high group ethos and cohesion whereas the second group have weaker ties with others and a strong sense of individuality. On the basis of this observation, a typology of individual/group responses to risk was developed by Wildavsky and Dake (see Table 1.1). This typology is an ideal type and provides us with a way of analysing how individual/group perceptions of risk tend to be shaped by their socio-cultural situation. They range from those who avoid (hierarchists), adapt to (fatalists) or seek to control the risk environment (individualists).

John Adams suggests that everyone has a propensity for risk but that this varies from one individual to the next depending upon the potential rewards of risk taking and on previous experience (losses or gains, one's own or that of others). Taking risk decisions is therefore a delicate balancing act between potential loss or gain. It is crucial, in Adam's opinion, that risk and risk management takes into account these behavioural responses to risk.[67]

Thus one of the most significant developments in the 1980s and 1990s was a gradual shift away from a perception of risk in cost effective terms utilising an insurance/probability approach to one which analysed the impact of socio-cultural factors on risk perceptions and management. These two schools of thought on risk provided the foundations for contemporary sociology to redefine the nature of risk once again.

Contemporary sociology and risk

> Risk then [in pre-modern times] meant the probability of an event occurring combined with the magnitude of the losses or gains that would be entailed ... now risk refers only to negative outcomes.[68]

The global changes in the second half of the twentieth century – the rise of television, computers, mobile phones and the Internet, the global impact of Coca-Cola, McDonalds, Disney and Sony, the decline of the nation state, the collapse of the Berlin Wall and Communism, the emergence of a borderless world, the failure of global governments, and many other events too numerous to mention – created a new stage in the development of society.[69] The transition from an industrial society (concerned with wealth and one in which conflict was based on the division between labour and capital) to a risk society (in which there was a shift from the 'distribution of good ... to the distribution of 'bads' or dangers',[70] so the costs and risks of social development became more evident) meant that trends in society could no longer be interpreted using classical sociological approaches towards risk. The uncertainty which characterised the new reality, the instability of social processes and the penetration of risk into different spheres of society, all predetermined the emergence of new risks which could only be evaluated using a new disciplinary approach. Social theory and sociology offered new interpretations of instability, uncertainty and risk.

In this context, the notion of the sociology of instability was put forward by the Russian sociologist Bekarev who argued that sociology must turn its attention towards the study of the socio-cultural mechanisms that regulate individual and group behaviour as well as the functioning of society as a whole under unstable and crisis conditions.[71] Bekarev points out that there are two extreme conditions: the first is characterised by mechanical and fatal order in the functioning of society and so individual/group behaviour is strongly programmed and consciousness is unified and easily manipulated. Social institutions keep order which maintains social stability but in a stagnant form, which, according to Bekarev, is best described as 'frozen'. The second extreme is characterised by a high degree of instability in which people have freedom of expression but their opinions are ignored and so they don't influence the real world. Reflection tends to be abstract in character and divorced from reality. Because of this, individual/group behaviour is less predictable depending on the situation. This particular extreme, according to Bekarev, can be described as 'boiling' but there is no exit point. Both these situations are extreme forms of uncertainty. Sociology is at home between these two extremes as it can function according to the laws of 'social physics' in so far as sociology is concerned with two parallel processes, namely integration (i.e. what holds different parts of society together) and differentiation (i.e. the causes of conflict). In addition, sociology also analyses rational choice (behaviouralism, exchange theory) and diagnoses individuals from the perspective of cultural prerogatives (symbolic interactionalism, ethnomethodology). Unfortunately, under extreme conditions in society, social physics is powerless.[72]

The well-known French sociologist Alain Touraine is also interested in the impact of social change on modern society. In his seminal work, *The Post-Industrial*

Society (French edition 1969, English translation 1974) Touraine argued that societies were driven by a desire for profits and economic growth and as a consequence the new technocratic (industrial) society controls and determines our way of life, behaviour and needs.[73]

Every society has to cope with uncertainty and risk. Classical sociology can make a contribution in so far as it has accumulated sufficient knowledge and experience of the process of disintegration, crisis and conflict. Russian and Soviet scholars, building upon this tradition, are particularly interested in investigating unstable societies and have successfully studied the process of disintegration, crisis and conflict in a theoretical and empirical way. For instance, Bekarev argues that under conditions of instability and the impact of globalisation, it is possible to gain a more systematic view of the nature and causes of risk. We also concur with Touraine that it is necessary to find new concepts and approaches in order to study unstable societies.[74] This is why we will utilise the ideas of key Western (Ulrich Beck and Anthony Giddens) and Russian scholars (Y. Babosov, S. Nikitin, N. Smakotina, A. Ursul, K. Feofanov and O. Yanitskii) concerning the sociology of risk in the rest of this chapter.

A successful attempt to make a theoretical reconstruction of modern society is offered by Natalya Smakotina in her book, *The basis of the sociology of instability and risk* (1999). Smakotina provides a detailed analysis of the problem of rational behaviour and choice during periods of crisis and concludes that there is a loss of a sense of social reality. Developing Giddens' idea of reflexivity, which centres around the limits and contradictions of the modern order, Smakotina suggests that rationalism co-exists with uncertainty and is widespread enough to explain social phenomena. Moreover, Smakotina argues, uncertainty has a much greater creative potential than irrationality.[75] In order to reduce irrationality under conditions of uncertainty and risk, it is necessary to ascertain the unrealised element in our activity and to consider it within the context of synergetic synthesis (i.e. in the spirit of collaboration and co-operation).

This is possible if an inter-disciplinary approach is used and Smakotina advocates a combination of sociology and psychology so that social and psychological attitudes – expectations, beliefs, fear, trust – towards risk can be discovered. These attitudes in Smakotina's view regulate people's behaviour and help determine choices.[76] The process of the construction of a non-classical view of risk is closely connected with the introduction of the principle of uncertainty and in particular with the impact of major socio-cultural shifts on perceptions of uncertainty and risk.[77] In situations of uncertainty, 'risky behaviour' or 'creative instrumental thinking' becomes more commonplace. Risk can therefore be viewed as a way of measuring and calculating uncertainty and as a means of assessing what action is taken on the basis of individual/group expectations, beliefs, trust, fear, opinion and mood.[78]

Nikitin and Feofanov argue that for the sociology of risk to be effective and useful, it must firstly, work at the junction between different social sciences and humanities subjects and not simply focus on narrow aspects of risk, such as its economic, psychological, political, ethical or cultural aspects; secondly, it must not be too abstract and finally, the sociology of risk, must be relevant to the real world and address issues of importance to individuals, groups, communities and societies by taking into account different aspects of peoples lives and activity.[79]

It can be seen then that some common methodological and theoretical aspects to the understanding of the sociology of risk have emerged in recent years in Western and Russian sociology. This culminated in the use of the term 'risk society' throughout the 1980s and especially during the 1990s.

The concept of a 'risk society'

The problems connected with the crisis of modern industrial society, the collapse of the USSR and the shift towards a uni-polar world has acted as the basis for new types of uncertainty under the influence of the globalisation of risk. This means that we need to develop new mechanisms and technologies to make the world a safer place, to reduce risk and, if it is not possible to eliminate risk, then it is essential that societies devise ways to help individuals and groups adapt to the new conditions of risk and uncertainty.

Present day sociological thinking on risk has been strongly influenced by the ideas of Anthony Giddens and Ulrich Beck. Their ideas are discussed in depth because they offer new insights into the nature of modernity, on the one hand, and a risk society, on the other. Both these notions underpin much of the sociological framework used in this book.

A detailed analysis of the works of Giddens and Beck shows their uniqueness and how their ideas have generated a total re-thinking of the nature of risk. They emphasise the urgent need for a re-assessment of the impact of modernity on contemporary society. It is also clear that although they worked independently of each other, Giddens and Beck complement each other by viewing modernity and risk in different ways. Thus, although they both acknowledge the existence of 'risk', it has different consequences for each sociologist. For Giddens, risk can be reduced and perhaps resolved; whereas for Beck 'risk' poses a much greater threat to society and above all to the progress of modernity.

In his book, *The Consequences of Modernity* (1991), Giddens argues that modernity refers to post-seventeenth century Europe. By the twentieth century modernity was said to be the product of the consequences of modernisation, both its positive and negative aspects, and various phrases have been used to describe this period: the 'information society', 'consumer society', 'post-industrial society', 'post-capitalism' or more recently 'post-modernity'. Modernity, according to Giddens:

> is a double edged phenomenon. The development of modern social institutions and their world-wide spread have created vastly greater opportunities for human beings to enjoy a secure and rewarding existence ... But modernity also has a sombre side which has become very apparent in the present [twentieth] century.[80]

These negative sides include alienation, poverty, social exclusion, unemployment, rising crime, environmental pollution and so forth. This is why in analysing different sociological concepts of the shift from traditional to modern society, Giddens relies on the idea of reflexive organisation and the reorganisation of social relations.[81] For Giddens, an individual's awareness and ability to maintain a constant understanding of their own activity is best seen as a process of reflexivity.[82] There are two forms of reflexivity: self monitoring by individuals or self monitoring of a social system.

The risks that inevitably exist in that kind of a society can be minimised by reflexivity, which functions on the basis of trust. In Gidden's understanding, trust has to be separated from the notions of safety, danger and risk, although they are all closely inter-connected. Trust is seen by Giddens as the desire to minimise the danger and hazards within the boundaries of what might be termed 'acceptable risk'. As for the notion of danger, it reflects the process of taking risks which might eventually threaten desired outcomes.[83] Giddens adds that 'what risk presumes is precisely danger (not necessarily awareness of danger)'.[84] This particular formulation means 'trust' not in individuals, but in the 'proper' functioning of the system and so in taking a risk, we demonstrate an awareness of potential threats to specific courses of action. Giddens refers to this action as taking a 'calculated risk'.[85] When talking about 'trust' Giddens points to two types: trust in systems (*faceless commitments*) and trust in individuals (*facework commitments*). Furthermore, Giddens points out how individuals and groups need the grounds to trust in the system in which they live (i.e. believe they receive benefits from it or trust experts/governments to reduce the risks they face). The key to maintaining this delicate balance between trust in individuals and the system is what Giddens calls *ontological security* or:

> ... the confidence that human beings have in the continuity of their self-identity and in the constancy of the surrounding social and material environments of action.[86]

Whether or not ontological security becomes a reality depends upon the environment. In this context, Giddens concludes that we have witnessed a shift from the pre-modern 'environment of trust' centred on locality to the modern 'environment of risk' centred on a more global arena.[87]

A similar approach to modern society can be found in the works of Ulrich Beck on modernisation and risk especially in his seminal work *Risk Society: Towards a New Modernity* (1992). Aiming at an analysis of the nature of post industrial society or late modernity, Beck successfully overcomes the drawbacks of existing approaches to the definition of classical industrial society by suggesting the use of an alternative term '(industrial) risk society'.[88] In this sense Beck draws a distinction between first (industrial society) and a more complex second modernity (or a risk society).

There is a fierce academic debate concerning the shift from pre-modernity to the reflexive stage of modernisation, which according to Beck, is not the end, but the beginning of modernity.[89] By contrast to Giddens, who believes that the risk reducing elements outweigh the new risks,[90] Beck points out that modernity poses a major threat to society in so far as modernisation is the cause of incomplete development and in turn has led to the emergence of a risk society. The new modernity involves three stages of social change: pre-modernity, simple modernity and reflexive modernity.

Both Beck and Giddens concur that the negative aspects of risk can be dealt with by reflexivity which involves structural changes in the relationship within and between social structures and agents, freeing them from any constraints and allowing them to shape the modernisation process. Beck uses the term 'reflexive modernisation' to describe this process.

The transition from an industrial society, with its division between capital and labour and its class determined distribution of goods and services to a risk society leads to the distribution of risks ('bads' in Beck's term) which are individualised. A risk society in Giddens' view means a:

> [shift] away from the institutions of modernity towards a new and distinct type of social order.[91]

whereas in Beck's opinion it refers to a society in which:

> the probabilities of physical harm due to given technological or other processes [are evident].[92]

Giddens appears to be more flexible than Beck in so far as he doesn't see a risk society as a new type of socio-economic formation, but instead argues that the existing social order becomes the object of its own forces in the sense that society must confront the issues raised by modernisation and globalisation. For Giddens, the nature of reflexivity also changes. In the pre-modern, traditional phase, reflexivity is limited to the reinterpretation and classification of tradition, but once we have made a transition to a risk society, then reflexivity becomes the basis for social reproduction in the sense that thought and action are constantly refracted back on each other. Finally, Giddens also points out that there is a globalisation of the risk environment. Thus he concludes that:

> Risk is not just a matter of individual action. There are *environments of risk* that collectively affect large masses of individuals.[93]

Drawing together the different notions of modernity, Giddens divides its institutional dimensions into four parts – capitalism, surveillance, military power and individualism – arguing that the aforementioned features are gradually transformed into world capitalist economy, nation-state system, world military order and international division of labour.[94] Globalisation manifests itself through the strengthening of social and international ties which link distant localities in such a way that local events are shaped by global changes and vice versa.[95] Thus the degree of danger, safety and risk that prevails in any given society take place within a global context. Globalisation therefore means that it is virtually impossible to make accurate 'calculated' risks.

At this point, Giddens and Beck's views overlap. Humankind systematically faces different kinds of risk, such as poverty, illness, ecological and nuclear risks and so on. Beck argues that we are not always able to calculate their consequences, as was the case, for instance, with Chernobyl in 1986. One consequence is that earlier probability theories of risk no longer work. Thus Turner aptly notes:

... the transformations of modern society are so profound that risks in modern society can no longer be adequately calculated according to existing paradigms.[96]

Reflexive modernisation, which comes from science, the intelligentsia, pressure groups, social movements etc., can play the role of a panacea of risks and facilitate an increase in the level of trust in a society.

The main difference between classical and reflexive modernisation is shown in Table 1.2.

Table 1.2 Classical versus reflexive modernisation

Classical modernisation	Reflexive modernisation
wealth production	risk production
traditional patterns – class, family, work	opposite starting to disintegrate, consequence of success not crisis of modernisation

Source: Adapted from U. Beck, *Risk Society: Towards a New Modernity*, SAGE, London 1992, p. 38.

Beck argues that it is not the distribution of wealth which is of over-riding significance, as Weber emphasised, but the production of risks and hazards, which need to be minimised and managed, and if possible prevented. At this stage, Beck offers a more qualified definition of risk as:

> [the] systematic way of dealing with [the] hazards and insecurities induced and introduced by modernisation itself.[97]

Giddens also sees the danger as induced by modernisation itself. However, for Giddens there is a possibility to overcome risks by making improvements in the socio-economic sphere.

Beck focuses on the political context of risk whereas Giddens emphasises the socio-economic aspects. They therefore complement each other well.

Although it may appear that we face the same problems today as we always have, such as physical hazards, climatic change and so on, what seem to be the same 'features' have 'different' consequences.[98] The conflict between local and global when our ties to local communities (in terms of the kinship system, religion, personalised trust etc.) have broken down under the pressure of globalisation is one such consequence. The globalisation of the risk environment which means the extension of risks beyond nation/state boundaries is another outcome of this situation. Under these conditions, all attempts to control risks locally inevitably fail. A third consequence is the increase in individual and group awareness and knowledge of the world in which they live and the risks they face. Unfortunately in the process, the level of their faith in prevailing expert systems is undermined. The outcome, according to Giddens is 'uncertainty' coupled with 'the imperfect operation' of integration mechanisms.[99] Individuals, groups and societies deprived of the possibility of resisting these problems have little choice but to adapt and accept the inevitable by living with risk.

In Giddens' view modernity can be compared to a high speed juggernaut which is out of control. We are forced to be passengers even though it has no clear direction and often crushes all in its path. Under such conditions the future is unpredictable.[100] The consequence is that:

> the mix of risk and opportunity is so complex in many of the circumstances involved that it is extremely difficult for individuals to know how far to vest trust in particular prescriptions or systems, and how far to suspend it.[101]

This situation produces four different responses or 'adaptive reactions':

1 *pragmatic acceptance* namely surviving and stressing day to day living. This person tends to be either pessimistic, optimistic or both;
2 *sustained optimism* which is typical of a person who believes that providence will always work no matter what current risks exist;
3 *cynical pessimism* which is common amongst those who are nostalgic about the past and negative about the future; and finally,
4 *radical engagement* whereby individuals do not simply stand by and watch but prefer instead to protest against perceived threats and mobilise themselves and others in order to reduce the impact of, or if possible transcend, risks. This attitude prevails among members of social movements and is evident, for example, among today's anti-globalisation protesters.[102]

Which one or combination of these responses prevail varies over time. But they can all strengthen or reduce the level of risk in any given society.

In contrast to Beck, Giddens believes that risk reduction is a possibility but depends on whether or not we are able find ways in which we can harness the juggernaut or in other words reduce risk and control modernity. The key is walking the tightrope between mininising the dangers and maximising the opportunities of modernity.[103] Our ability to control modernity depends upon several factors according to Giddens: firstly, the effectiveness of the system (*design faults*); secondly on the degree of system or individual operator errors (*operator failure*); thirdly on the level of unintended consequences; and finally, on whether or not knowledge is used to correct the first two problems or at least to try and create a more stable society.[104] Giddens refers to these strategies as 'steering mechanisms' designed to control the juggernaut[105] and argues that our success in achieving this goal relates to the type of society we wish to create and the role of social movements (fighting for free speech, peace, labour, ecology etc) within it.[106] Social movements, in Giddens' view, provide glimpses of possible futures and are vehicles for their realisation.[107] If they are successful, this new post-modern order will have the following components: a post-scarcity system, multi-layered democratic participation, demilitarisation and humanisation of technology as well as the following global characteristics: socialised economic organisation, co-ordinated global order, system of planetary care; and transcendence of war.[108] However, given changes in the risk environment, there can be no guarantees that we will move in the direction of a post-modern order. As a consequence, at the start of twenty-first century we still face the following risks: global inequalities, nuclear conflict, increased warfare, ecological catastrophe, the collapse of markets and so forth.[109]

Whilst each state is an individual risk society, the nations of the world constitute a global risk society. We have seen that risks range from the personal (anxiety, stress, hardship, poverty) to regional (unemployment), national (recession) through to global (ecological catastrophe, nuclear disaster, terrorism as recent events in the USA, Afghanistan and illustrate).

We would now like to consider the usefulness of Giddens and Beck's theories for our understanding of Russian modernity given the fact that it is taking place under different circumstances. Particular attention will be devoted firstly to the way in which risk theory can be developed further so that account can be taken of the specifics of Russian modernity; secondly, we will examine what the role of the individual, on the one hand, and the state, on the other, should be in managing risk and then finally, we will outline the flaws in Giddens and Beck's theories of modernity before offering our own working definition and theory of risk which will be applied to Russia in the following chapter and to global youth from chapter 3 onwards. This will enable us firstly, to provide the grounds for a sociological assessment of risk in Russia and among youth in particular and secondly, to challenge current theories concerning Russia and Russian youth using risk theory.

The Pros and Cons of Risk theory

Many insights can be gained from Giddens and Beck's works on late-modernity and risk societies. Firstly, they emphasise that risk is not simply a matter of personal fate, instead risk is central to the nature of modernity itself. This is why Beck uses the term 'risk society' to describe the nature of modernity. The second key point made by these two thinkers is that risk is no longer a collective issue instead individuals must accept the responsibility for dealing with risk and not expect the state to protect them. In this sense risk is also part of individualism, on the one hand, and of the impact of the market, on the other. The third aspect of Giddens and Beck's analysis centres on the control of risk as well as perceptions of it. In this sense, the structures and patterns of knowledge coming from experts as well as governments are important in influencing public awareness of risk, on the one hand, and in terms of the state and expert systems trying to reduce risk, on the other. This leads us to the fourth and final useful insight emanating from Giddens', *Consequences of Modernity* and Beck's, *Risk Society*, namely, the risk environment in which we live. Risk is not therefore simply local or national in character, it is global.

Whilst, it must be acknowledged that Giddens and Beck have made a major contribution to current understanding of the reasons for the decay of modernity, many writers have criticised them for not highlighting the legacy left to them by the likes of Mary Douglas who developed a cultural theory of risk. Furthermore, other scholars, such as Bryan Turner, disagree with Beck's view that modernity has altered the nature of the risks which we now face, arguing instead that:

In the context of high modernity within an advanced capitalist system, risk follows from the production of wealth itself. Whereas risks in traditional and early modern society were *primarily personal*, now *they are global and they threaten the entire system of human societies*.[110]

Beck in particular can be criticised for downplaying the diffusion of risk according to social class, power and wealth as he appears to suggest that risk is not the result of social position but the consequence of a lack of knowledge.[111] Douglas disagrees with Beck on this point and argues instead that exposure to risk varies according to social group – rich, poor and minorities. In this context, Douglas points out that 'in an individualist culture, the *weak* are going to carry the *blame* for what happens to them'.[112]

Although we can see the value of Giddens and Beck's work, and will utilise aspects of it in *Youth, Risk and Russian Modernity*, we also feel that their work has a number of drawbacks. Firstly, they are largely Western in scope, with Beck basing most of his conclusions on the situation in Germany, which is not typical of Western Europe, let alone other parts of the New Europe since the fall of communism. Secondly, many of their remarks are far too general in nature and their texts often lack concrete examples. This applies more to Beck than Giddens. Thirdly, neither authors provide a detailed breakdown of the types of risks we face apart from general references to nuclear wars and ecological disasters. Fourthly, Giddens in particular, argues that modernity is largely a Western project.[113] Fifthly, very little distinction is made by Beck's or Giddens' works between the differences in the nature, scope and degree of risk prevailing in stable/unstable societies. We will argue in *Youth, Risk and Russian Modernity*, that risk varies according to country and that every country has its own specifics which strongly influence the types of risk prevailing, the ability to adapt to risk and the types of mechanisms available for resolving risk. Finally, very few studies have been made of the impact of risk on specific groups in society. This book looks at the risks facing one group in post-communist Russia – youth.

Defining a 'risk society'

What are the main features of a risk society then? As Beck points out a risk society emerges because of the demise of an industrial society and the emergence of new uncontrolled risks throughout the new society which replaces it. If an industrial society tends to rely on traditional social norms, patterns of family relations, social class and gender roles, then the development of a risk society radically changes the nature of the social structure, in particular the meaning attached to class, family, gender, marriage, occupation and so on. The outcome, according to Beck, is that traditionalism and collectivism have been replaced by individualisation. As Turner puts it:

> Risk society is associated with a new form of individualism in which the self becomes the project ... risk brings about a multiplication of the problems and contradictions which beset modern institutions ... because Beck sees industrial society as an incomplete project

of radical modernity, he places a special emphasis on the *individualising process of late modernisation*.[114]

On the question of whether or not we still live in class-based societies, Beck argues that patterns of social inequality have remained relatively stable, but standards of living have dramatically changed. This has resulted in the loss of class identity and given rise to the individualisation of social inequality. Thus nowadays, individuals are blamed for their failures (unemployment, poverty, exclusion from the education system and labour market etc.). In Beck's view, attachment to social class has weakened; whilst at the same time, individuals are becoming increasingly separated from their traditional support networks (family, neighbourhood etc.). Beck concedes, however, that this process is not just negative, it also has positive aspects in so far as individuals have the possibility of gaining greater control over money, time, living space, the ability to plan their own educational course and career, entry into labour market and so on. In the past, these trends were largely determined by class, family, and neighbourhood ties amongst other things. On the negative side, however, Beck acknowledges that growing competition between individuals (over, for instance, skills and qualifications) still takes place. All in all because class identity in the traditional sense of word is being gradually eroded, individuals seek alliances centred on specific issues (feminism, ecology, pacifism, anti-globalisation etc.) during their search for a new social/personal identity in a de-traditionalised culture. As a result, nowadays conflicts arise over issues of race/ethnicity, colour, gender, age, sexuality and physical disabilities. Beck refers to these factors as 'ascribed characteristics'.[115]

Let us consider just one example, the gender issue. For Beck, the mid–late twentieth century provided new opportunities for women, including the possibility to enter the education and labour markets in larger numbers. As a result in the post-1945 period, women had a greater sense of independence, but they still had to deal with all-pervasive gender stereotyping, on the one hand, and the fear of unemployment, the shift from full to part-time (or casual) employment and the erosion of lifelong job security, on the other. These new opportunities and challenges, brought on by major changes in the economic and political contexts of various risk societies, put pressure on relations between the sexes and on the family. This meant that the latter was either undermined or in extreme cases destroyed. Thus whilst individualisation frees males/females from their traditional roles, both sexes, still might have to make the difficult choice between work (career) and parenthood. This means that other problems arise over child-care, sexual intercourse, use of contraception and so forth because of the lack of institutional provision and solutions. Although fatherhood is no longer an obstacle to the male pursuit of a career, males still suffer in custody battles and more often than not lose out. Thus Beck argues that 'children [are] seen as [an] impediment to [the] individualisation process'.[116] He concludes that in future we will see the return of the nuclear family, male/female inequality and a move beyond traditional male/female roles.

Following Beck, it is possible to argue that a triple individualisation takes place in a risk society:

1   So-called liberation or the removal of traditional constraints made by class, family etc.
2   Disenchantment which arises due to the loss of traditional society; and
3   Reintegration which is founded on new types of social commitment.

The industrialisation process involves both objective (life situation) and subjective (consciousness, identity, personalisation) aspects. However, this process is not free of the contradiction associated with increased risk. Alongside the breakdown of traditional family and class ties, our way of life also becomes institutionalised. As part of this process, in the risk society phase we also witness the gradual replacement of the notion of 'bread winner' with that of the 'earner/provider', as well as increased vulnerability across traditional boundaries, such as class. The consequence is individualisation of life process, in the sense that each persons life biography becomes 'self reflexive', with individuals determining wage, labour, education, employment, consumption and other factors. This is why '[an] entire generation [has] drift[ed] to [the] margins of society'.[117] We will show later that this is certainly the case with regard to young people.

The transformation of the meaning of work is another key feature of a risk society.[118] In an industrial society, work had status and occupation defined an individual or groups social position and acted as a key 'identification pattern'.[119] However, since the 1980s work has lost its previous value and significance, is less secure and offers less protection. For nearly two decades now we have been witnessing a gradual transition from employment to unemployment. People's job, career, wage, are all at risk. At the start of the twenty-first century there are no longer any guarantees of 'lifelong work'. The development of a job 'contact system', which limits the workplace and hours, has made work more standardised. In addition, due to the increased proportion of people working from home, the boundaries between work/non-work have become more fluid. This is largely the consequence of the emergence of an information society but it also symbolises a process of decentralisation. At the same time, besides open unemployment, there is also the problem of underemployment (i.e. work without pay).

Before modernity, our situation was more stable and our career and wages were more secure. But under modernity, the level of risk has substantially increased. Each individual now needs to be more flexible and willing, if the situation demands it, to transfer from full to part-time work, and to undergo periods of unemployment. The difficulty in these cases is increased vulnerability. Thus part-timers, for example, tend to be temporary, unprotected and unorganised workers (i.e. non-trade unionists).

The solution to this contradiction is firstly, to *open up politics and economics* and secondly, to *monitor the 'market'*. This requires a change in governing the workplace, a change in job structures and a change in the nature of the organisation of labour. The main obstacle here is a blurring of the boundaries between industrial/ familial production; service/informal production; market/non-market and production/consumption. All of the former are 'hybrids'. The consequence is reduced mass production; de-standardisation of markets; transformation of labour and production; politicisation of labour organisation and operations (which have become de-standardised and pluralised); increased pressure for legitimation and greater moralisation of industrial development.

Perceptions of risk and the solutions to it also vary. In the business sector (some public; most private) risks are seen as positive. They are viewed as part of market opportunities, so the oligarchs walk a tightrope between revealing and concealing risks. On the surface, there is the outward appearance of preventive risk management, but the latter is a myth, because no real risk management strategy is actually in place. This phase of risk is characterised by an escalation in the level of conflict between science and society. The problem is that technical experts define the agenda and risk discourses, but at the same time there is growing scepticism about the ability of science to resolve risk and this undermines public trust in scientists and gradually destroys their credibility. This is the product of a contradictory process in which science is supposed to control risk (for example, the degree of environmental pollution, BSE, CJD, Genetically Modified foods and so on) but actually also causes risk. This leads to a battle over knowledge. Thus officialdom and their experts blame their critics for causing the risk or accuse them of being alarmist, instead of realising that they might be to blame. This battle, and people's better awareness of risk, eventually leads to the collapse of the idea of a 'scientific monopoly'. Nevertheless, governments, in most risk societies still continue to argue that the hazards caused by exposure to risks are low or not proven, stressing instead that the gains outweigh losses. Risk is therefore falsely portrayed as part of the price of progress.

Although the scientific monopoly on risk is founded on lies and deceit, the general public still by and large rely on science. Nevertheless, the outcome, according to Beck, is that:

> the reality of risk threatens and grows, knowing no social or national differences anymore. Behind the walls of indifference, danger runs wild.[120]

It must be pointed out, however, that not only science is to blame for risk because there is also the problem of 'economic blindness to risks'. Thus as profits fall, risks are denied; but if profits are made, then a myth of 'acceptable levels' of risk (say in relation to pollution) is created. Although the 'polluter pays' principle exists, this is rarely acted upon. The solution to this problem, according to Beck, is to *demystify science and change the degree of intervention*. This means questioning the authority of science and introducing through the process of 'reflexive modernisation' a critical debate regarding 'risk'. In this way, although risks increase over time, there is also a corresponding increase in risk consciousness, so the spell of 'invisibility of risks' is finally broken.

Another feature of a risk society is the growing attention given to democracy. Beck emphasises in his later book, *The Reinvention of Politics: Rethinking modernity in the Global social order* (1997) that risks depend on decisions, are individually produced and politically reflexive. Under risk society conditions, the politics of industrial democracy is undercut by a new sub-politics of technical expertise and market-based progress. Thus the political system which existed in an industrial society (political parties, parliament, government, law and policies) is said to have functioned at the expense of the individual who was forced to bow to the majority. Individual sovereignty was also tied to the boundaries of state and nation.[121] This caused a crisis because politics suffered from immobilism and the circulation of elites. In order to resolve this situation we need, according to Beck, to *reinvent* politics so that it protects the rights of citizens, and this requires the decentralisation of politics.[122] This involves a bisection of democracy, the introduction of the separation of powers, freedom of mass media, observation of civil rights and so on.

The key to the gradual establishment of 'democratic rights' and 'concrete democracy', according to Beck, is *participation*. In the *Reinvention of Politics* Beck points out that if we focus on the *sub-political level* (i.e. the role of agents outside the political system (such as judiciary and civil service)) then individuals will have a greater opportunity to shape the political process and in this way *subpoliticisation* (or *communitarianism* as it is referred to in the United States) might act as a means of resolving the dilemmas of late modernity.[123] As Beck notes:

> Sub-politicised society is, or more cautiously, could become (among several other possibilities) the civil society that takes its concerns into its own hands in all areas and fields of action of society.[124]

For this to become a possibility, Beck argues that we need a transition from *rule-directed* (or official) politics to *rule-altering* (or a stress on sub-politics). The former can be creative and non-conformist but operates within the existing rule-system; whereas the latter alters the rules of the game and allows a switch towards reflexive modernity.[125] In other words a new political system run by different politicians needs to be introduced so that society can think globally and act in different ways about risk. Our ability to do this, depends on three dichotomies, according to Beck:

1   *safe/unsafe*, which concerns our attitude towards uncertainty
2   *inside/outside*, which relates to our view of strangers; and
3   *political/unpolitical*, which centres on the possibility of shaping society.[126]

These three aspects are constantly struggling against each other, but only a new model of politics based on an active, devolved civil society will sustain an inherently democratic modernity in Beck's view.

Giddens shares some of Beck's views and also argues that politics needs to be transformed. Giddens talks in particular about a third way in which the old left/right divide is rejected in favour of a more active middle force, which Giddens terms the 'radical centre'. This force is central to our ability to negotiate the impact of the rise of a risk society, globalisation and the individualisation of risk.[127]

Thus the aforementioned analysis shows that the emergence of a risk society creates new uncertainties and as a result of the impact of individualisation and radical changes in the way political and social institutions function, a gradual shift back to an industrial society takes place. This involves three processes:

1   *Re-industrialisation* which refers to greater realism, criticism of anti-modernists and an awareness of industrial society as semi-modern etc. The problem is that the antagonism between industrial society and modernity

remains unrecognised. Therefore, despite increased risk, governments have no desire to research it, and furthermore any risk intervention drives wedges in the business camp, but there are still winners and losers. Denial does not reduce risk, instead it produces de-stabilisation.

2   *Democratisation of technology transfer*, here modernisation is considered rational and industrial society is seen as democratic. In order to resolve this dilemma, Beck argues that decision-making needs to be more open and accessible; science and research must be placed under political control and the welfare state must try to combat risks (poverty, mass unemployment, destruction of nature, technological threat etc.). The downside is scientific authoritarianism and excessive bureaucracy; and

3   *Differential politics*, namely the need for a different epoch of modernisation – reflexivity, risk co-operation (to resolve conflict), flexibility, a greater stress on the sub-political level, structural democratisation, and the reduced monopoly of science on rationality, men on profits, marriage on sexuality, politics on policy together with the increased equality, freedom and self-expression as promised by modernity.

All in all this constitutes a 'different understanding of politics'. The outcome is that the 'age of excuses is over', there will be no faits accomplis, instead we will witness increased self-criticism and the promotion of a different evaluation of risk (i.e. controversial and alternative definition/discussion of risk).

Summarising our analysis of the existing approaches to risk, we can see that: firstly, most theories see uncertainty, the need to make a choice and a personal evaluation of consequences (moral as well as ethnic ones) as common to most definitions of risk. Secondly, taking all of this into consideration, Al'gin defines risk as:

> an activity connected with the need to overcome uncertainty in a situation of unavoidable choice when there is a possibility to make qualitative and quantitative evaluations of the probable result, failure and deviation from one's original goal.[128]

Thus the possibility of estimating probable outcomes is the main condition for overcoming uncertainty.[129] Such a possibility, however, does not simply exist at times of uncertainty, it also appears in the process of transition from certainty to uncertainty and vice versa. During this phase choice as well as the evaluation of outcomes occurs. Our working definition of risk differs from that of Al'gin in so far as *we see risk* as:

> an activity carried out during the transition from uncertainty to certainty and vice versa and where there is a possibility to estimate the probability (in quantitative and qualitative terms) of achieving the expected outcome or to measure the degree of deviation from the original goal, whilst taking into account existing moral and ethical norms.

Such a flexible definition is especially important in societies in crisis and/or transition and this is why risk merits further attention especially in relation to Russia's current phase of modernisation. This definition is also better suited to the situation of risk among young people, as it adequately allows for the transitory character of youth which is shifting from the relative certainty of the past, provided by their parents, to greater uncertainty in their own lives in the present and future. Contemporary young people in general are more pragmatic than their parents. This is why the younger generation are more or less willing to rely on chance when calculating risk. The socio-cultural bases of risk also have greater significance in relation to youth. On the one hand, society cannot escape its responsibility for the situation of risk in which young people find themselves. On the other hand, however, in calculating risk and taking action, we must not forget the moral implications and consequences of any decisions made. This is why our definition of risk includes a vital aspect left out in Al'gin's own definition of risk and also why our analysis has much in common with that of Douglas and Smakotina. Our analysis shows that risk calculation carries with it the potential for social conflict and it is also the case that decisions on risk cannot be separated from the potential damage to others.

Risk theory, Russia and its youth

The concepts of 'risk' and 'modernity' have not yet been fully explored in relation to countries in 'transition'. However, we shall argue throughout this book that 'risk theory' allows for the development of new forms of understanding and provides a new sociological discourse on Russian modernity and on Russian youth. We shall outline of own typology of risk in greater detail in subsequent chapters, so for the moment using Beck's theory, it is possible to highlight the following distinctions between the pre and post-modern phase of development (see Table 1.3).

Table 1.3 Shift from pre and simple to reflexive modernity

Classical/traditional modernisation	*Risk society/Reflexive modernisation*
Stability	Instability
Wealth production	Risk production
Strong social class	Importance of social class diminishing
Stable family	Disintegrating family
Traditional labour relations	De-traditionalisation
Social differences	Social inequality
Collectivism	Individualism
Conflict based on class and capital division	Growth of social movements fighting over specific issues

The difficulty with Table 1.3 is that it is useful in explaining Western experience, but it does not take into account the situation in post-Soviet societies. Beck argues that the decay of modern order can be attributed not to the class struggle but to the success of capitalism. In the case of former communist states, such as Russia, the demise of the Russian Empire and the Russian nation state was due not to progress towards a communist ideal, but to a crisis within communism which eventually led to the disintegration of the USSR. Thus in both instances, we may have witnessed the transition from an industrial to a risk society, but the origins of this path to a new or counter-modernisation are different, according to the context and country to which we are referring.

Some examples of the characteristic features of Russian modernity are given in Table 1.4 which has something in common with Table 1.3, but in many respects is also fundamentally different because each country has its own specifics and levels of development at any given moment in time.

Table 1.4 Aspects of Russian modernity

Classical/traditional Russian modernisation	*Russian Risk society/Reflexive modernisation*
Stability	Instability
Certainty	Uncertainty
Wealth production	Risk production
'Classless' society	Emergence of class divisions
Stable family	Family in crisis
Planned/command economy	Market economy
Totalitarianism	Pseudo liberal-democracy
Communist party represents society's interests	Rise of social movements and multi-party system
Collectivism	Individualism
Social guarantees (job, education, welfare)	Virtually no social protection
Minimal poverty	Widespread poverty
Traditional labour relations	De-traditionalisation
Limited social differences.	Widespread social inequality
Reliance on state and government regulation	Self-regulation and search for self-identity
Internal and external threats	Globalisation of risk
Sense of identity	Deformation and crisis of identity

Following Beck and Giddens, it is possible to argue that the motors of social transformation in Russia's case include the breakdown of traditional forms of solidarity as well as challenges to legitimacy of past rulers as a result of what Beck calls *vertical* and *horizontal* aspects of the Russian embryonic democracy, which became more reflexive from the mid-1980s onwards, if not earlier.

At this stage, it is necessary to note that there are at least three categories of risk – economic, political and social – all of which overlap with one another, as we shall see in the next chapter. What happens in one area can adversely affect the other variables. Thus uncertainties in the post-Soviet political sphere can have negative affects on Russian economy and society and similarly economic and political democratisation also go hand in hand. Finally, it must also not be forgotten that changes in social forces can strongly influence the process of economic and political reform.

Table 1.4 shows that Russia has undergone tremendous changes in the late twentieth century especially during its last two decades. Such changes in the environment of risk in Russia have not simply influenced the nature of the risks prevailing, they have also adversely affected Russia's ability to adapt to the new risks arising in the post-communist phase at two levels – the micro level (individual, group) and the macro level (society as a whole). This has led to the division of society into winners (former nomenklatura, oligarchs, business class, new Russians, bureaucracy and police) and losers (students, pensioners, one parent families, poor, well qualified and educated etc.). However, the ongoing crisis is even making these distinctions meaningless, so Russia is becoming a society in which everyone is at risk.

The fact that the goals pursued by successive Soviet and post-Soviet leaderships have changed (partly as a consequence of internal struggles for power but also as a result of the rise and increased pressure of globalisation) together with constant changes in the rules of the game, has led to increased uncertainty and chaos, and this in turn has led to new risks in Russia. This situation has made it virtually impossible for individuals or groups in post-Soviet society to adapt to or manage risk. This has produced a situation of increased social tension and conflict between specific groups and society. As our case study of Russian youth shows, risk has produced conflict among different sections of youth and thereafter increased conflict between young people and society thereby engendering an escalation in the level of risk and making the conflict-risk relationship an on-going process. However, like Giddens, we believe that these conflicts can be resolved, enabling Russia to control its juggernaut.

Conclusion

In *Youth, Risk and Russian Modernity*, we will be using aspects of both Beck's description of the nature of a risk society – using Russia as an illustrative example – as well as Giddens' theory of modernity to suggest possible ways of resolving risk. But we will also, in analysing trends among Russian youth, extend Giddens and Beck's sociological theories in various respects by:

1. Analysing Russia as a risk society, which has never hitherto been attempted.
2. Developing our own typology of risk in relation to Russia, on the one hand, and youth, on the other.

3 Providing insights into ways in which conflicts within a risk society, particularly in the youth sphere, might be resolved;
4 Finally, following Bryan Turner, we will be assessing whether or not the risks facing Russia and its young people have increased or decreased with the transition to capitalism since the mid-1980s.

The analysis presented in the following chapters will allow us to consider whether the evidence we have collected using longitudinal data from 1990–1999 supports Giddens' earlier claim that the risk-reducing elements substantially outweigh the new array of risks or whether, Russia is just as much an apocalyptic risk society as the rest of the globe.

Notes

1 B.S. Turner, *Orientalism, Postmodernism and Globalism*, Routledge, London, 1994, p. 167.
2 D. Lupton, *Risk*, Routledge, London, 1999, p. 5.
3 A. Giddens, *The Consequences of Modernity*, Polity Press, London, 1991, pp. 14–15.
4 J. Bradbury, 'The policy implications of differing concepts of risk', *Science, Technology and Human Values*, Vol. 14 (4), 1989, p. 382.
5 See V.Oigezikhm, *Problema riska v grazhdanskoi prave*, Dushambe, 1972, p. 5
6 N. Luhmann, *Risk: A Sociological Theory*, Aldine de Gruyer, New York, 1993, p. 9.
7 Ibid.
8 Lupton, *Risk*, 1999, p. 9
9 Ibid, p. 18.
10 Luhmann, *Risk*, 1993, p. 13.
11 M. Douglas, *Risk and Blame: Essays in cultural theory*, Routledge, London, 1992, p. 13.
12 M. Douglas, *Risk acceptability according to the social sciences*, Russell Sage Foundation, New York, 1986, p. 43.
13 One exception here, and a major difference between Western Europe and the USA, on the one hand, and Russia, on the other, is Russians reluctance to pay car insurance. Unfortunately, this makes Russian drivers extremely vulnerable and the subject of great risks. During a research trip made by Christopher Williams to Russia in July 2001, it was discovered that the latest criminal scam in Moscow was to use minor car crashes as a way of swindling money from unsuspecting drivers. Thus two criminals would gather behind an innocent driver, one criminal would flash in the driver's rear view mirror for him to move over whilst the second criminal would switch lanes and bump into the innocent driver. As this had already happened on numerous occasions, the criminals car would appear to be seriously damaged. In order to avoid any risks (the police and a possible driving ban) such innocent drivers can pay anything between $50–200 dollars in 'damages'. If they refuse, by-standers (actually friends of the criminals) would just happen to pass by to say they witnessed everything (in the criminals favour, of course). If this failed, a violent incident might follow. Organised gangs in Moscow have made thousands of dollars in Moscow and other large cities in this way between 2000–2001 and it had become so common newspaper articles and TV programmes had publicised the problem. The militsia (police) meanwhile did nothing. Why? Because they took a cut of the action. In the West, most drivers have car insurance and money never changes hands as the insurance companies of the parties involved deal with any car accidents.
14 Luhmann, *Risk*, 1993, pp. 20–21.

15 Ibid, pp. 21–22.
16 Douglas, *Risk Acceptability*, 1986, p. 46.
17 Luhmann, *Risk*, 1993, p. 22.
18 Douglas, *Risk and Blame*, 1992, p. 23.
19 Lupton, Risk 1999, p. 18.
20 A. Al'gin, *Risk i ego rol' v obshchestvennoi zhizni*, Moscow, Mysl', 1989, p. 19.
21 *Psikhologiia Slovar'*, Moscow, Politizdat, 1990, p. 344.
22 Ibid, pp. 344–345.
23 R. Bellan, *Beyond belief: Essays on religion in a post-traditional world*, Free Press, New York, 1970, p. 6.
24 V. Gott and A. Ursul, *Opredelennost' i neopredelennost' kak kategorii nauchnogo poznaniya*, Kishinev, Shtinita, 1971, p. 54.
25 Ibid, p. 56.
26 S. Eisenstadt, *Revoluitsiia i preobravanie obshchestv: sravnitel'noe izuchenie tsivilizatsii*, Moscow, Aspekt Press, 1999, p. 59.
27 This definition is strongly influenced by Al'gin's view of risk as 'the opportunity to realise at least one possible variant' (see A. Al'gin, *Risk I ego rol' v obshchestvennoi zhizni*, Moscow, Mysl', 1989, p. 19).
28 I. Wallerstein, 'Uncertainty and creativity' cited at http://fbc.binghampton.edu/iwuncer.htm.
29 For a useful discussion of the main issues here see S. Miles, *Social theory in the real world*, Sage, London, 2001, chapter 4.
30 On this issue see U. Beck, *Ecological Enlightenment: Essays on the politics of the Risk Society*, Humanities Press, Atlantic Highlands, New Jersey, 1994 and his *Ecological Politics in an Age of Risk*, Polity, Cambridge, 1995; S. Lash, B. Szerszynski and B. Wynne, *Risk, government and modernity: Towards a new ecology*, Sage, London, 1996; S. Yearley, *The Green case: A sociology of environmental issues, arguments and politics*, Routledge, London, 1991 and his *Sociology, environmentalism, globalization: Reinventing the Globe*, Sage, London, 1996.
31 For a fuller discussion of these issues see R. Almas, 'Food trust, ethics and safety in risk society', *Sociological Research on line*, Vol. 4 (3), 1999 cited at www.socresonline.org.uk/ocresonline/4/3/almas.html; B. Adams, 'Industrial food for thought: Timescapes of risk', *Environmental Values*, Vol. 8 (2), 1999, pp. 219–238; H. Campbell and R. Fitzgerald, 'Food scares and GM: Ambivalent technologies, fear and the politics of nostalgia'; and R. Fitzgerald and H. Campbell, 'Bleeding/Cutting into Nature/Culture: Frankenfoods and science fictions', papers presented to the *New natures, new cultures, new technologies* conference, Fitzwilliam College, Cambridge, UK, July 2001.
32 Ulrich Beck, *Ecological Enlightenment: Essays on the politics of the Risk Society*, Humanities Press, Atlantic Highlands, New Jersey, 1994, p. 2.
33 Turner, *Orientalism, postmodernism and globalism*, 1994, p. 178. Our emphasis.
34 U. Beck, *Risk Society: Towards a New Modernity*, Sage, London, 1992 p. 21. Our emphasis.
35 D. Kellner, 'Globalization and the postmodern turn' cited at www.gseis.ucla.edu.
36 Ibid.
37 On these groups see A. Cockburn, J. St. Clair and A. Sekula, *5 days that shook the world: Seattle and Beyond*, Verso, London 2000 and B. Shephard and R. Hayduk (ed.), *Urban protest and community building in the era of globalisation*, Verso, London, forthcoming.
38 This view is typified, for example, by the group *Globalise Resistance* (see BBC 2 Newsnight programme, 8 August 2001).
39 U. Beck, *World Risk Society*, Polity, Cambridge, 1999, especially, chapter 2.
40 D. Kellner, 'Globalization and the postmodern turn' cited at www.gseis.ucla.edu.

41 D. Bell, *The Coming of the Post-industrial Society*, Basic, New York, 1973.
42 M. McLuhan and B.P. Powers, *The Global Village*, Oxford University Press, Oxford, 1989.
43 F. Webster, *Theories of the information society*, Routledge, London, 1995, pp. 6–29.
44 M. Cassells, *The Rise of the Network Society, The information Age: Economy, Society and Culture*, Vol. 1, Blackwell, Oxford, 1996.
45 S. Lash, 'Informationcritique' paper presented to the UK–Nordic meeting, 9 April, 1999, cited by Virtual Society? at www.brunel.ac.uk/research/virtsoc/nordic/cbslash.htm
46 Giddens, *Consequences of Modernity*, pp. 36–44
47 For more here see T.P. Voronina, *Infomatsionnaia obshchestvo: sushchnost', cherty, problemy*, Moscow, IO TsAGI 1995 and R.G. Yanovskii, *Global'nye izmeniia i sostial'naia bezopasnost*, Moscow: Akademia, 1999.
48 On this issue see for instance, Ye. Iu. Mitrokhina, 'Informatsionnaia bezopasnost' kak sotsiologicheskaia problema (Nekotorye metodologicheskie podkhody)', *Bezopasnost' (Infomatsionnyi sbornik)*, 1999, No. 7–9 (39); I. B.Novik, 'Informatsionnye aspekty riska', in *Sistemnaia kontseptsiia informatsionnykh protsessov: Sbornik trudov*, Moscow, VNIISI 1988; I.A. Sosnova, 'Informatsionnia ustroichivost' i informatsionnaia bezopasnost' sotsial'nykh sistem', in *Analiz sistem na poroge XXI veka: Teoriia i praktika. T. 2*, Moscow, Intellekt, 1996; R.G. Yanovskii, 'Dukhovno-nravstvennai bezopasnost' Rossii', *Sotsiologicheskie Issledovaniia*, 1995, No. 12.
49 Ye. Iu. Mitrokhina, 'Informatsionnaia bezopasnost' lichnosti kak sotsiologicheskaia problema' *Kandidat Sotsiologicheskikh nauk*, Moscow, ISPR, RAN, 1999, p. 48.
50 Lupton, *Risk*, 1999, p. 38.
51 M. Douglas, 'Risk as a forensic resource', *Daedalus*, Special Issue on *Risk*, Fall 1990, p. 4.
52 Ibid, p. 5.
53 Ibid, p. 9.
54 N. Smakotina, *Osnovyi sotsiologii nestabil'nosti i riska*, Moscow, 1999, pp. 210–211.
55 Lupton, *Risk*, 1999, p. 38.
56 Douglas, 'Risk, as a forensic resource', 1990, p. 11.
57 Douglas, *Risk and Blame*, 1992, p. 16.
58 Douglas, 'Risk as a forensic resource', 1990, p. 12.
59 Lupton, *Risk*, 1999, p. 20.
60 Douglas, *Risk Acceptability*, 1986, pp. 5, 23.
61 Ibid, p. 29. Our emphasis.
62 Douglas, *Risk and Blame*, 1992, p. 46
63 Douglas, *Risk Acceptability*, 1986, p. 30.
64 Ibid, pp. 37–39.
65 A. Wildavsky and K. Dake, 'Theories of Risk perception: Who fears what and why?', *Daedalus*, Special Issue on *Risk*, Fall 1990, pp. 42–44.
66 M. Douglas and A. Wildavsky, *Risk and Culture: An Essay on the selection of technological and environmental dangers*, University of California Press, Berkeley, 1982, p. 138.
67 J. Adams, *Risk*, University College London Press, London, 1994, chapter 2.
68 Douglas, 'Risk as a forensic resource', 1990, pp. 2–3.
69 For more on some of these issues see S. Miles, *Social theory in the real world*, SAGE, London, 2001, chapters 2–4, 6. Giddens argues the main trends here are the end of history, a use of the past to help shape the present, alternation in the regional distribution of power, the rise of new social movements, new novel political agendas and 'the declining grip of the West over the rest of the world' (Giddens, *Consequences of Modernity*, 1991, pp. 50–52). In their book, *A Future Perfect: The Challenge and Hidden Promise of Globalisation* (2000), John Micklethwait and Adrian Woolridge argue that

there are five false myths regarding globalisation, namely that it leads to the triumph of big companies, ushers in global products, means the end of the traditional business cycle, involves a zero-sum game in which some win and others lose and finally, globalisation supposedly means that geography doesn't matter (J. Micklethwait and A. Woolridge, *A Future Perfect: The Challenge and Hidden Promise of Globalisation*, William Heinemann, London 2000, p. 100).
70   S. Lash and B. Wynne, 'Introduction' to Beck, *Risk Society*, p. 3.
71   A.A. Bekarev, 'Sotsiologiia nestabil'nosti', *Biulleten' Akademii gumanitarnykh nauk*, Nizhnyi Novgorod State University, 1997, No. 4, p. 34.
72   Ibid, p. 35.
73   Summarised in A. Touraine, *Vozvrashchenie cheloveka deistviushchego. Ocherk sotsiologii* (Translation from French), Moscow Nauchnyi mir, 1998, p. 36.
74   A.A. Bekarev, 'Sotsiologiia nestabil'nosti', *Biulleten' Akademii gumanitarnykh nauk*, Nizhnyi Novgorod State University, 1997, No. 4, p. 37 and Ibid, p. 40.
75   N. Smakotina, *Osnovyi sotsiologii nestabil'nosti i riska*, p. 29.
76   Ibid, p. 22.
77   Ibid, p. 39.
78   Ibid, p. 84.
79   S. Nikitin and K. Feofanov, 'Sotsiologicheskaia teoriia riska: v poiskakh predmeta', *Sotsiologicheskie Issledovaniia*, 1992, No. 10, pp. 120–127.
80   Giddens, *Consequences of Modernity*, 1991, p. 7.
81   Ibid, p. 21.
82   A. Giddens, 'Elementy teorii strukturatsii', in *Sovremenaia sotsial'naia teoriia: Bourdeau, Giddens, Habermas*, Novosibirsk State University Press, 1995, pp. 41–2. See also J. Franklin (ed.), *The Politics of Risk Society*, Polity, 1998, p. 20.
83   Giddens, *Consequences of Modernity*, 1991, p. 35.
84   Ibid, p. 34.
85   Ibid, p. 35.
86   Ibid.
87   Ibid, Table 1, p. 102.
88   Beck, *Risk Society*, 1992 p. 9.
89   Ibid, p. 10.
90   Giddens, *Consequences of Modernity*, 1991, p. 16.
91   Ibid, p. 46.
92   Beck, *Risk Society*, 1992, p. 4.
93   Giddens, *Consequences of Modernity*, 1991, p. 35. Our emphasis.
94   Ibid, Figure 1, p. 59 and Figure 2, p. 71.
95   Ibid, p. 92.
96   Turner, *Orientalism, postmodernism and globalism*, 1994, p. 177.
97   Beck, *Risk Society*, 1992, p. 21.
98   Giddens, *Consequences of Modernity*, 1991, p. 108.
99   Ibid, p. 128.
100 Ibid, pp. 139–146.
101 Ibid, pp. 147–148.
102 Ibid, pp. 126–137.
103 Ibid, p. 151.
104 Ibid, pp. 151–153.
105 Ibid, p. 154.
106 Ibid, Figure 4, p. 160.
107 Ibid, p. 161. For more on the role of the social movements see E. Lara-a, H. Johnson and J.R. Gusfield (eds), *New social movements: From ideology to identity*, Temple University Press, Philadelphia, 1994. On their role in a risk society see M. Hajer and S. Kesselring,

'Democracy in the Risk society? Learning from the new politics of mobility in Munich', *Environmental Politics*, 1999, No. 3, pp. 1–23 whereas on their transformation into 'risk movements' see J. Halfmann, 'Community and life chances: Risk movements in the United States and Germany', *Environmental Values*, Vol. 8 (2), 1999, pp. 177–197.

108 Giddens, *Consequences of Modernity*, 1991, Figure 5, p. 163 and Figure 6, p. 166.
109 Ibid, pp. 172–173. Giddens remarks refer to the end of the twentieth century but are still applicable today.
110 Turner, *Orientalism, postmodernism and globalism*, 1994, p. 177. Our emphasis.
111 Beck concurs with Douglas that risks are unequally distributed, but he makes it absolutely clear that he is not simply referring to the existence of different risks, according to social class. For Beck the diffusion of risks transcend social classes regardless of their power and wealth. He does concede, however, that there is concentration of risks among the poor and weak but argues that 'even the rich and powerful are not safe from them (risks)' and adds that in long-term, 'perpetrator and victim sooner or later become identical'. As a consequence 'risk positions are *not* class positions'. Risk therefore becomes more generalised and crosses the class structure. (Beck, *Risk Society*, 1992, pp. 37–39. Our emphasis.)
112 Douglas, 'Risk as a forensic resource', 1990, pp. 15–16. Our emphasis.
113 Thus Giddens writes 'modernity is a distinctly Western project' because of 'the diffusion of Western institutions across the world'. (Giddens, *Consequences of Modernity*, 1991, pp. 174–175. Our emphasis.)
114 Turner, *Orientalism, postmodernism and globalism*, 1994, p. 179. Our emphasis.
115 Beck, *Risk Society*, 1992, pp. 37–39.
116 Ibid, p. 115.
117 Ibid, p. 133.
118 Ibid, p. 144.
119 Ibid, p. 46.
120 U. Beck, *The Reinvention of Politics: Rethinking modernity in the Global social order*, Policy, London, 1997, pp. 44–46.
121 Ibid, p. 97.
122 Ibid, p. 104.
123 Ibid, pp. 133–134.
124 Ibid, pp. 149–150.
125 Ibid, p. 175.
126 Beck, *Risk Society*, 1992, p. 229.
127 A. Giddens, *Beyond Right and Left: The Future of Radical Politics*, Cambridge, Cambridge University Press, 1994; A. Giddens, *The Third Way: The renewal of Social Democracy*, Polity, London, 1998 and A. Giddens, *Runaway World: How globalisation is reshaping our lives*, London, Profile books, 1999, chapter 5.
128 Al'gin, *Risk i ego rol' v obshchestvennoi zhizni*, Moscow, Mysl', 1989, pp. 19–20.
129 Probability, following Spirkin, is defined as 'the degree to which certain actions can be realised under certain conditions'. (A. Spirkin, *Osnovy filosofii*, Moscow, Politizdat, 1988, p. 218.)

Chapter 2
Russia's Risk Society

Building upon the previous chapter's review of various theories, concepts and schools of thought concerning the evolution and development of risk, modernity and a risk society, this chapter outlines the risks existing in Russia and examines ways in which contemporary Russia can be viewed as a 'risk society'.

Risk in a society in transition

The reform of Russia and its transition to a modern society in turn requires the reform of the entire system of social relations, including the modernisation of productive forces and the relations of production. This process is connected to innovations in different spheres of society but the latter cannot be easily predicted and innovation always carries with it an element of risk. In other words, every act of innovation produces innovational risk. Risk has become the norm of social relations as Russian society is dramatically changing and undergoing a new stage of modernisation. Thus, the transition from a modern industrial society to a risk society produces certain types of modernisation and development and engenders new types of risk.

Every stage in a society's development is characterised by a certain type of risk. If pre-modern societies were characterised mainly by risk engendered by natural factors and by people's inability to resist the natural elements then the transition to a post-modern industrial society also brings about new types of risk. They come into existence because of the human factor and as a result of mistakes made. This is what Giddens referred to in the previous chapter as flaws in the effectiveness of the system and unintended consequences of any decisions or policies introduced.

The rapid development of information technology, which accompanies the transition to a post-industrial society, strengthens the likelihood of individual or group disorientation in the information space (i.e. the problem of pressure of virtual reality). Thus during the process of societal development, different types of risk are being produced. Consequently innovational risk might be characterised as individual/group vulnerability in the face of different risks of the type outlined in Chapter 1 produced by Russian modernisation itself. Following Beck, it is possible to note that these hazards arise due to the irrational use of science and technology.

In societies experiencing transition, risk has its own peculiarities. Individuals and groups face the loss of old patterns of social relations and the demise of old social mechanisms, which have lost their effectiveness. However, the new forms of social relations and social mechanisms have not yet been fully worked out. This situation gives rise to greater uncertainty and risk. It means that risk in a society in transition occurs alongside other social, economic and political contradictions, which are also on the increase. This reflects a certain period of transition as society moves from one stage of development to another. The extent of risk is defined by the scale and degree of contradiction prevailing.

As a rule, risk is latent in character in societies evolving without social shocks due to the effectiveness of integration mechanisms and the high level of social cohesion. By contrast, long-term instability, deep social contradictions, conflicts and unclear social goals lead to the escalation of risks. In these cases, the entire society becomes a field of risk (a risk society) in which escape from one risk situation does not lead to reduced risk but gives rise to an even riskier situation. Thus one difficult situation is overcome, but another quickly replaces it. This escalation of risk becomes a key feature of societies in transition. Following Beck, the Russian sociologist Oleg Yanitskii has argued that the transition to a risk society involves the production and reproduction of risk in different spheres of the economy, politics and society. It also means that contemporary risk societies are difficult to evaluate, so risks are hard to calculate and, as a rule, risks are also difficult to address. As their reflexivity is weakened, societies have fewer opportunities to neutralise the effects of different forms of risk on their sources of livelihood. The environment itself becomes a generator and distributor of risk. As a result of the accumulation of risks in different surroundings (both natural and social), the present determines future risks. Finally, Yanitskii points out that the production of risk often supplants the production of wealth and welfare.[1]

Thus in general, risk is a set of hazards which threatens peoples life and activity. The escalation of risk, and its permanence, is the main attribute of a risk society. Certain types of risk exist in societies undergoing transformation, such as Russia. As we saw in the previous chapter, the analysis of the nature of risk and descriptions of a risk society, have so far been largely confined to economically advanced Western countries, which have passed through different stages of modernisation. In this chapter, we will attempt to examine contemporary Russian society in terms of risk theory whilst bearing in mind the fact that Russia was a latecomer in the modernisation process.

The peculiarities of Russian modernisation

The period of rapid and large-scale social change and long-term instability has determined the process of modernisation of Russian society. The desire for democratisation of social relations and a modern way of life found their expression in the total rejection of totalitarianism, particularly among the younger generation. As a result of the command-administrative system of management (planning), a large number of contradictions exist in Russia. The resolution of existing problems was possible only through further modernisation and so the current social changes being undertaken reflect the next (routine) stage during the transition from totalitarianism to a post-modern society in Russia.

However, this process has its own peculiarities in Russia's case. It is impossible to understand Russia's current phase of modernisation and the role of young people in this process without taking this factor into consideration. First of all, this *process of change is determined by thousands of years of history*, marked by many different kinds of 'modernisation' which took place at different stages in Russia's historical development from Peter the Great through to Lenin, Stalin, Khrushchev, Brezhnev, Gorbachev in Soviet times then Yeltsin and Putin in the post-Soviet era. Of course, each phase of modernisation was different from the preceding one, but they all had something in common, in the sense that they promoted the reproduction of originality, independence and integration of Russia into the world system. The fact that modernisation in Russia is perceived as a process of renaissance and is linked with historical transitions, demands a careful choice of a transformation model. Russia's experience over the last decade and a half proves that the 'transplantation' of any pre-prepared models, such as Westernisation, Europeanisation and/or Americanisation, can have adverse consequences by producing more risk.

Secondly, it is necessary to take into account the *peculiarities of the historical consciousness of Russians*, including the younger generation, which also influences the process of modernisation. 'Jealousy' of the West has always been a part of the Russian psyche, but the need to make certain historical choices has also played a key role. Russian attitudes towards the West has always oscillated from rapprochement (close relations) to confrontation. This trend is rooted in the debates and divisions in Russian philosophy and sociology between those seeking to emulate Western patterns in Russia (westerners) and their (Slavophile) opponents favouring a more Russian approach. This is why attempts at the imitation of the West, sooner or later, conflicts with traditional Russian values and meets with some form of resistance. Experience shows that these values are well ingrained in Russian consciousness. We must also remember that the majority of Russia's younger generation, whose parents and grandparents were brought up believing in a socialist view of justice, had most of their rights guaranteed by the state, not just in theory, but in practice as well. Generations for which, the *labour right* (right to work, free education and medical care as well as other forms of social protection) was part of the reality of their daily lives, are unlikely to be inclined to unconditionally accept a new form of modernisation which would not provide past social guarantees. Furthermore, the Soviet generation still retains their past 'genetic code' and has transmitted some of their motivations to the post-Soviet generation. At this stage reproduction of this kind of motivation exists. The positive affect of socialist values on peoples' view of reality as well as on existing modernisation theories is obvious. However, we must not ignore the negative aspects of socialist practice which are frequently marked by subjectivism and voluntarism as they are equally as important. In this sense, it must not be forgotten that the collapse of the former socialist model has to a large extent determined the character of Russian modernisation throughout the 1990s.

Thirdly, Russia's totalitarian past has also influenced the present. Russia suffered from a lack of freedom, virtually total repression and from a high degree of state control. As a result, inertia was widespread. This meant *dependency*, a tendency not to express strong opinions and to rely on any kind of power and state. Nowadays, Russia is suffering from the so-called 'post-totalitarian syndrome',[2] which has resulted in intolerance and a strong desire to fasten one's ideas. This situation can be reversed when the notion of collectivism is stronger than the idea of individualism, when ideological unity is replaced by a lack of ideology and when morals are stronger than immorality. The latter is a product of the changes in the fundamental views of Russians in the last decade but is also the consequence of the reproduction of post-totalitarian consciousness in a very destructive form. All of this, of course, does not coincide with the normal understanding of modernisation, which stresses individual autonomy and freedom. This is why Russia's modernisation process is closely linked to the need to overcome the aforementioned contradictions.

Fourthly, there is the *question of globalisation*. According to Vladimir Boxer, Russia views globalisation as a threat for several reasons: firstly, it is 'foreign to the Russian elite and new middle class'; secondly, globalisation is seen as being pro-American in orientation, so being 'anti-global' is equated with 'anti-Americanism'; thirdly, globalisation has so far produced more disadvantages than advantages and hence finally, globalisation is said to conflict with 'Russia's *vital* national interests'.[3] Against this backdrop, it is hardly surprising that Russian modernisation is largely based on the premise that Russia must shorten the extent to which it lags behind the West. At the same time, Russia does not want to repeat errors of the past (i.e. become over-reliant on the West) as this is not in Russia's geopolitical interest. This stance is not necessarily anti-Western in orientation, it is simply that Russia wishes to protect her national interests. How effectively, Russia is able to pursue these interests will vary from one risk stage to the next, but they are nevertheless a crucial part of the reform process and vital to the reproduction of Russia and its society. Thus the transition to a risk society also has implications for future Russian foreign policy. Russia's modernisation is best described as 'late' modernisation. The latter involves an extended transitional period and is only being realised, not in leaps and bounds, but in a gradual manner, and then not without systematic shocks. The degree to which the Russian population feel that they have 'gained' or 'lost' tells us a great deal about the effectiveness of Russia's current process of modernisation. Public opinion in Russia has to a large extent been shaped by the adverse results of Russia's privatisation process under Yeltsin. This has led to various legal, economic and social barriers being put in place throughout Russia, but these mechanisms have proved too weak to prevent a private sector monopoly from emerging. The latter is no better and no more effective than its old Soviet state counterpart.

Risk production in Russia during the reform period

Russia is a rich country. Rich in natural resources with 45 percent of world gas supplies, 23 percent of the world's coal and 13 percent of its oil. These resources are worth, according to conservative international estimates, around 32–35 trillion dollars. Per-capita wealth suggests Russia should be a well-developed country.[4] Russia also possesses great intellectual potential. Its scientists were responsible for many major scientific developments and inventions throughout the last century. Nowadays only the United States has more scientists and engineers per 10,000 population than Russia.[5]

During the transition from the ineffective Soviet socialist system to a Western market economy, a new process of modernisation began in Russia. The experience of the years of Gorbachev's perestroika and Yeltsin's reforms shows that there are better ways to modernise societies. These two leaders totally ignored all of the aforementioned peculiarities as well as past Russian experiences of modernisation. This has generated many new mistakes and caused the de-stabilisation of Russian society. As a result, the socio-economic base of its society, which was created by past generations, and which allowed Russia to make a successful transition from a backward to modern industrial society, was destroyed.

Despite the obvious backwardness of Russia in comparison to the advanced Western countries as judged by a range of criteria (the tempo of socio-economic progress, labour divisions, the degree of mechanisation, the qualifications of the labour force and so on), it is still possible to refer to Soviet society as an industrial society. This means that the late Soviet phase should not have been addressing industrialisation, but dealing with the modernisation of a developed socialist society. When Gorbachev's reform strategy was being considered and implemented, there was a fierce struggle between old patterns of policy and behaviour and new ones. This led to a state of permanent instability in which reform was only partial or else past and current leaders introduced reforms which destroyed most of the social system. The only reforms which might prove successful and constructive for Russia are those in which innovation is possible alongside renovation so that the social structure and relations can be renewed. The coup of August 1991 failed to restore the balance and simply constituted an attempt to substitute the Gorbachev model of risk management with a pre-Gorbachev one. Russian society in moving away from totalitarianism under Gorbachev only experienced the influence of pseudo-alternatives. Russia found herself facing a chaotic situation which lay somewhere between the new patterns of social relations and the demise of the old ones, which were now considered obsolete. For Russian democrats this was the only way to reform. For instance, Russia was moving towards the greater economic choice provided by a liberal market economy but to a large extent was not holding onto the social guarantees provided by a socialist system. This is why the pseudo choice make by so-called democrats put Russia and its citizens at risk. The choice was supposed to be between the personal freedoms typical in Western liberal democracies and the social protection provided by Soviet socialism. In the end, Russian democrats asked people to choose between freedom and protection, which was nonsense. Unfortunately, in the process, the important democratic principle of 'justice' was not taken into account. Social justice should have been one of the prizes Russia received in its transition to democracy and in its latest phase of modernisation, but this failed to happen.

An in-depth analysis of the main trends in the 1990s is beyond the scope of this chapter, so suffice it to say that the following are some of the main gains and losses since the collapse of communism. Among the gains are:

- the improved availability of a wide range of consumer goods;
- an increase in private investment (produced by easing restrictions on the size of land-holdings, the percent of foreign ownership in local firms and on the repatriation of profits);
- a thriving private sector (which consists of a mix of kiosk capitalism and large department stores);
- falling inflation (from 900 percent in 1992 to around 19 percent by 2000) and
- the emergence of a small affluent business class.

However, such progress (if we can call it that), has been achieved at great cost and risk. There is a broad consensus that Russia's transition to the market economy has so far been unsuccessful. On the downside, the losses include:

- a decline in Russia's GNP since 1989 (by around 53 percent in the last decade);
- plummeting production;
- limited trade with the East (largely due to a lost East European export market) and the West;
- local industries which are still adversely affected by a weak domestic market;
- enterprise closures have led to rising unemployment (currently at around 10 percent of the economically active population);
- a huge budget deficit for most of the 1990s;
- high interest rates (around 5 percent per month) which threaten Russia's ability to service its external debt (13 percent of Federal expenditure);
- the fact that many people do not get paid, so over one in three Russians are living below the poverty line and finally;
- Russia has accumulated huge debts at home (US$60–80 billion) and abroad (around US$147 billion).

All of these trends are evident in Table 2.1.

In August 1998, the bubble finally burst. Russia was forced to devalue the rouble, the banking system collapsed, inflation skyrocketed, imports fell, output declined still further and most of society was badly affected. It was not so much that Russia now consisted of a society of 'rich' and 'poor', but was largely composed of 'have-nots'.

Although it was felt that this situation might de-rail Russia's experiment with the market, it eventually signalled the demise of Yeltsin and the rise of Putin. We shall explore this transition to a new risk situation below.

As a result, changes in the socio-economic and political system and in ideological and moral norms were accompanied by the collapse of economic, political and social structures. This situation influenced Russia's entire system of social relations. The last attempt at modernisation undertaken in the late twentieth century by Gorbachev and Yeltsin failed and now Russia finds itself in a deep systemic crisis at the start of this century.

Risk production factors in Russia

At least three variables have determined Russia's transition to a risk society.

Economic collapse and social crisis

The first factor associated with the crisis is connected with the social and economic consequences of the reforms. The disintegration of the USSR and with it the collapse of Russia's economy, the breakdown of its established economic links (with other former Union Republics as well as with the former Socialist Bloc) and the virtual standstill in most branches of industry, has led to a dramatic decline in production. For instance, by 65 percent in the food and chemical industry, 62 percent in machine tools, 65 percent in construction and 86 percent in light industry since the mid-1980s.[6] During the course of Russia's reforms, her GDP has decreased by 38 percent; industrial output has fallen by 53 percent on average and production in other sectors of the economy has declined by between 60–70 percent. By the late 1990s (1998), Russia was ranked sixteenth in the world after India, Brazil, Indonesia, Mexico and South Korea.[7] This has meant firstly that the Russian economy has not been able to feed all of its population and secondly that there has been an unprecedented fall in real incomes among the majority of the Russian population leading to a rapid decline in their standard of living. This in turn has led to falling consumption. Thus by the late 1990s consumption in Russia stood at the level it was two decades before.

Table 2.1 Economic trends in Russia, 1991–2001

Indicator	1991	1993	1995	1997	1999	2000/1
Pop. (millions)	148.5	148.6	148.3	147.5	146.6	144.9
No. of unemployed (as % of econ. active pop.)	–	3.95	9.5	11.8	12.9	9.2[a]
GDP growth (annual % change)	-5.0	-8.7	-12.6	0.8	5.4	4.9[b]
Wage arrears (as % of GDP)	80.9	978.5	184.3	26	n.a.	n.a.
External debt (billion US$)	67.0	112.7	120.4	130.8	138.8	147
Inflation (% of prev. year)	92.7	896	132	11	36.5	23.7[c]
Budget deficit as % of GDP	2.9	-7.4	-5.4	-7.0	-1.6	3.5
Number living below official poverty line (% of pop.)	n.a.	31.5	24.7	20.6	40.0	n.a.

Key: [a] May 2001   [b] January 2001   [c] June 2001
Sources: *Sotsial'noe polozhenie i uroven' zhizni naseleniya Rossii 2000*, Goskomstat, Moscow, 2000, pp. 21, 30, 65, 180; *Bank of Finland, Russian Economy: The month in Review*, June and July 2001; Business Central Europe, 28 August 2001; Central Bank of the Russian Federation, 26 August 2001; *Economist*, 4 May 2001.

Current wages largely correspond with the official definition of the 'poverty line' for most Russians. According to official data, nearly 30 percent of Russians live below the poverty line, but independent estimates suggest that around 40 percent suffer from extreme poverty.[8] The situation in 1998 is shown in Table 2.2.

Table 2.2   Russian population in 1998 according to income levels

Category	Percent of total population	Average monthly income (in dollars, $)
Rich	3–5	more than 3,000
Well-off	15	1,000–3,000
Average	20	100–1,000
On poverty line	20	50–100
Poor (i.e. below official poverty line)	40	less than 50

Source: V. Ivanov, 'The social protection of the population as a factor of social security', in *Sotsial'noe znanie v Rossii: Nasledie, vyizovy, perspektivy (Materialy simpoziuma Moskva, 28 Fev. 1998g)* (UNESCO Bulletin No. 3, Institute of Socio-Political Research, Moscow, 1998), p. 11.

One in two young people are in danger of losing their main source of income at any given moment in time. The risk of unemployment is one of the main social consequences of the deepening social and economic crisis in Russia. By May 2001, there were just over 9 million unemployed in Russia, but this figure does not include large-scale latent unemployment. Groups of so-called 'semi-unemployed' who work in state enterprises for 2–3 days a week or else are on compulsory holiday as their enterprises have not closed are not included in the previous category. At the start of 1998, no fewer than 13 percent of the population were said to be completely or semi-unemployed. In some regions only half the population work.[9] The collapse of the system of state paternalism and the emergence of new commercial and other types of economic structures has influenced the size of the economically active population because employers are now demanding different things than they did in the past. This has occurred alongside the deterioration in the working conditions and technological degradation of the Russian economy. As a result, Russia's accumulated labour potential is not being fully utilised. Under these conditions, the so-called 'survival model' of behaviour has become the only means of adaptation for Russians in the light of the difficulties brought about by the transition to a risk society. This roughly corresponds to Giddens' pragmatic acceptance category.

In order to survive, Russians, especially those who live in rural areas, are forced to rely on small pieces of land (their dachas) to help meet their food needs or to take a secondary job (i.e. most Russians have more than one job and often work at several places at the same time). This is typical of about a third of the population and is particularly common amongst the middle aged and younger generation. The consequence is that a large proportion of well-qualified workers are at risk of either never finding reasonably well paid work, of becoming 'disqualified' or of not finding a job at all. This is partly the outcome of de-traditionalisation in contemporary Russia.

The deep polarisation of incomes evident in Table 2.2 has resulted in the strengthening of social differentiation in Russian society. The 'shock therapy' policy, corruption and illegal privatisation of state property have led to hyperinflation and increased the gap between rich and poor. According to different estimates, the Dino income coefficient ranges from 10 to 25 times in Russia nowadays. It is well known that the growth in the rate of the Dino income coefficient increases the likelihood of the degradation of society by up to eight times and blocks upward social mobility and social participation. All of these phenomena exist in contemporary Russia.

Income polarisation and differences in life chances has led to the emergence of 'two Russia's', two different worlds. Russia's population is divided according to living standards, lifestyles, orientations, types of behaviour and patterns of consumption. These two groups of the Russian population are not similar in size. The smallest group consists of the very rich, the 'New Russians' whilst the largest group (the 'New Poor') includes most of the population. Poverty has increased because the number of state enterprises subsidised via the state budget has declined leading to the closure of factories and chronic shortages of income. The large majority of the scientific and cultural intelligentsia, including well-qualified engineers and white-collar employees, are also included in this group. Most of Russian youth are also poor. The new rich are not oriented towards production but instead focus on the redistribution and consumption of their own material wealth. Moreover they are willing to engage in criminal activities in order to enhance it. At the same time, this group has accumulated a great deal of finance, which under the conditions of an underdeveloped democracy, means that they are able to usurp economic and political power. This leads to the risk of deformation of social reproduction when production is in decline, but the redistribution and non-stop consumption of wealth produced by earlier generations still takes place.

There have also been significant changes in the position and social function of the Russian middle class. As a consequence according to the Russian sociologist, Zinaida Golenkova, Russia has replaced its former middle class of intellectuals and members of the intelligentsia with a new middle class of entrepreneurs.[10] This new middle class has not, however, brought about stability, instead it has lined its own pockets and significantly improved its own status at the expense of the rest of the population which has been marginalised and put at greater risk.

The extremely low level of wages does not correspond to the rising cost of living (the increase in food, transport, housing and medical costs), which means that many people have had to do without the latter. Thus a 2001 OECD report entitled *The Social Crisis in the Russian Federation* shows that those with smaller incomes cannot afford to pay for drug prescriptions, have laboratory tests carried out or pay for essential hospital or dental care.[11] At the same time, unemployment has placed restraints on labour market opportunities. Uncertainty about how to resolve these problems, means the degree of risk intensifies. All these factors taken together increase the possibility of risk and with it rising social tensions and social instability.

Furthermore, rapid changes in the physical, mental and health conditions of the population have resulted in the continuing de-population of Russia. This is the result of an increased death rate, a major outcome of which is falling Russian life expectancy (see Table 2.3). This rapid decline in health status and conditions has been further exacerbated by the introduction of a fee paying medical service. The fact that most enterprises have closed, together with their labour protection departments, has meant a higher level of industrial injuries, poisonings and accidents in Russian factories. This has also pushed the death rate in an upward direction. All in all, Russians have paid a heavy social price for reform.

Malnutrition and decreased access to medical care, preventive measures and medical treatment has put the majority of Russians' health at risk. Current data shows that 30 percent of Russia's water supply is not up to WHO standards; that diets contain only a quarter of the required proteins; a half of vitamin C and a fifth of vitamin B requirements; that most diseases, infectious, heart, respiratory etc. are rising and that the death rate has exceeded the birth rate for many years now meaning that the birth-rate is insufficient to guarantee reproduction of the population and that this trend is likely to continue for some time yet (see Table 2.3). The WHO believes that 30 percent of Russia's illness arises out of environmental pollution. Russian data indicates that 17 percent of the territory of Russia falls into the category 'ecologically damaged'. The degree of air pollution is five times the permissible level and three-quarters of Russia's natural reservoirs are so contaminated that cleaning operations are virtually impossible.[12]

Table 2.3 Health status in the Russian Federation, 1991–2000

Indicator	1991	1993	1995	1997	1999	July 2000
Birth Rate (per 1,000 pop.)	12.1	9.4	9.3	8.6	8.3	9.0
Infant mortality rate (per 1,000 live births)	17.8	19.9	18.1	17.2	16.9	20.4
Death rate (per 1,000 pop.)	11.4	14.5	15.0	13.8	14.7	15.3
Life expectancy (years at birth)	69.0	68.0	64.6	66.8	65.9	67.2

Sources: A.G. Vishnevskii (ed.), *Naselenie Rossii 1998*, Moscow, 'Knizhnyi dom Universitet' 1999, p. 78; *Sotsial'noe polozhenie i uroven' zhizni naseleniya Rossii 2000*, Moscow, Goskomstat 2000, pp. 31, 60 and www.photius.com/wfb2000/countries/russia_people.html.

The key to dealing with these problems is early diagnosis. Unfortunately, poor links between the different medical establishments and uncertainty about the role of the new commercial and private medical establishments, constitutes major obstacles to improvements in illness diagnosis and prevention. The relationship between doctor and patient has also fundamentally changed. It is now based largely upon commercial considerations. However, the growth in expensive medical services has taken place at the same time as the large-scale impoverishment of the population. This means that most people are forced to do without medical care, even if it is urgently needed. Despite an increase in medical facilities, Russia's health needs are far from being satisfied. Most medical establishments face severe financial difficulties and so they often do not possess the necessary equipment and medicines to treat their patients or the food to feed them whilst they are in hospital. In many regions, financial constraints, have led to hospital closures.

All in all, Russia faces a range of different risks, some of which are typical of developing countries and others which are being experienced by more advanced nations. The aforementioned analysis shows that Russia has made a transition from a socialist society based on the production of welfare to a risk society in which there is significant economic and social degradation.

Human Rights

The second aspect of Russia's crisis has arisen because human rights have been ignored and there is no system of social protection in place. It is important to point out here that we are using the term 'human rights' in a very broad sense so this term refers not simply to the violation of political rights but also includes the lack of social guarantees and protection.

Freedom House surveys, as shown in Table 2.4, demonstrate the record of various countries in terms of the degree of political rights and civil liberties prevailing. According to Freedom House classification, countries whose combined averages for political rights and civil liberties range from 1.0–2.5 are designated 'free'; those between 3.0–5.5 'partly free' and those between 5.5–7.0 are 'not free. It is evident that Russia is within the category 'Partly Free' and well behind other East-Central European states in transition. Russians have suffered a steady decline in the level of their political rights and civil liberties since the collapse of the USSR at the end of 1991 in comparison to West Europeans or Americans. This situation arises because existing laws do not correspond with the process of modernisation and because many Russian citizens ignore the norms of society and possess a low level of knowledge about and a corresponding low level of respect for the rule of law. These variables are becoming important factors in the individualisation of risk.

The lack of social guarantees and protection is particularly noticeable in the labour sphere where breaches of the law, relating to workers rights, social guarantees, leisure and rest exist on a large scale. As a consequence, according to the Russian Ministry of Labour and Social Development data, nearly 43 percent of Russians work in conditions were there is no respect for health and safety. Not surprisingly, Russia occupies first place in terms of its high level of industrial accidents with fatal results. Thus in 1998, there were 9,564 industrial accident cases, of which over half (5,423) resulted in death.

The violation of rights does not however stop here. There are also breaches in terms of the non-payment of wages which ranges from 3–10 months. In this context, one recent OECD report on *The Social Crisis in the Russian Federation* (2001) points out that official Russian estimates put the level of wage arrears as high as 55 billion roubles in October 1999.[13]

Table 2.4 Comparative measures of 'freedom' in various countries in the New Europe, 2000 (1= Free; 7= Not free)

Country	Political rights	Civil liberties	Freedom Rating
Albania	4	5	Partly Free
Austria	1	1	Free
Belarus	6	6	Not Free
Belgium	1	2	Free
Bulgaria	2	3	Free
Czech Republic	1	2	Free
Denmark	1	1	Free
Finland	1	1	Free
France	1	2	Free
Germany	1	2	Free
Greece	1	3	Free
Hungary	1	2	Free
Italy	1	2	Free
Norway	1	1	Free
Poland	1	2	Free
Portugal	1	1	Free
Romania	2	2	Free
Russia	*5*	*5*	*Partly Free*
Slovakia	1	2	Free
Spain	1	2	Free
Sweden	1	1	Free
Ukraine	4	4	Partly Free
United Kingdom	1	2	Free
USA	1	1	Free

Key: a Political rights   b Civil Liberties   c Freedom rating
Source: *Freedom House survey results for 2000* cited at freedomhouse.org/research/freeworld/2001/table.html.

But it is not just a question of non-payment of wages. Due to inflation and the mismanagement of economic affairs, wages in real terms are low. In 1998, for instance, they stood at 48 percent of their 1990 level and by 1999 had declined to 30 percent of their late Soviet level. An estimated 140,000 Russian enterprises are faced with frequent, chronic wage non-payment. As a result because a third of those who work do not have sufficient money to live on,[14] many people in Russia are forced to sell possessions on the streets or in underground subways near metro stations. These can either be new items, such as blouses bought in the market for 100r and then sold at a profit, or other items, such as books. In Soviet times, this was called 'speculation', but in the new market economy, it is tolerated. In addition, people's property rights are also being constantly breached. Furthermore, no guarantees at all are given to small bank account holders, who constitute the large majority of bank users in Russia. Breaches of the 1995 'Law on the protection of savings' shows that the Russian state has stopped regulating this sphere and is constantly shirking its responsibilities. The existence of corrupt legal mechanisms and agencies means that this situation is unlikely to change in the near future. This applies as much to commercial as it does to state banks. For instance, one survey carried out by the Centre for the Study of the Sociology of Human Rights, ISPR, RAN in 1999 asked the question: 'Do citizens have the right to have their human rights protected and to be free?'. The replies were as follows: no one said 'yes', 44 percent said 'partly', 54 percent replied 'no' and 2 percent gave 'no reply'. Such subjective feelings of vulnerability and lack of protection produces a state of uncertainty and anxiety. Any kind of activity involves the risk of being discriminated against, deceived or offended.

Finally, the growing in-flux of refugees, has compounded this problem, as many refugees are also being deprived of their proper social and economic rights (see below).

Political instability

The third aspect of risk is connected with political instability. For most of the Communist era, 1917–1990, the Communist Party (CPSU) was responsible for managing the level of risk. Unfortunately, it managed this process badly and was in fact a source of risk. By the time Gorbachev took over power in 1985 political inertia was widespread and a major overhaul of the Russian political system was deemed necessary. In Spring 1990, Gorbachev abolished Article 6 of the 1977 Constitution, giving the CPSU a leading and guiding role in Soviet society. This was supposed to reduce the level of risk but instead the multi-party elections and the creation of a Russian President post significantly increased the degree of risk and uncertainty. As a result, the political changes from 1985–1990 failed to solve Russia's problems, this increased the degree of risk and eventually culminated in the disintegration of the USSR in late 1991. Thus it was not the mass of the population, but political leaders who were to blame for all the shocks and turmoil faced by society.

Since the political changeover, little has changed. For the sake of simplicity, the post-communist period can be split into four stages: the first phase (January 1992–September 1993) saw a continuing executive-legislative conflict; the second phase (December 1993–December 1995) witnessed the emergence of a Presidential

Republic alongside a new parliament dominated by Yeltsin's opponents; the third phase, December 1995 to June 1996, saw the rise of a new parliament dominated by Yeltsin's opponents and his re-election as President; and the current phase (July 1996 to the present day) has seen the appointment and dismissal of 5 different Prime Ministers (Viktor Chernomrydin, Sergei Kiriyenko, Yevgenii Primakov, Sergei Stepashin and Vladimir Putin, the ex-FSB chief, who was appointed on 9 August 1999, and subsequently elected the new President of Russia in March 2000).

This constant shift in PMs, governments and the bickering between the President (executive) and the parliament (legislature), as well as unsuccessful parliamentary votes of no confidence in Yeltsin and the fact that Yeltsin was forced to storm the 'White House' and dissolve and dismantle the parliament in October 1993 meant that neither the Russian President nor its parliament has been strong enough to dominate post-Soviet politics in the 1990s. This has increased the level of political instability and risk.

The December 1993 parliamentary elections added to the crisis as Yeltsin and the centrists suffered a major defeat at the hands of Zhirinovsky's Liberal Democrats. Luckily, it turned out that the new Russian political system was adaptable and flexible enough to survive. However between 1993–1995 Yeltsin was unable to mobilise sufficient resources or the political will to counteract Duma attempts to block major economic and political decisions, such as the President's reform programme, changes to the Federal Budget, etc. This was hardly surprising as only 92 out of the 450 Duma members were supporters of Yeltsin and 56 out of the 172 people elected to the Council of the Federation opposed Yeltsin's reform strategy. Such a situation left Yeltsin with little choice but to try and reduce the level of risk (in economic, political, social and personal terms) by ruling 'by decree'.[15]

On 17 December 1995, Russia's second democratic elections to the Federal Assembly were held. Once again the level of risk and political instability increased as Yeltsin and the centrists suffered their second major defeat of the post-communist era, this time at the hands of Gennady Zyuganov's Communist Party which received 22.3 per cent of the vote as opposed to Zhirinovsky's LDPR with 11.1 per cent; Chernomyrdin's Our Home Is Russia with 9.7 per cent and Yavlinsky's Yabloko with 7 per cent. This time the CPRF potentially produced risk, the risk if it was increasingly successful that Russia might be isolated in the world, that further rebellion and sabotage of communist opponents might occur and so on. The situation might have worsened and from this point of view risk could be increased.

On the eve of Russia's 1996 Presidential elections, the level of political inertia and economic instability (corruption, rising crime, declining living standards, civil war) was extremely high. On 16 June 1996 Boris Yeltsin, the existing President of Russia since 1991, was forced to fight for power with Gennady Zyuganov, Vladimir Zhirinovsky, Grigory Yavlinskii and Alexandr Lebed. Although most people, except the New Russians, had not benefited from Yeltsin's reforms and in the run up to the first round he was still involved in an unpopular, bloody war in Chechnya, it was still widely felt that Yeltsin's victory would possibly mean less risk than if Zyuganov, head of the Communists, was voted in as President because he was viewed as a nationalist, appeared to be in favour of a return to Russia's glorious communist past and wanted to reverse Yeltsin's market reforms. The media (in particular RTR and Kiselev's NTV) painted a very black picture of Zyuganov and he became an anti-hero. As a result, put rather crudely, the choice was either a continuation of the current level of risk or political instability or greater risks if some form of the old order was restored. In the second round on 3 July 1996, Yeltsin won by gaining 53.8 percent of the vote as against Zyuganov's 40.3 percent.[16] The media once again did a very successful job in discrediting the CPRF, constantly repeating the message that if Zyuganov gained power Russia would see a return of the gulag and of widespread shortages.

Yeltsin's re-election as President did little to restore political innovation, to reverse the high degree of instability (frequent shifts of personnel) or to eradicate the aforementioned economic and social crisis or human rights violations. Over the next few years the situation went from bad to worse as Russia encountered one risk after another.

The August–September 1998 crisis was a turning point. It meant that the new (rich) Russian oligarchs who financed Russia's market transition for the last few years, suffered major financial losses. This had an adverse effect on Russia's political situation: firstly, by generating greater rivalry between Russian political elites (centred around the President; the mayor of Moscow (Luzhkov) and the PM) and secondly, by contributing to the rise of regional elites. This in turn intensified the political struggle and level of risk in the run up to the December 1999 regional and parliamentary elections and the June 2000 Presidential elections.

In the end, the choice in December 1999 was between centrists and pro-market reformers, on the one hand, and the communists and nationalists, on the other, who advocated a strong Russia. They did not necessarily adopt an anti-Western stance but instead wanted to prevent Russia from suffering downward mobility in the sphere of its economic and other relations with the outside world. What they wanted was to encourage Russia to rely on its own potential, not continue borrowing ideas and money from the West without taking into account the consequences. The results are shown in Table 2.5.

Table 2.5 Results of the December 1999 Russian Duma elections

Name of Political Party	Percent of Vote	No. of seats in Duma
Communist Party of the Russian Federation	24.29	113
Unity	23.32	72
Fatherland All Russia	13.33	67
Union of Right Forces	8.52	29
Zhirinovsky bloc	5.98	17
Yabloko	5.93	21

Source: Central Electoral Commission data cited in *Novye Izvestiya*, 30 December 1999, p. 2; *Nezavisimaya Gazeta*, 30 December 1999, p. 1; *Sevodnya*, 30 December 1999, p. 2 and *Izvestiya*, 30 December 1999, p. 3.

No matter who won, the degree of risk was likely to increase. It did not take long before the latter occurred as the tragic bombings throughout Russia in September 1999 showed. These so-called 'terrorist' bombs created a tense atmosphere during Russia's third set of elections and increased the degree of anxiety and uncertainty.

Given the transition to a risk society and the great turnaround in peoples lives, it is hardly surprising that the average Russian supported the likes of Zyuganov and also Primakov who they hoped would guarantee a return to the 'Golden Age' of the Soviets (i.e. classical modernisation). In reality, though, *Unity's* victory in December 1999 (see Table 2.5) and Putin's subsequent election as the new President of Russia in March 2000 (see Table 2.6) altered very little.

Since Putin's rise to power there has been a protracted struggle between the executive and regional leaders, media moguls and others. This has heightened the degree of uncertainty concerning the political situation in Russia and accelerated the level of different types of risk.[17]

Table 2.6 Outcome of March 2000 Presidential election in Russia (main four candidates only)

Candidate	Percent of votes
Vladimir Putin	52.9
Gennady Zyuganov	29.2
Grigory Yavlinsky	5.8
Vladimir Zhirinovsky	2.7

Source: Central Election commission results cited at www.fci.ru.

Year on year we have witnessed the elimination of the political rights of Russian citizens. Although most exercise their democratic right to vote, this has not led to greater accountability for those in power. Voters have in fact been badly manipulated by the government controlled media who have used 'dirty tactics' (including the exclusion of some voters, interfering with the registration of some candidates and their parties (such as those of Zhirinovsky and Yavlinsky), replacing respectable candidates with mafia types and misusing campaign funds (some of which went or came from abroad)), all in order to distort the election result and render them virtually worthless and 'undemocratic'. It appears that the electorate themselves have started to recognise this situation as fewer are voting and an increasing number of Russians are tending to cast their votes 'against all candidates'.[18]

In this way Russian citizens are at risk of being deprived of their constitutional rights and politicians have also failed to realise that they are undermining the social base of their reforms and endangering the possibility of more effective political management of the process of change in Russia's risk society.

Unfortunately Russia's 'democracy' is imagined or decorative in character. She possesses a political regime which is rather arbitrary in nature. Although many hoped that Putin's rise to power would put a stop to this, little, if anything, has really changed since March 2000 because Russia has become more authoritarian, especially in relation to media power. The recent clamp-down on NTV, *Itogi* and *Segodnya* are cases in point. The same is also true of the tougher stance on the regional elites. This process has not simply affected centre-periphery relations and the power wielded by regional leaders, it has also impacted on every Russian citizen.

Yeltsin's motto was 'Take as much freedom and property as you can' and regional elites and political leaders quickly cottoned onto this. Putin's reforms have been geared towards preventing regional authoritarianism and thereby retaining Russia's territorial integrity. But regional rulers are reluctant to give up power, as the July 2001 vote in the Council of the Federation demonstrated. However, the regional elite were simply trying to protect corporate interest not that of the ordinary people. The regional elite, of course, took Yeltsin's slogan literally and tried to live like kings, to ignore the Russian Constitution and to transform Russia into a Confederation. This almost put Russia in the same position as Yugoslavia. Hence, the regional elites (many of whom are former nomenklatura) have sought to act in their own interests, by for instance, making business activity dependent upon them, and by forcing local and regional business elites to converge with them.[19] Thus the regional administrative elite are not adherents to democracy and its underlying principles.

The manipulation of and passiveness among the regional population has partly facilitated this process and as a result created three types of risk: firstly, ineffective control of the chief administration which might inadvertently legitimate them; secondly, the danger is that this might reinforce their dependence on finance capital and finally, the risk is that there will be a gradual replacement of legal with oligarchical power. These risks will not be overcome until the power of regional parliaments and the legal system is strengthened and until an independent mass media exists. The mass media has played a key role in shaping public opinion, thereby ensuring that a third of those surveyed, according to Vilen Ivanov, are for the Russian government's strong stance on the regions, but another third also approve of granting independence, even though they don't live in these ethnic areas.[20] This is leading to a rethink on the nature of Russian Federalism under Putin.[21] Unfortunately, all of this might mean that young people get caught up in the fight between centre and periphery and in possible subsequent demands for separation.

Furthermore, the process of the realisation of political rights has proved difficult and contradictory. This is particularly noticeable during elections, especially Presidential ones. Thus certain voters are excluded from voting, such as those Russians living in the CIS, whilst others eligible to vote are forced to give other people their proxy (this applies to electoral candidates representing the Mafia). Other tactics used include foreign funding of certain candidates; manipulation of the mass media for political ends (this includes state as well as so-called 'independent' television and newspapers, such as NTV and *Itogi*)[22] and the rigging of voting in smaller districts and wards. All of these situations are evidence of the violation of political rights of citizens in Russia.

The political situation in Russia is strongly influenced by changes in the socio-economic sphere. Social and economic stability have not been achieved because of the aforementioned political instability. The large number of political parties and movements do not represent the *real* social interests of the majority of the population. As a result, people are developing a negative attitude towards politicians. The Russian political system is now perceived as being 'anti-people' in character. Therefore, more than 40 percent of Russian citizens totally reject the current political regime. All of these factors have meant less support for more socially oriented reforms, on the one hand, and a shift towards authoritarian forms of political management, on the other. It is obvious that contemporary Russia has all the attributes of a formal theoretical 'democracy', but this 'democracy' largely exists on paper, not in reality.

Another major factor generating risk in contemporary Russia is *ethnic conflict* within the Russian Federation[23] and of an international nature. The biggest area of ethnic conflict recently has been in the Northern Caucasus[24] where extremist groups have successfully manipulated ethnic leaders and hence the civil war in Chechnya has escalated because of separatist demands for independence. This has led to a tougher stance by the Russian government and retaliations by Chechens elsewhere in Russia.[25] This has been an extremely costly process and resulted not only in the loss of countless lives on both sides but also led to the destruction of the economic, political and social infrastructure of Chechnya itself. There is a widespread fear in Russia today that this ethnic conflict will spread to other areas of the Russian Federation and so the risk of further ethnic division and possible wars seems increasingly likely.

Linked to ethnic conflict is an increase in the proportion of *terrorist acts* and terrorism in Russia. This is not simply criminal in orientation, it is also driven by social, economic and political goals. Terrorist acts have already occurred in Moscow and elsewhere and have thereby escalated the level of conflict between rival criminal groups. This has only served to destabilise the social, economic and political situation and created a climate of fear among Russians and of Russia among foreigners. It is extremely difficult to obtain precise data on the number of terrorist acts carried out in Russia during the post-Soviet period, but increasing incidents of major conflicts between rival groups, which have risen from 64 in 1994–1995 to 700 in 1999, are clear indications of the underlying trend. If we dis-aggregate the 1999 figure, the darker side of Russian modernity emerges because these conflicts led to 75,237 threats to kill, 47,664 serious health threats, 31,140 murders and attempted murders, 523 acts of banditism and to 1,554 cases of kidnapping.[26]

This situation is closely connected, of course, to Russia's rising crime problem[27] and to the emergence of *Russia's Mafia Capitalism*.[28] In media circles, contemporary Russia is now frequently compared to Chicago in the 1920s or to Sicily. Russia's organised criminals like their Western counterparts control prostitution, drugs and gambling. There are an estimated 9,000 criminal gangs in Russia today. According to Russian estimates, criminal groups invest about 80 percent of their money in legitimate businesses, control 25 percent of the banks and 40 percent of Russia's GNP. The state is powerless to stop them. The police (*milisia*) is over-stretched, underpaid or corrupt because an estimated 90 percent of

Russian officials are said to be on the take. As a result, one in four crimes remain unsolved.[29] The August 1999 Bank of New York Russian mafia money laundering scandal is only the tip of the organised crime iceberg which stretches across the globe. All in all, the future looks bleak and an expansion in the size and power of the mafia looks likely.

This situation of growing ethnic conflict, terrorism and rising crime, especially of an organised nature, is likely to add to the level of risk and uncertainty now and in the future. These factors do not simply pose a risk to Russia itself but to each individual's life, to that of their children, family and friends and to people's ability to lead a normal life. But most importantly in terms of this book, such a situation of risk negatively shapes relations between those who live in such a risk society.

All of the aforementioned risks enter different spheres of society thereby creating sustainable risk conditions.

Russia's risk society: Common and specific trends

Our review suggested that the aforementioned features were typical of Russia's risk society during the current modernisation phase. However, although Russia possesses many similarities to Western risk societies, it also has its own unique characteristics. Due to the peculiarities of Russia's reforms since the mid-1980s, the mechanisms of social reproduction have broken down. This has led to a chain of events driving Russia towards risk. This state of uncertainty, which breaks and deforms the social reproduction mechanism, is central to any understanding and definition of Russia's risk society. It is also crucial to realise that this process varies from one society to another and this is partly what distinguishes different risk societies. Thus it is the way societies are organised, the way social links are established and the process of social interaction under conditions of uncertainty which makes Russia a unique risk society because the reproduction of life conditions and the physical, cultural and other resources which determine the latter tend to fluctuate, thereby creating a risk production process. This book, therefore suggests that the following risk factors are central to any definition of risk and to the nature of Russia's risk society.

Risk Factors

The aforementioned analysis of the consequences of Russian modernisation shows that Russia has all the typical characteristics of a risk society (see Figures 1.3 and 1.4). We can sub-divide these indicators (or factors) of risk into three main categories.

Socio-Economic

Included in this risk factor category are the collapse of the industrial, technical and scientific potential of Russia; an over-reliance on imports, Russia's technological lag behind the West, Russian reliance on Western credits' commercial bank speculation, a lack of investment in industry, the misappropriation (redistribution) of state property, and the creation of numerous financial schemes with no basis in reality. The consequence of this risk factor is an unprecedented fall in living standards, widespread economic, social and political differentiation and rising social tension.

Socio-Legal

This risk factor is linked to the lack of, and breaches of, various types of legislation as well as to the absence of a well-developed system of legislative and social protection of citizens. As a consequence, there has been a sharp divergence between rights in theory and practice. This issue concerns all Russians, but especially youth. Unfortunately, the lack of respect for the rule of law provides firm grounds for the development of the criminalisation of society in different spheres of social life as well at different levels of the power structure.

Socio-Political

This risk factor is the product of the contradictions between the separation of powers. Presidential power is not sufficiently constrained. Russia almost has a 'monarchy' and successive Russian governments seem incapable of doing their job, the parliament (Duma) in particular is weak and it seems that all politicians have no clear idea in which direction Russia is heading. This unpredictability is compounded by the actions of the President, especially during the Yeltsin era, when Yeltsin became a key source of risk in Russia. The present political regime which is based upon the 1993 Constitution is actually protected against major change. Thus any attempts at change are blocked by existing laws or by the President as arbiter of the Constitution. At the same time, as problems build up and attempts to resolve them fail, this produces a situation of constant uncertainty. This risk knows no social boundaries and affects the entire population, especially the younger generation.

Conclusion

All of these risk factors and the ever-changing environment of risk have adversely affected the social management sphere. The lack of a unified legal system and law under the circumstances of weak Federalisation and deficiencies in the stable management of politics, has paved the way for the rise of an uncontrolled bureaucracy as well as oligarchical and criminal elements. At the same time, none of these groups – bureaucrats, oligarchs and criminals – are held accountable for their actions. This especially applies to law enforcement agencies who largely serve Russia's corrupt political regime and their corporate interests.

Our analysis of Russia shows that its risk environment is different to that of the West. It is virtually impossible due to the three risk factors outlined above, for people in Russia to take a 'calculated risk'. Trust in systems (*faceless commitments*) and trust in individuals (*facework commitments*) are constantly shifting and the degree to which individuals feel a sense of *ontological security* also varies. Most

Russians are still searching for their self-identity in a new post-communist society undergoing transition. We have also challenged Giddens' view that modernity is a largely Western project in arguing that modernisation is also occurring in Russia. Although we would concede that the spreading of Western values and institutions has accelerated Russia's transition to a risk society, this chapter also points out that Russia has its own unique factors which would make it a risk society, even without the influence of external Western variables. This chapter therefore shows that we must always take into account the specifics of a country's situation because the degree of risk, the extent of disembedding, the effectiveness (or otherwise) of integration mechanisms and the reactions to risk (pragmatic acceptance, sustained optimism, cynical pessimism and radical engagement) will vary from country to country. The origins and causes of risk (design faults, operator failure, unintended outcome etc.) and a country's ability to cope with risk will also vary accordingly.

The outcome is that the main characteristic of Russian society at the start of the twenty-first century is that the degree of risk and the number of risk factors are getting stronger. In fact risk is becoming a permanent feature in Russia today. In Russia's case, risk has been produced by two factors: the collapse of communism and the transition to a new form of society, on the one hand, and by the shift from pre and simple modernity to reflexive modernisation, on the other. Unfortunately, under Russian conditions most changes can be described as de-modernisation hence risk has a rather distorted, irrational character. Thus the threats outlined in this book transcend social boundaries and affect all the population's social and personal lives.

Having outlined various sociological theories of risk in chapter 1 and assessed in what ways Russia might constitute a risk society in this chapter, the following two chapters focus on the impact of risk on one particular group in society, youth. Our aim is to show how young people have coped with growing up in different risk societies.

Notes

1. O.N. Yanitskii, 'Rossiya vseobshchego riska', in *Sotsiologiia i Obshchestvo. Tezisy dokladov Pervogo Vserossiiskogo Sotsiologicheskogo Kongressa*, St. Petersburg, 2000, p. 4. See also his 'Sotsiologiia i riskologiia', in *Rossiya: Riska i opasnosti 'perekhodnogo obshchestva'*, Moscow, Instituta Sotsiologii, 1998.
2. On this see S. Averintsev, 'Overcoming the totalitarian past', *Russian Magazine*, 27 June 2001.
3. V. Boxer, 'Who will "find" Russia? How suspicions of globalization could push Russia towards the East', *Russia Watch*, No. 5, March 2001, pp. 25–31.
4. G.V. Osipov, S.K. Levashov, V.V. Lokosov and V.V. Sukhodeev (ed.), *Rossiya v poiskakh strategii: obshchestvo i vlast'. Sotsial'naia i sotsial'no-politicheskaia situatsiia v Rossii v 1999 godu*, Moscow, PiTs, ISPI, RAN 2000, pp. 17, 19.
5. Ibid.
6. Ibid, p. 4.
7. Ibid, p. 5.
8. *Sotsial'noe polozhenie i uroven' zhizni naseleniya Rossii 2000*, Goskomstat, Moscow 2000, p. 180.

9 I. Ya. Bogdanov, A.P. Kalinin and Yu. N.Rodionov, *Ekonomicheskaia bezopasnost' Rossii: tsifry i fakty*, Moscow, 1999, pp. 18, 55.
10 Z.T. Golenkova, *Transformatsiia sotsial'noi struktury i stratifikatsiia Rossisskogo obshchestva*, 3rd edition, Moscow, Institut Sotsiologii, RAN, 2000, chapter 5. For more on this see V.E. Bonnell, 'Russia's New Entrepreneurs', in V.E. Bonnell and G.W. Breslauer (eds), *Russia in the New Century: Stability or Disorder?*, Westview, Boulder Colorado 2001, pp. 175–200.
11 OECD report, *The Social Crisis in the Russian Federation*, OECD, Paris, 2001, p. 21 and Table 1.4, p. 35.
12 C. Williams, 'Russian health care in transition' in C.Williams, V.Chuprov and V.Staroverov (eds), *Russian Society in Transition*, Dartmouth, Aldershot 1996, pp. 198–199 and I.A. Grundarov, *Demograficheskaia katastrofa v Rossii: Prichiny, mekhanizm, puti preodleniya*, Moscow, URSS, 2001, pp. 25–27.
13 G.V. Osipov, S.K. Levashov, V.V. Lokosov and V.V. Sukhodeev (eds), *Rossiya v poiskakh strategii: obshchestvo i vlast'. Sotsial'naia i sotsial'no-politicheskaia situatsiia v Rossii v 1999 godu*, Moscow, PiTs, ISPI, RAN 2000, p. 109 and *Sotsial'noe polozhenie i uroven' zhizni naseleniya Rossii 2000*, Goskomstat, Moscow, 2000, p. 98.
14 *The Social Crisis in the Russian Federation*, OECD, Paris, 2001, p. 21 and Table 1.4 on p. 76. Thankfully this situation is gradually improving.
15 I. Ya. Bogdanov, A.P. Kalinin and Yu. N. Rodionov, *Ekonomicheskaia bezopasnost' Rossii: tsifry i fakty*, Moscow, 1999, p. 109.
16 *Vybory Prezidenta Rossiiskoi Federatsii. 1996. Elektoral'naya statistika*, Moscow, Ves'mir, 1996, pp. 128, 130.
17 On these trends see C.Williams, 'The New Russia: From Cold War strength to post-communist weakness and beyond', in P.J. Anderson, G. Wiessala and C. Williams (ed.), *New Europe in Transition*, Continuum, London and New York, 2000, pp. 248–266.
18 Ya. Bogdanov, A.P. Kalinin and Yu. N. Rodionov, *Ekonomicheskaia bezopasnost' Rossii: tsifry i fakty*, Moscow, 1999, p. 111.
19 Ibid, p. 110.
20 Cited in ibid, p. 120.
21 See J. Hughes, 'From Federalisation to Recentralisation' in S. White, A. Pravda and Z. Gitelman (eds), *Developments in Russian Politics 5*, Palgrave, Basingtoke, 2001, pp. 128–146.
22 On the fight against the media see 'The future of the free media in Russia', Carnegie endowment for international peace meeting report, Vol. 3 (13), 1 May 2001 and 'Russia's embattled media', *Russia Watch*, No. 6, June 2001, pp. 1, 4–14. This struggle has recently been extended to include the Internet. There are an estimated 30 million Internet users in Russia most of whom are students, college graduates, professionals or managers (E. Kiselyov and M. Castells, 'Russia in the information age', in V.E. Bonnell and G.W. Breslauer (eds), *Russia in the New Century: Stability or Disorder?*, Westview, Boulder Colorado, 2001, pp. 142–143). On the grounds that the Net is a key focus for 'computer piracy, viruses, thefts ... crime and perversion', the Russian government issued a series of laws in 1998–2000 which allows the Federal Security Service (FSB) to monitor use, including private, of the internet ('Russia's internet lags', *RFE/RL Press release*, 3 August 2001).
23 For more on this issue see C. Williams and T.D. Sfikas (eds), *Ethnicity and nationalism in Russia, the C.I.S. and the Baltic States*, Ashgate, Aldershot, 1999.
24 On this see G. Yemelianova, 'Ethnic nationalism, Islam and Russian Politics in the North Caucasus (with special reference to the Republic of Dagestan)', in ibid, pp. 120–147.
25 On the situation in Chechnya see V. Bennett, *Crying wolf: the return war to chechnya*, Trans-Atlantic publications, 2001; J.B. Dunlop, *Russia confronts Chechnya: Roots of a seperatist conflict*, Cambridge University Press, Cambridge, 1998; C. Gall and T. De

Waal, *Chechnya: Calamity in the Caucasus*, New York University Press, New York, 2000; S. Knezys and R. Sedlickas, *The War in Chechnya*, Texas and A & M University Press, 1999; A. Lieven, *Chechnya: Tombstone of Russian power*, Yale University Press, 1998; Yu. K. Nikolaev, *Chechnya Revisited*, Nova Science Publishers, 2002; A. Politovskaya, *A dirty war: A Russian reporter in Chechnya*, Harvell Press, 2001; S. Smith, *Allah's Mountains: The Battle for Chechnya*, St. Martin's Press, New York, 2001.

26 I. Ya. Bogdanov, A.P. Kalinin and Yu. N. Rodionov, *Ekonomicheskaia bezopasnost' Rossii: tsifry i fakty*, Moscow, 1999, p. 79.

27 On this issue see I. Illynsky, 'Law and Order', in C. Williams, V. Chuprov and V. Staroverov (ed.), *Russian Society in Transition*, Dartmouth, Aldershot, 1996, pp. 219–240.

28 On the mafia see A. Gurov, *Organizatsiia prestupnost' – Ne mif, a real'nost'*, Moscow 'Znanie' 1992; A, Gurov, *Krasnaia Mafia*, Moscow 'Kommercheskii vestnik' 1995; S. Handelman, *Comrade Criminal: The theft of the Second Russian Revolution*, Michael Joseph, London, 1994; A. Vaksburg, *The Soviet Mafia*, Weidenfeld and Nicolson, London, 1991.

29 I. Illynsky, 'Law and Order', in C. Williams, V. Chuprov and V. Staroverov (eds), *Russian Society in Transition*, Dartmouth, Aldershot, 1996, p. 225.

Chapter 3

Coming of Age in Different Risk Societies

In order to understand the role and place of young people in the process of social reproduction, namely the process by which societies reproduce their social institutions and social structure, we first need to have some idea of how important the younger generation are. Some basic features of the countries we shall be analysing here are given in Table 3.1 overleaf. It is evident that the size of the youth population in European countries varies from as low as half a million in Norway to 3.5 million in Romania through to between 6–7 million in France, Italy, Ukraine and the UK before finally constituting 22.6 million in Russia and a staggering 37.5 million in the United States. In the European Union (hereafter EU) in 1995, young people aged 15–25 years totalled 50.2 million or 14 percent of the total EU population. If we defined youth as those aged between 15–29 then the size of this group would increase to 80 million or 22 percent of the population of the EU.[1] By comparison, in Russia in 1999, the proportion of the population aged 15–29 years totalled 32.2 million, of which 11.5 million were aged 15–19 years, 10.6 million 20–24 years and 10.1 million between 25–29 years.[2] These statistics demonstrate that young people are a sizeable social group representing a significant social force across the globe.

As a result of the replacement of one generation by another simple or expanded reproduction of the social structure takes place. During this process, the particular social functions of youth itself become more prominent. The most important function is young people's role in society's reproduction due to which the younger generation inherits and reproduces the existing social structure and relations. In realising this function, every younger generation contributes to the maintenance of society's integration and development by bringing about innovation. Thus in this way youth development and the reproduction of society are closely inter-linked.

In general when using the term *social reproduction* we will be referring to the on-going process of societal reproduction which is essential for the evolution and development of society and the social groups within it. Depending upon the context, this process can either be destructive (retarded development), simple (repetitive) or broadening (renewal of all on a large scale). Social reproduction involves not only changes in economic variables, but also the reproduction of all kinds of social ties and relations. That is why it is possible to talk about the evolution of the system of social relations and groups in terms of cyclical reproduction.

Correspondingly, the social development of young people can also be destructive (disintegration; social exclusion), act as a form of continuity of past social experience accumulated by older generations (simple reproduction) and/or become expanded via a process of renovation or renewal of life conditions and the entire system of social relations.

Taking part in this process every younger generation is integrating themselves into the social structure. Reflecting the cyclical reproduction of the system of social relations, this process brings about changes in the place that youth occupy in the social structure.

Table 3.1 Youth in different risk societies, 2000

Country	Total pop. (million)	Youth pop. (million)	Youth in labour force (as percent)
Albania	3.5	0.6	27[a]
Austria	8.3	1.0	17.0
Belarus	10.3	1.5	n.a.
Belgium	10.3	1.2	20[a]
Bulgaria	8.3	1.2	14
Czech Republic	10.2	1.6	n.a.
Denmark	5.3	0.6	18[b]
Finland	5.2	0.7	11.2
France	59.1	7.7	9.6
Germany	82.7	9.6	12.3
Greece	10.6	1.4	12.3
Hungary	9.8	1.4	15.0[c]
Italy	57.2	6.7	14.1[d]
Norway	4.4	0.5	13.5[b]
Poland	38.7	6.5	13.2[b]
Portugal	9.8	1.4	16.4[d]
Romania	22.5	3.5	16.7[b]
Russia	*146.2*	*22.6*	*13.9[b]*
Slovakia	5.4	0.9	16.9[b]
Spain	39.8	5.6	17.3[b]
Sweden	8.9	1.0	11.5[b]
Ukraine	50.8	7.5	n.a.
United Kingdom	58.3	7.2	21[a]
USA	277.8	37.5	16.2[b]

Key: n.a.=data not available   a 1985   b 1996   c 1995   d 1994
Source: United Nations Youth Information network, 2000.

This is closely linked to patterns of social mobility. The positive nature of the changes in the quantitative and qualitative characteristics of youth is evidence of the social development of this particular socio-demographic group. The degree of social maturity is an indicator of the level of social development among young people. Social maturity of the younger generation is connected with achievements and changes in a young person's social status during the process of their integration into the social structure as well as with the nature of their identification with different social groups. This process, which is often called 'the transition into adulthood', has different meanings at different times. Approaches to the *definition* of 'youth transition' can be sub-divided according to the way in which scholars characterise the interaction between youth with its social surroundings and by their understanding of the typical consequences of the transition to adult life.[3] Thus, the transition from school to work plays a decisive role in determining their eventual coming of age.

The nature and process of achieving social maturity varies greatly according to country and the period of time.[4] In the 1960s, for example, the definition of 'youth transition' referred to the way in which young people were integrated into society relatively rapidly as they occupied a particular 'social niche' and, in line with the popular functionalist approach, researchers emphasised their acceptance of the norms of society. In this way, young people were guaranteed a place in society and made a swift transition into adulthood. In relation to the world of work, three explanations have traditionally been offered to explain rapid youth transition into the labour market, namely higher education; professional training, apprenticeships and different sorts of activities starting from white-collar to unqualified work, with the latter meaning weak prospects of occupational and social mobility.[5]

Of course, there was always a fourth option after the period of obligatory education had finished, namely unemployment, because youth transition was also becoming more complicated. Post-compulsory education was becoming more common and many young people in order, not to become unemployed, tried special professional training and took any chances to find a job. As a result of this, the process of social reproduction was also becoming more complicated. The long-term transition in the labour sphere reflected new concepts that widened functionalist understanding of the transition to adulthood. Concepts such as 'bridge', 'routes' and 'pathways' were now used to describe the transition from education (school, college, university) to work.

After the hardships of the 1970s and 1980s, Western sociologists started to use different terms in the 1990s to describe the new risks and situation such as 'trajectories'. This reflected the growing influence of structuralism. These youth trajectories also varied according to social class, gender, ethnicity, level of education, labour market conditions, the individual characteristics of the labour market entrant and young people's interests. These were the main factors but they were often beyond young people's control.

The development of post-structuralism in the 1990s, brought about significant changes in sociological analyses of the occupational self-determination of youth. The latter was now described in terms of 'navigation'. It is clear that this process refers to an individual's ability under risk society conditions to navigate the transition from education to work and thereby overcome any barriers, risks and threats along the way. Following Giddens, it is possible to argue that young people grab whatever opportunities come their way.[6] In other words, in contemporary societies young people, just like sailors, are forced to navigate their way through waves of uncertainty.

In personal terms, social mobility is an expression of young peoples' desire to achieve the same status as their parents, older siblings and friends. Conversely, the failure to achieve one's life plans or goals can lead to disappointment and a search for other ways of self-realisation.

Achievements as well as the search for alternatives are closely connected with risk and risk-taking. In the first instance, risk is determined by the limited opportunities for upward mobility among young people provided by society. As a consequence of the prevailing risk environment, young individuals in many countries, including Russia, are permanently at risk of missing out, of not achieving their desired goal in life, be it a proper vocational education, a job (let alone an interesting one), good career and promotion prospects, a good salary (adequate enough to be able to start a family) or a nice home. In cases where young people fail to realise these ambitions, they naturally search for alternatives but this also brings risks of failure and of being disadvantaged. This can lead to alienation and social exclusion and in turn start the search for other ways to a better life and a new start, such as crime.

Thus, *risk is characterised by the transition from certainty to uncertainty of the outcome among youth and the possibility of unfavourable outcomes in cases of failure.*

As the younger generation enters into social relations and starts participating in the social reproduction of society, certain demands are placed upon them. The sources of such demands, on the one hand, are the historical, social and cultural traditions of particular society; whilst on the other hand, they stem from societal goals and dominant ideas of what the future ought and should look like. Thus, society manages the direction of the social integration of youth, taking into account the necessity of certain patterns of relations and structures providing they sustain and develop society. In this way, society controls the direction of youth integration as the main task is to take responsibility for reproducing different social elements in order to maintain and sustain that particular society. However, in a risk society, as a rule, there is no, or very little notion of social goals. All of the social processes within the society become spontaneous as socialisation institutions and agencies lose control of them. The integration of young people into society becomes much more chaotic. From then on, integration is driven by the reproduction of the very elements and structures that stand in the way of the development of society. Many young people are drawn into this process either on purpose or by chance and find themselves at risk of losing their career, family, security, life, etc.

It is well-known that the nature of the process of social reproduction reflects existing social relations. In the former Soviet society ideological principles determined social expectations. Loyalty to Communist Party policy and communist ideals, enthusiastic participation in politics, the drive towards creating socialism, patriotism (understood as one's love of the motherland), internationalism and collectivism; the desire to work, social optimism and enthusiasm were the basic elements of the USSR model of citizenship and youth integration. The notion of the 'good citizen' itself meant energetic and enthusiastic participation in Soviet social and political life. Slogans such as 'Everyone is responsible for everything' or 'if not me, then who?' were typical of symbols of the previous Soviet historical epoch. At the same time, every type of youth activity was strictly regimented by ideological boundaries. Any attempt to escape from this framework was considered an act of deviance and punished. This ideological cul-de-sac was defined by the alliance between state and individual interests. However, state interests always prevailed over personal ones, it was the people for the state, not vice versa.

This model of integration was partially successful under the previous totalitarian regime. However contemporary post-Soviet society has left behind most of the aforementioned ideals and in the process also changed the expectations of the younger generation as well as youth policy. We can assess these new expectations by examining how they correspond to the specific social requirements of a modern risk society.

The neo-liberal reforms arose from an attempt to break down the former patterns of youth integration. However, some mistakes were made. Reformers failed to take into account at least two very important points. Firstly, the collapse of the old model and rejection of social control were not replaced by new mechanisms of self-regulation and self-control commonly found in other modern societies. It is no coincidence that there is the risk of collapse of society as a whole in Russia today. Secondly, the inertia associated with the old patterns of citizenship in youth consciousness was ignored. These persisted and became perverted in nature. Soviet society's dream of an active citizen remains. The question is what direction should this activity take? Yeltsin's slogan 'take as much freedom as you can' has mutated into a looting of the state. Thus in the absence of the new mechanisms of empowerment all these changes have created a different type of citizen who, conversely, lives at the expense of society.

The mechanisms of social reproduction (i.e. *the reproduction of the means necessary for life and reproduction of human forces*) appear to be equal in all modern societies, but this does not mean that the reproductive processes as a whole are similar. On the contrary, stable, transitional and crisis societies experience totally different processes of social reproduction. As can be seen in the case of Russia, a period of radical change has put youth in a different situation. Patterns of socialisation and transition differ not only from those experienced by their parents but also from older members of their own generation. Thus, although they belong to the same generation, they are very different in terms of image, experience and life-style.

Sudden social differentiation, changes in the structure of social relations and the consequent intensive level of contact between young people and the new socialisation agencies (market, employer–employee relations, fee paying education and so forth), which are not conducive to the socialisation of future generations, render inter-generational and in some cases intra-generational differences more and more significant. During periods of social transformation young people tend to reject the experience accumulated by previous generations rather than accept it. This changes the process of social reproduction at the earliest stage – the continuity stage – and increases the *risk of an unequal start in life*. Young people from different social backgrounds have different chances in life in terms of educational opportunity, career choices, starting a family and so on.

The social and economic crisis in Russia has led to a deterioration in the position of the most vulnerable groups, including young people, and brings them into conflict with society (see chapter 4). This deterioration has created another risk situation connected with *the uncertainty of life-course*. It has also affected the process of social reproduction.

Society plays a decisive role in determining strategies of social reproduction. In order to formulate specific goals and criteria, society creates the most acceptable models of socialisation. Therefore it is unrealistic to expect young people to be aware of their role in social relations or that they are the subject of social reproduction. This is more a matter of social rather than individual consciousness. When young people experience difficulties growing up and making a transition to adulthood, their only desire is to achieve a certain level of independence, to plan their life in their own way, without pausing to reflect on the social role that they play in society.

In addition, an individual's assessment of the surrounding social reality is based upon their own interests in the areas of education, career, material well-being, etc. and upon *opportunities for one's self-realisation*, i.e. whether they can realise their goals and achieve the desired status. This critical view leads to agreement with some standards and the rejection of others. Everything that contradicts an individual's goals generates not simply protest, but also leads to possible attempts to change the existing system. As a result of these innovations, young people gradually become aware of their significance (i.e. ordinary or simple reproduction) and this gives way to a renewal of the patterns of social relations (i.e. expanded reproduction). However a certain level of risk – the *risk of the new*, always accompanies any innovation. This is a phenomenon that particularly affects youth in the period of transition and during their search for a place in society. This phase is often accompanied by rejection of previous experience and innovative actions.

This strengthening of their own social position by means of such rejection may have both positive and negative consequences. Russian society was given a positive momentum by the rejection of the obsolete forms of social values and patterns of relationships (which were characteristic of the era of administrative socialism) entered into by the majority of the younger and older generation, although as experience has shown, there is still the risk that these relations will continue to be reproduced under the new post-Soviet conditions. On the other hand, rejection of the past without thinking eventually breaks down the historical traditions and consciousness of the younger generation. All of this leads to uncertainty in value systems and standards and to the *risk of either a deformed or lost identity*.

As for the concept of new models of social reproduction and citizenship, this depends upon finding an answer to two main questions. Firstly whether all structures and relations can be reproduced by the younger generation. The key issues here include: What kind of structures are young people being integrated into, what will their goals be and, finally, what will they identify with? These are crucial questions because these processes will affect not only youth itself, but society as a whole. The fact is that Russian society has not yet defined the main goals of the reforms except in very general, vague terms. Neither reformers nor their opponents under Yeltsin (and so far under Putin too) had any clear idea of what types of reforms Russia really needed. This meant that the existing reproductive mechanisms lost their ideological content, and the former have not yet been replaced by properly functioning alternatives. This gave rise to numerous contradictions between the stated, sensible ideas, and the real course of transformation in Russia during the 1990s and beyond.

We must acknowledge that neither society, the various socialisation agencies, nor parents have any notion about the social and moral values nor behaviour patterns which they expect from the younger generation. Thus Russian society finds itself in a situation of *uncertainty of values and standards*, i.e. *anomie*, experiencing feelings of alienation, and yet unable to resist the risk of reproduction of this alienation. Society cannot cope with the reproduction and spread of negative situations, crime, and the failure to prevent an increasing number of young Russians from falling into this situation.

It is well known that successful social reproduction largely depends upon the individual's ability to participate in this process and on the degree of their participation. Thus the second question, which needs to be resolved, refers to the ability of young people to develop innovative activity/strategies. This requires them not to be passive observers and a manipulated object of the social integration strategies, but instead an active participant in the process. Attitudes towards integration (passive or active) will be indicative of the level of social participation of young people.

At the same time, contemporary Russian society is characterised by an infringement of each element of the mechanism of social reproduction. First of all, the place and role of young people in this process is being distorted. Young people are being alienated from its main social function (to accept, reproduce and improve the social system). Eventually young people are becoming alienated from society. In this way the younger generation is losing its important inter-group identity, youth is being transformed from a *social* group into a *demographic* group and rapidly losing its social meaning in the process.

Reproduction of risk

The results of a Eurobarometer survey carried out by the European Union between 20 April and 7 June 1997 among a representative sample of 9,400, 15–24 year olds from the 15 Member states of the European Union showed the two sides of European modernity.[7] On the possibilities, young people expressed confidence in tomorrow's Europe and were enthusiastic about the concept of mobility; but on the downside, they were also very concerned about unemployment.

The problems facing European youth in the 1990s included firstly, the *problem of adapting* to rapid technological change in the 1970s and 1980s, the impact of which are now being felt. Hence young people now need to be more flexible in their patterns of work, are forced to make complex choices regarding education, training and employment and finally, as a consequence, they face *uncertainty* about future job prospects. Secondly, as Giddens pointed out in chapter one, late modernity has led to the *eradication of traditional types of social order*. In the case of youth, this means the breakdown of traditional ways/means of achieving adulthood. Thus the 'rites of passage' of all European teenagers as they make a transition from being a youth to becoming an adult, and thereby experience the roles, rights and responsibilities of adults, have now been extended. Thirdly, young people are having to grow up facing *increased risks*. Thus the decline of the manufacturing sectors in some parts of the USA and many European countries has led to the availability of fewer youth apprenticeships (see below). This, coupled with other variables, has increased the prospect of higher youth unemployment and had a major impact on working and family life. Fourthly, and finally, difficulties in the education sector has meant that many young people fail to acquire the essential skills necessary to negotiate the transition to adulthood successfully and experience *exclusion*. The outcome is that some sections of youth are excluded from certain areas of occupational life and from acquiring full citizenship rights, and so in the end, some young people become alienated from adults and the socialisation agencies.

In these and other areas of life, young people in the USA and Europe were supposed to make a swift transition from dependent childhood to independent adulthood. However, in many cases this has failed to happen. There are several reasons for this, the most important of which are firstly, increased reliance on the family as a source of income (but this in itself is difficult because many families are in crisis) and secondly, the fact, as we saw in chapter 1, that young people are growing up in risk societies.

In this context, the UN report on *The Global Situation of Youth: Trends and Prospects, 2000–2025* (2000) acknowledged that 'many countries have formulated strategies, policies, programmes and projects for young people' but resolving the risks facing youth is far from easy because 'young people are living at a time when profound economic, political, social, cultural and environmental changes are occurring, resulting in both *opportunities and constraints*'.[8] Factors on the constraints include globalisation, poverty, unemployment, social exclusion, external debts and financial crises; whereas on the opportunities side, better chances for trade and development, the deepening of democracy and more chances for youth participation in a range of activities which provides more opportunities for growth and learning (by and from young persons) and for youth empowerment. On balance, the UN report concludes that 'much of the potential of youth is yet to be realised'.[9] The main reasons for this are that 'seniority is valued' and so 'younger persons are often excluded from discussions and decision-making that influences their lives'. The UN argues that 'societies need to develop mechanisms for bridging this gap' and to ensure that young people don't get 'trapped in circles of exclusion' if they want to overcome poverty, unemployment and the processes of marginalisation.[10]

All in all, the dilemma facing young people today is, integration into the existing order versus mobilisation for change and development. Whereas some young people, including Russians and East Central Europeans, the Chinese and their counterparts in the rest of the world, have been 'at the forefront of movements for democracy and social justice'; others 'choose to *exit* and protest the status-quo by remaining on the outside'. This dichotomy and its resolution is one of the key issues addressed throughout this book.

The UN report goes on to emphasise that 'providing opportunities for young people contributes to social stability and cohesion'.[11] Unfortunately, constraints and insufficient youth opportunities in the education system, labour market and elsewhere has led to a disproportionate number of young people being affected by poverty, unemployment and social exclusion. Although young people have the right to have access to good education and employment prospects and to good health care, these rights are either not properly implemented or even if the appropriate legislation exists, the laws are broken far too often. In order to prevent a repeat of this situation in future, UN youth experts advocate 'better targeted social policy and understanding [of] the situation of specific groups of youth'.[12]

Thus for all the reasons outlined above, young people in Europe and America are experiencing prolonged dependency on adults. This means that youth only become 'quasi-citizens' whose rights and responsibilities are withheld or else they are exercised through their parents. Another key point is that the emergence of a risk society has made the predictability of youth transition to adulthood more uncertain than it was in the past. Furthermore, a major consequence of increased differentiation, social exclusion and marginalisation is the increased vulnerability of young people. This is especially true of young people from disadvantaged backgrounds, single parent families, the ethnic minorities and those living in inner cities or rural communities.

All of these factors when taken together mean that some young people in the new twenty-first century Europe are becoming part of a growing 'underclass', which Patricia Allatt defines as those 'groups [of young people] society casts to its margins'.[13] The consequences are that some young people are dropping out of education and the labour market, whereas others are unable to find adequate housing or they are turning to crime in order to survive. Although new youth cultures and sub-cultures are developing and these to some extent constitute survival strategies, one outcome of the emergence of the former is that young people are seen as 'risk takers'. Part of the difficulty here, however, is that no distinction is drawn between what is transient and what is permanent in so-called youth 'risk activity' (delinquency, drug taking, alcoholism, mental illness, suicide).[14] Government and public opinion alike often neglects the relationship between youth lifestyles, identity and citizenship. Following on from the previous point, even though some young people are involved in the aforementioned activities, this does not necessarily mean that all young people, some of whom are increasingly apathetic and cynical, are not interested in liberal democracy and politics. It is perhaps more a question that they are disillusioned with existing politicians. If young people vote, then they think that it doesn't have any *real impact*, so many young people simply follow the political choice of their family or parents. However only a marginal few turn to political extremism as a result of their disillusionment.

In terms of Giddens theory outlined in Chapter 1, young people are finding it increasingly difficult to make a 'calculated risk' on essential issues which affect their lives. Some sections of youth have greater faith in systems (*faceless commitments*) whilst others rely more on individuals whom they have known for long periods of time (i.e. *facework commitments*). The balance between trust in individuals and systems varies according to the nation state and so few young people have what Giddens calls *ontological security*. This is partly due to the conflict between local (nation state), European and global factors which have put youth ties to their local communities (in terms of the kinship system, religion, personalised trust etc.) under increased pressure. Some young people have merely accepted this situation or remain optimistic about the future. They would fall into Giddens' *pragmatic acceptance* or *sustained optimism* categories but other sections of youth have either become *cynical pessimists* or started to involve themselves in *radical engagement* and joined various issue based social movements in order firstly, to try and reduce the impact or transcend some of the risks mentioned earlier in this chapter, or secondly, the more fortunate sections of youth have attempted to maximise the opportunities offered to them by late modernity. However, young peoples' ability to influence their life opportunities lies largely outside of their control because of what Giddens terms *design faults* and *operator failure* by adults (neither of which young people had a part in), but the unintended consequence is that their lives, like that of many adults, are still affected.

Beck's *Risk Society* is also pertinent to any analysis of European and American youth in so far as the emergence of a risk society has not led to increased choice for young people. Instead many young people suffer from poverty, hunger and overcrowding. These risks affect all sections of youth, but they vary according to country and according to social class, family, gender, ethnicity etc. Another relevant point from Beck is that young people in the West are themselves expected to face up to risks. Thus young people are blamed for their failures (unemployment, poverty etc.). This is what contemporary social theorists call the individualisation of risk.

It is also possible to argue following Beck that the transition to risk societies in Europe and America is not just negative, but also has some positive aspects. Some of these benefits were highlighted in the 1997 Eurobarometer survey quoted earlier. It is clear that in these cases some sections of youth have managed to gain greater control over their income, time, living space, education and career, entry into the labour market and so forth even though there is still fierce competition between individuals (over skills, qualifications etc.).

However, the process of triple individualisation (liberation, disenchantment and reintegration) referred to by Beck varies according to the nation state. Some countries have had greater successes than others. Furthermore, the degree to which traditional constraints of class, family etc. have been removed and the level of disenchantment, is also uneven. Moreover, not all sections of youth have been reintegrated and developed new types of social commitment. Another difficulty is that class and family ties have partly disintegrated in Europe, but this applies to some societies (Germany) more than others (the UK for example). In many instances, young people are still heavily reliant on these traditional contacts rather than on the national education systems, the welfare state and the labour market which are at different stages of development and decay throughout the various American states as well as in the EU. Thus some countries, such as Germany and the UK, have well-established welfare systems, whereas other countries, such as Spain and Portugal, have relatively new welfare states, which only emerged in the transition from dictatorship to the democracy phase. Thus a country's ability to provide support networks for its young varies greatly in terms of its provision and effectiveness. It is therefore hard in the light of the evidence presented in this chapter to disagree with Beck when he concludes, as we saw in chapter 1, that the younger generation seems to have drifted to the margins of society. In support of this view, the aforementioned UN report points out that in most Western countries all significant prospects for young people (job, career, salary, starting a family etc.) are under threat. But the degree of risk varies in each society.

It is important to point out here that all young people experience some degree of social exclusion, discrimination and so on. Levels are higher among ethnic minorities, the poorly qualified and among new entrants to the labour market than among ethnic majorities, the well-qualified and older, more experienced sections of the population, who already have years, perhaps decades, of work experience behind them.

Young people in America and Western Europe are in many respects far better off in terms of living standards than their Russian and East-Central European counterparts. The causes of risk in the USA and Europe and the factors which determine its level and duration among youth in these countries also differ. Standards which are viewed as 'normal' in the USA and EU and in the former USSR determine many things, such as life expectancy, and young people's attitudes towards it. The relatively high welfare standards prevailing in the EU has resulted in higher life expectancy in Western Europe. Thus in 1960, 17 percent of the EU population were aged 60 years and older but by 1997, this figure had increased by 21 percent. By 2030 it is estimated that the proportion of the population over 60 will reach 30 percent.[15] Without taking into account such standards in every society it is impossible to provide reliable estimates of particular youth problems. Thus although young West Europeans emphasise the benefits of greater geographical mobility this is largely offset by a high prospect of unemployment. On top of this risk, young people today are also faced with poverty. The determinations of the benefits and the problems engendered by a risk society therefore vary according to country. Thus the reasons for youth unemployment and poverty in the USA and EU are different to those in the post-Soviet countries.

Even though the aforementioned analysis shows that young people in different risk societies appear to be facing the *same problems* in actual fact the reasons behind them and the responses available *differ greatly* between countries. The main trends in young people's social position in the West and Russia reflects the outcome of the impact of general world risk factors together with specific national ones.

The reforms in Russian society, which were undertaken in the absence of strategies, with the latter confirming to the narrow corporate and political interests of specific groups, makes social and economic policy totally uncertain and hence unpredictable for the entire population. The spontaneity and impulsiveness caused by the aforementioned situation makers itself felt in all spheres of social life.

In Russia's case, the three types of risks outlined in the previous chapter (socio-economic, socio-legal and socio-political) have all had a significant impact on the entire population, especially on young people's role in the process of social reproduction.

Over the last few years, the most dramatic change has been in the rapid decline in the socio-economic status of Russian youth. The drop in their material position, which is occurring alongside an overall trend towards impoverishment among the population, has led to a deeper differentiation among youth. Uncertainty in socio-economic policy has not helped young people's confidence in the future or reassured them that they will be able to sustain their position in the economic system and also does not assist them in having a clear picture of their future. Whilst the socio-economic and political situation is rather unpredictable, young people simply want to 'live each day as it comes' because this may not be possible tomorrow.

At the start of perestroika and the legalisation of the initial market activities from the mid-late 1980s, there was a popular rephrasing of an old Russian proverb 'strike whilst Gorbachev is in power' which originally meant 'strike whilst the iron is hot'. In this way, risk gradually becomes part of youth transition due to an uncertain social policy.

Even now, no one, from politicians through to ordinary citizens, knows how long they will have access to power, financial resources, material well-being, etc. However, any instability will inevitably have an adverse effect upon public opinion and action. Most young Russians live for today and prefer not to think what tomorrow will bring. In this situation they do not care about the consequences of their actions and are losing a sense of responsibility for their actions. Under these conditions, risk becomes a measure of the way that young people have adapted to instability.

Youth is always a particularly risky group. Their behaviour patterns are always extraordinary, but particularly so under conditions of uncertainty. On the one hand, these conditions promise the earth, but at the same time they might also lead to cruel failure. In most cases, young people are doomed to gamble, as they do not have the necessary life experience, financial backing, power etc. Hence they find themselves in an unequal position in comparison with more experienced and powerful adults with whom they just cannot compete.

Meanwhile this unequal position and the desire to overcome this disadvantage causes young people to take risks. Young people frequently show more readiness than adults to take risks. As a rule, young people do not own their own property or have any savings. They have not had a chance to be integrated into the system of social relations. This all means that they have nothing to lose and have no established social ties to break down. This is another source of risk.

At the same time, the state fails to deal with the total risk, and in fact inadvertently promotes the escalation of risk. Although the state is unable to provide for successful youth integration into the economy, it continues to assist various types of shady enterprises, such as financial pyramid schemes and so on. Young people were amongst the tens of thousands of Russians encouraged to speculate in these schemes and ended up being deceived by crooked entrepreneurs. Inexperienced people were seeking to enhance the last of their savings and lost everything.

The fact that young people expect good things to come from their risk taking makes the results extremely unpredictable. Very often young people stake everything they have on the turn of a metaphorical card, even their lives, and as a rule they lose. Very few of them are lucky enough to achieve the desired success. However, those who do succeed, the so-called advanced groups, are seen as role models for other young people, setting them an example and throwing down the gauntlet, a challenge. Young peoples' desire to be integrated into this group is one of the main catalysts for the reproduction of risk.

The mass media constantly portray images of risk and lucky gambles, giving support to these trends and expectations amongst Russian youth. However, in most cases young people experience disappointment as the driving forces of a forward looking social and economic policy are beyond their control. This gives them a feeling of hopelessness and a lack of control over their lives. Now, as before, young people have hardly any influence over the decision making process. Moreover they have almost stopped participating in political life (and make no pretence of doing so).

In the late 1980s–early 1990s, and during the second Presidential election in 1996, the new Russian political elite used young people who believed in democracy and hoped that politicians would act in their interest.[16] In this context, it is important to remember that Russian youth had already played a key role in breaking down the socialist system in 1991–1993[17] and since that time the only consideration given to youth had been during the run up to the 1996 elections and then only as a likely candidate for political manipulation. Such political slogans as 'vote or you will lose out' have attracted a large number of young voters, but they have nothing in common with the youth movement.

Young people are seen by Russian politicians only as a potential electorate. Such a utilitarian approach to young people and the relatively successful attempts to push them away from real political power is nothing other than 'juvenilophobia' which is typical of all political regimes in the former Soviet Union as well as in contemporary Russia. For the powerful elites, youth has always been seen as a source of instability, as a threat to their power. That is why young people have always been kept under strict control. Excessive political pressure on young people, attempts to make political advances to them and winning over youth leaders were tried and tested measures used to keep them within certain boundaries. Nowadays these measures are accompanied by terrible stories about Russia's socialist past, which the new government propaganda identifies solely with shortages, the gulag (camps) and the possibility of a future communist socialist revanche.

Due to these influences, the younger generation of Russians has been transformed into a politically apathetic, barely integrated group, which is unable to develop their inter-group interests independently. This has been a crucial factor in the decline of the youth movement. The hundreds of officially-registered youth organisations do not reflect the views or interests of young people, only those of their leaders.

At the very beginning of the market reforms young businessmen were provided with different facilities and advantages, and as a result these youth organisations were quickly transformed into small commercial structures. Their interests coincided with those of the contemporary political regime, which led to closer interaction and explains why most of the youth organisations are in agreement with recent reforms.

As a result of the collapse of social and legal protection of young people and the absence of any real youth organisations capable of defending youth interests and resisting the arbitrary conditions faced by young people, their basic constitutional rights are being destroyed. Young people constitute one of the most vulnerable groups within the Russian population, a victim of every possible kind of lawlessness and arbitrariness, which are becoming typical of contemporary social relations in Russia.

A combination of the undeveloped legal mechanisms and the autonomy of the socialisation agencies greatly increases the risk of contradictions between these agencies and young people, with regard to young people's civil rights in the areas of education, work, leisure, and their rights to live their own lives. As they have no way of overcoming these obstacles, young people are forced to take a risk, with the possibility of failure. This inevitably brings the younger generation into conflict with society (see chapter 4).

Changes in the position of youth in Russia's risk society of the 1990s

The results of the research presented in the rest of this chapter and in subsequent ones stems from a collaborative project between the authors concerning 'The social development of Russian youth in a risk society'. We have described the methodical and theoretical framework underpinning this research elsewhere[18] and so here we will utilise four separate surveys of young people in Russia aged between 15–29 years. Sample sizes varied as follows: in 1990, 10,412; followed by 2,612 in 1994, 2,500 in 1997 and 2,004 in 1999. This research was co-ordinated by Professor Chuprov and Dr. Julia Zubok of the Sociology of Youth Division of the Russian Academy of Sciences, Moscow and by Professor Christopher Williams of the University of Central Lancashire, Preston, UK, partly through a Nuffield Foundation grant. Particular attention was devoted to young peoples place in the social structure, their consumption and leisure patterns, job prospects and so forth because they illustrate different aspects of social reproduction.

Employment trends and realisation of occupational goals

Since the start of Russia's reform process under Gorbachev and its continuation under Yeltsin then Putin, Russia's economy has faced serious problems, as we saw in the previous chapter (see Table 2.1). This situation has also had an adverse affect upon youth employment prospects. Although the proportion of young people (aged 16–29 years) in the Russian labour force increased from 9.5 percent in the last quarter of 1992 to 20.7 percent in the last quarter of 1998,[19] thereafter the 1998 collapse had a significant impact.[20] According to our calculations by 1999 only 44.2 percent of young people were working, that is almost half of the 1990 level. This has led to the risk of young people in Russia not fulfilling their occupational goals. At the start of the 1990s, for example, the large majority of Russian youth (more than 80 percent) were able to reach occupational maturity and gain economic self-sufficiency by the time they were 30 years old. This meant that they had a high occupational status, were well qualified and well paid. But ever since then, the proportion of young people in this position has steadily declined. Thus by 1999, there were 1.5 times fewer young people in high status, well paid jobs which required good qualifications in comparison to 1990.

This process started much earlier than the 1990s, of course. In the early Gorbachev era (1985–1987) relatively few young cadres were being adequately trained.[21] As a consequence by 1990, the number of qualified young workers fell by 1.4 million and the number of specialists in the average work unit were reduced by 22,000.[22] This had knock on effects. According to our research, by 1994 there were 15 percent fewer highly qualified young people (under 30 years) in the Russian labour force. Vladimir Gimpelson and Douglas Lippoldt attribute this situation to:

the lack of resources for training activities; [to] managers rather poor vision of future developments [and their lack of] clear ideas of whom and how to train.[23]

Furthermore changes in the Russian labour market itself, such as:

> shrinking employment and the general lack of formal job ladders [has] left many employees with a perception of little opportunity for upward mobility, [thereby] decreasing their motivation to seek training.[24]

Our surveys of Russian youth in the 1990s show that one in two (51 percent) young people were unable to work in their own specialism and one out of three (34 percent) stated that there was no prospects for promotion. Although adverse changes in economic policy and in the Russian labour market were primarily to blame, Gimpelson and Lippoldt also point out that:

> [holders of firm skills] actually sought to *oust young newcomers whom they saw as potential threats.*[25]

Poor training and hostility impacted on the labour motivation of Russian youth. It made them feel 'unwanted' and as a consequence labour turnover amongst young people was high in some areas.[26] In other instances Russian youth found it extremely hard to find a job. This has influenced youth living conditions. Thus according to our research findings in 1990 in Russia, 78.5 percent of Russian youth who worked did not have enough to live on in comparison to only 15 percent of American youth in 1988. As Russia's reform process has gathered momentum some young people found it hard to realise their job goals and more found it even harder to find a job which meant that they could live relatively comfortably. Those lucky enough to secure jobs, found it was hard for them to either improve their qualifications or gain higher wages (see Table 3.2).

Table 3.2 Young people's chances of improving their qualifications and wages in Russia (on a 7 point scale), 1990–1999

Possibility of	*1990*	*1994*	*1997*	*1999*
Improving qualifications	4.46	3.43	2.35	4.54
Better pay	3.29	2.70	1.81	3.66

Source: Authors 'Social development of Russian youth' survey data, 1990–1999.

It is clear from the above table that young people had little chance of improving their qualifications until the late 1990s. It is no coincidence that at the same time the importance attached to these variables rose by 5 places in young peoples instrumental attitudes. Alongside the growing importance attached to better qualifications and pay, young people also attached greater significance to skill and professionalism (up from sixth place in 1990 to first place in 1999), to hard work and a challenging job (up from ninth to fifth place between 1990–1999) and to earnings (up from ninth place in 1990 to third place by 1999). Only the freedom to change jobs and labour ethics declined in significance from fifth to eighth place in the same period. Changes in Russia's labour market situation largely explains these attitudinal shifts towards work among Russian youth.

But things are not quite as simple as they first appear. For some Russian youngsters, if they can't find anything better, they would still be willing to work for a small wage; whilst for others, the opportunity of improving their qualifications and knowledge (by gaining a degree for instance) is viewed as far more important than good wages in the short-term. Finally, there are other sections of Russian youth, especially those working in the private or business sector, were money comes before everything else. The market transition in Russia is clearly influencing the labour motivation and goals of young people in post-Soviet Russia in very different and often contradictory ways. For some youngsters, this process is having a civilising effect whereas on others it is having the opposite effect.

The labour education and training of teenagers and other future workers in post-Soviet Russia is likely to have a significant impact on future attitudes towards work. One of the major changes in the 1990s was the rapid decline in the proportion of young people working in the state sector. Nowadays young people are not equally divided between the state and non-state sectors. This has not simply adversely affected output, especially in industry, it has also influenced young peoples integration into the economy. The reasons why young people find state sector employment unattractive are clearly visible: withdrawal of state subsidies, decay, low wages (often paid in arrears or not at all if a firm has gone bankrupt), poor working conditions and so forth. Young people desire stability, but the state sector cannot guarantee it. Thus among our sample in 1990, 52 percent said they wanted to work in the state sector of the Russian economy, but by 1999 this figure had fallen to 24 percent (or only 1 in 4). In general, at the start of the twenty-first century, our research showed the following employment trends among young people: 90 percent were hired labour, 4 percent worked on their own and 6 percent were employed in small companies. At best 1 in 10 of our sample (or 10 percent) worked as entrepreneurs.

Future employment

Young people have suffered firstly, because of the crisis in the state sector, secondly, due to changes in the financial and banking system, thirdly as a result of the rapid decline in the level of services and finally because of the difficulties with supplies and sales. All of these areas have witnessed a 10–fold decline since the first half of the 1990s. How should we evaluate these tendencies though? The first point is the decline of the state sector. This has occurred because the market economy in Russia has not functioned normally. The basic reason for this is the role of Russia's middle-class. This group is a bad role model for Russian youth because unlike the situation in other countries it has failed to encourage innovation and spontaneity. This has left young people with no option (and in some cases they have simply copied their middle class counterparts) but to engage in non-productive types of activity that give little back to the Russian economy. Good examples here include young peoples involvement in rackets, extortion, swindling and fraud. These activities take away from rather than replenish the economy. On the one hand, young people in Russia have a great deal of freedom of choice, but on the other hand, there is a lack of consideration given to the impact of these choices on society as a whole and on its morals. The worst excesses of individualism have already replaced some of the old collectivist values of the Soviet period. Thus since the early 1990s, the exercise of free choice has been uncontrolled. We are not against the principle of free choice per se, but when free choice means non-payment of taxes, a lack of respect for the law, the loss of basic social protection, widespread crime and criminal control of potentially legitimate businesses, then things have gone too far. Choice must be exercised, in our view, with due consideration to the consequences for others and especially to society. Such a situation, as Table 3.3 shows, has influenced the work values of Russian youth. It is evident that from the beginning of 1994 there was a shift in young peoples notion of a 'desirable job'. This has moved from a wish to work in the state sector (in the past stable, now less so) towards a desire to work in the private sector, including foreign firms and even abroad. Although the market transition in part is generating such goals, it must also be remembered that apart from economics, ethics also enters into things.

Table 3.3 Work orientation of Russian youth (as percent of sample), 1990–1999

Desired place of work	1990	1994	1997	1999
State sector/enterprise	52	25	24	26
Work alone	14	12	8	12
Co-operative	32	4	3	2
Private firm	–	18	19	10
Joint venture	–	26	19	13
Work from home	5	8	3	2
Foreign company	–	35	28	19
Contract work	10	4	4	4
Difficult priority areas	8	2	1	1
Job abroad	–	–	12	9
Family business	8	1	2	2
Property services	–	38	31	33
Commerce and trade	–	4	1	1
Army	–	–	3	2
Ministry of Internal Affairs	–	–	8	12

Source: Authors' 'Social development of Russian youth' survey data 1990–1999.

Thus the choice of 'commerce and trade' and other related categories might be influenced by personal motives, namely the possibility of significant future material gains. However, at the same time, the August 1998 crash seems to have had an adverse effect upon future occupational choice. Thus those young people wishing to work for a private firm, in joint ventures or for foreign companies, according to our research fell by 9.6 and 11 percent respectively. In other instances though, such as the desire to work on ones own or in property services the reverse is true (both up by 4 and 2 percent respectively). There was also a slight upturn in the number of young people hoping to work in the state sector (up by 2 percent in 1999 over 1997). What is clear overall is that job choice involves risk, with some occupations involving greater risks and fewer opportunities than others.

The wages of young people can also influence their attitudes towards work. Here the situation is particularly bad. Russian youth are often paid very low wages and in many cases this means below the statutory minimum. Our research shows that since 1977, young peoples wage levels have remained largely unchanged. Those paid particularly low wages tend to work in agriculture or light industry whereas youngsters employed in transport or construction tend to be better off. From this brief survey, it is clear that the occupational position of most young people in Russia is highly unstable, with great variations according to age and gender. Only technical, engineering and transport workers remained relatively secure in the late 1990s.

In real terms, according to our research findings, the situation was as follows in 1999 (see Table 3.4). Although these figures seem high, we need to remember that after the August 1998 economic crisis, the rouble was devalued, prices rose by 2.5–3 times and average wages only increased by 25 percent. So in actual fact there was a significant decrease in living standards and conditions among Russian youth in the last quarter of 1998 and into 1999.

Table 3.4 Young people's monthly wages in Russia (in roubles), 1999

Monthly wages	*Percent of sample of 2,004*
Less than 1,000r	44.4
1–3,000r	48.4
More than 3,000r	7.2

Source: Authors' 'Social development of Russian youth' survey data 1999.

Youth poverty

One of the biggest changes in the last decade of the twentieth century was the increase in the number of young poor. The proportion of young people officially designated 'poor' in 1990 stood at 27 percent. Since May 1992, poverty has been defined as the proportion of the population, in this instance youth, falling below the minimum wage. According to official statistics by October 1993, 29.2 percent of those aged 16–30 were living below the poverty line.[27] Since the early 1990s, the

Russian government budget has risen by approximately 4.8 times but at the same time the cost of living has increased by around 45.2 times making it extremely difficult for young people to avoid the poverty trap. Changes in the level of income and expenditure among Russian youth shown in table 3.5 indicates that after 1997, there was a slight increase in the income of Russian youth. Average expenditure rose by 1.2 times whereas income increased by 1.8 times. This trend did not have a positive impact on young peoples standard of living or their ability to avoid poverty because prices rose by 2.5–3 times. Therefore in 1997, 41.9 of respondents stated that their wages were only adequate enough to buy essentials. By 1999, 45.5 percent replied in a similar fashion highlighting in particular the negative impact of the 1998 crash.

Table 3.5   Changes in the level of income and expenditure amongst Russian youth (as percent of sample), 1997–1999

Average income (in roubles)	1997[a]		1999[b]	
	exp.	income	exp.	income
Less than 1,000r	85.6	89.5	68.1	49.9
1,000–2,999r	7.5	6.4	22.8	31.6
2,000–2,999r	1.3	1.6	5.4	10.4

Key: exp. = expenditure [a] Sample of 2,500 [b] Sample of 2,004
Source: Authors' 'Social development of Russian youth' survey data 1997–1999.

In the 1990s, there were 3 categories of Russian youth according to living standards and consumption patterns.

First type: survival   Which young people share with the large majority of the Russian population. This concerns attempts to try and obtain enough food to live on. This covers 60–75 percent of young people in Russia. Most in this category believe that three years on things have stabilised somewhat since the 1998 crash.

Second type: middle class consumption   which refers to that section of Russian youth who share the consumer values of the middle-classes. What they desire is stable and high living standards in Russian rather than Western (European or American) terms. Thus this group of young people do not simply want adequate food supplies, they also desire consumer durables (such as a video, TV), a good home library and a car. They also subsequently want to be in a position to be able to offer their children a good education in elite schools and to look after the welfare of their family. They make up around 20 percent of young people in Russia.

Third type: middle class attainments This group has already acquired middle class standards of living and consumption patterns. They do not simply possess a video, TV, a good home library and a car, but have also succeeded in building their own dacha. Their consumption pattern is that of the upper middle-class and in many ways is comparable to that of their Western counterparts. Little has changed for them since 1998. They constitute up to 5 percent of Russian youth.

Thus in general terms, consumption patterns and living standards vary from basic to well above average depending upon category. The above trends would also vary according to age, gender and region (urban versus rural, large cities versus provinces etc). It is also evident that only a small proportion of young people in Russia today have been able to maintain relatively high standards of living and levels of consumption. The large majority have seen their quality and standards significantly decline since the 1990s. The reason for this is not simply the localisation of risk (particular trends in Russia's economy and politics, first under Gorbachev, then under Yeltsin), it is also the product of the pressures of globalisation and the impact of greater exposure to mass media and Western trends which have influenced consumption patterns.

Education, culture and leisure patterns

Russian youth have positive attitudes towards education. In 1990, 33.7 percent of those we surveyed viewed the acquisition of knowledge as crucial but by 1997, this figure had increased to 38.3 percent and today it has risen further to around 42 percent. Not surprisingly education has climbed up the ladder from fourth place in 1990 to second place today in terms of young peoples priorities in contemporary Russia. Although Russian youth view educational status as important, the introduction of fees and other errors in Russian educational reforms has significantly influenced the degree of inter-generational mobility.

Table 3.6 compares a father's education with that of his children in the late 1990s. It demonstrates that in 1999, 25.5 percent of the sample of young people whose father's had incomplete education, 28.5 percent of those whose father's had a complete secondary education, 41.6 percent of those whose father's had a specialised secondary education and 25.6 percent of those young people whose father's possessed a higher education had obtained the same status. Every young person, apart from those whose father had an incomplete or complete secondary education, had stagnated in terms of their educational status and mobility between 1997–99. Columns 10–11 show the level of social mobility of father and son. The most upwardly mobile were those with incomplete secondary whereas those young people from good educational backgrounds (specialised secondary and higher education) suffered from downward social mobility in the late 1990s.

This concurs with Henryk Domanski's finding that mobility dynamics have been less intense in Russia compared with other East-Central European countries since the collapse of communism.[28] All in all, the educational attainments of young people vary, as does their level of social mobility, with the father-son link being looser.[29]

Table 3.6 Degree of inter-generational mobility in Russia (as percent of group), 1997–1999

Father's education	Incomplete secondary		Complete secondary		Specialised secondary		Higher Education		Level of social mobility	
	1997	1999	1997	1999	1997	1999	1997	1999	1997	1999
Incomplete secondary	27.0	25.5	27.8	28.6	32.3	37.2	11.3	8.7	+71.4	+74.5
Complete secondary	17.9	30.8	33.4	28.9	37.6	31.9	9.6	9.3	+29.8	+10.4
Specialised secondary	13.4	20.8	33.9	22.6	34.8	41.6	16.8	15.0	-30.5	-28.4
Higher Education	12.5	20.2	39.8	31.0	18.8	23.1	27.3	25.6	-71.1	-74.3

Source: Authors' 'Social development of Russian youth' survey data 1997–1999.

With regard to leisure trends, the data shown in Table 3.7 indicates that some types of leisure activity, such as love of nature, have remained fairly popular (third place) whereas other activities such as listening to classical or rock music have declined (the latter from eleventh to thirteenth place). It is also noticeable, despite greater religious freedoms, that few young people in Russia today seem interested in religion and going to church (20 percent) and instead are much more inclined towards visiting the cinema (stable at fourth place throughout the 1990s).

Table 3.7 Ranking of different types of leisure activity amongst Russian youth (on a 7 point scale), 1990–1999

Leisure activity	1990 Rank	1997 Rank	1999 Rank
Time with loved ones	1	2	1
Time with friends	2	1	2
Nature	3	3	3
Cinema	4	4	4
Non-musical Concerts	5	5	5
Sport	8	6	6
Poetry & Lit.	6	7	7
Theatre	7	8	8
Visiting monuments and churches	9	9	9
Painting, subculture	10	10	10
Classical music	–	13	11
Traditional music	–	12	12
Rock music	–	11	13
Religion/going to church	–	14	14

Source: Authors' 'Social development of Russian youth' survey data 1997–1999.

Table 3.8 groups young people in Russia into three broad categories according to their own subjective views regarding the extent to which they have realised various goals.

Table 3.8 Personal evaluation of degree of self-realisation among Russian youth (on a 7 point scale), 1999

Evaluation of level of self-realisation in terms of	a	b	c
Job	5.94	1	
Family	5.67	2	Type I
Income	5.57	3	
Communication skills	5.55	4	
Job satisfaction	5.45	5	
Enterprise	5.39	6	Type II
Sexual relations	5.31	7	
Honesty, integrity	5.02	8	
Relationship to parents	4.71	9	
Access to power	4.53	10	Type III
Individualism	4.39	11	
Physical prowess	3.74	12	

Key: a Coefficient   b Rank   c Type
Source: Authors' 'Social development of Russian youth' survey data 1999.

The *first type*, including the typical statistical Russian, desire a good job, income, a family and ability to communicate with others. They tend to think in terms of 'I' (*Ya*). The extent to which these goals are possible depends upon support from their family and on their material status. The *second type* of young person in Russia is more concerned about sexual relationships and honesty and integrity. This is typical of workaholics and very entrepreneurial individuals who tend to live each day as it comes. Those of the *third type* care more about their relationship with their parents, their physical condition, the pursuit of individual goals and access to power. These young people tend to be rather individualistic in approach, but not totally selfish, although they are rather self-confident.

It is also possible to perceive of Russian youth in terms of the notions of citizenship, level of patriotism and by the extent to which they identify with the Russian government and people of their own age. Here we are not necessarily referring to nationalistic tendencies but instead to a strong association with one's country (which is ranked second or third in young peoples sense of identity in Russia). This is natural. There has always been a strong link between people and nation in Russia. As a consequence, our young respondents argued that 'if you are not willing to stand up for your country, then you cannot be considered a Russian'. We found in 1999 that 69.3 percent of young people were willing to stand up for their country, 22.3 percent were not and 9.6 did not reply. These answers in part reflect two trends, on the one hand, continuity with the traditional values of the Soviet past, but, on the other, coming to terms with the new liberal values of contemporary post-Soviet society.

There are three fundamental contradictions: firstly, contradictions connected with the redistribution of young labour forces between different spheres of social reproduction (material and cultural production, distribution, exchange and consumption). This leads not to modernisation but to disharmony of the reproduction process as a whole. Secondly, the contradiction between continuity and innovation and between traditional and modern models of socio-historical experience, which are essential for further modernisation, and the break in the unity between these opposing trends, has led to a break in inter-generational ties and also hinders stability in society. Finally, the contradiction between spontaneous and controlled elements in the social reproduction function of youth, is becoming more pronounced in the absence of clearly defined goals and criteria in relation to social reproduction under the conditions of Russian modernisation. All in all, this produces risks both among youth and in society.

Young people themselves are not able to overcome the aforementioned contradictions. They are forced to take uncalculated risks and might fail. In this way, youth come into conflict with society.

Conclusion

This chapter has examined how youth transition has changed in the last two decades. It is clear that in Western Europe's risk societies young people have found it increasingly difficult to gain economic independence, find a job, buy a home, start a family and so forth. Youth transitions today are far more complicated and prolonged than they were in the 1950s, 1960s and even the 1970s. Young people are staying on in education, struggling to find a place in the labour market and even those young people who are successful tend to be concentrated in low-skilled and low-paid jobs. Others are less fortunate so many young people are unemployed. It is evident from our discussion that prolonged transition, as with risk society itself, has both benefits, such as more education, the possibility of combining study and work, and so forth, but these are more than offset by the tendency among young people to stay at home longer, marry later, and take longer to find a job. This has put a severe strain on relations within many Western families. The absence of strong state support for young people has made youth transition even more difficult. Thus the demise of the welfare state, in Europe for instance, has led to the erosion of safety nets, which in turn has produced high youth poverty, homelessness, marginalisation and social exclusion. As yet, despite good intentions, Western political and economic elites have failed to prioritise youth policy. Until they do so the problems highlighted herein will continue to exist unabated.

With regard to Russian youth, in particular, this analysis points to three conclusions: firstly, there has been a significant change in the material and moral well-being of young people in Russia, especially as regards income and consumption; secondly, today's younger generation is stuck in-between traditional old and new modern values. The possibility of conflict therefore remains. Finally, young people have difficulty achieving their goals in a number of spheres. For all these reasons, as we shall now see, young people in Russia, often come into conflict with state and society.

Notes

1. *United Nations Report on the Global Situation of Youth*, cited at www.unorg/events/youth98/dackinfo/report/globl-2.htm, 1999.
2. A. Lukov, V.A. Rodionov and B.A. Ruchkin (eds), *Molodezh' Rossisskoi Federatsii: polozheniye, vybor puti. Osnovye vyvod I predlozheniya Gosugarstvennogo doklada Pravitel'stvu Rossiskoi Federatsii/Gosudarstvenii komitet RF po molodezhnoi politike*, Moscow, 2000, p. 27.
3. K. Evans and A. Furlong, 'Metaphors of youth transitions: Niches, pathways, trajectories or navigations', in J. Bynner, L. Chisholm and A. Furlong (ed.), *Youth, Citizenship and Social Change in a European Context*, Ashgate, Aldershot, 1997, pp. 17–19.
4. The following discussion is based upon Evans and Furlong, ibid.
5. D.N. Ashton and D. Field, *Young Workers*, Hutchinson, London, 1976, p. 67.
6. A. Giddens, *Modernity and self-identity: Self and society in late modernity*, Polity Press, Cambridge, 1991, p. 76.
7. The following discussion of EU youth is based upon *Young Europeans*, Eurobarometer DG XXII report, 29 July 1997.
8. *United Nations Report on the Global Situation of Youth*, cited at www.unorg/events/youth98/dackinfo/report/globl-2.htm, 1999.
9. Ibid.
10. Ibid.
11. Ibid.
12. Ibid.
13. P. Allatt, 'Conceptualising youth: Transitions, risk and the public and the private', in J. Bynner, L. Chisholm and A. Furlong (eds), *Youth, Citizenship and Social Change in a European Context*, Ashgate, Aldershot, 1997, p. 89.
14. See C. Williams, '"Respectable fears" and "moral panics": Youth as a social problem in Russia and Britain!', in J. Riordan, C. Williams and I. Illynsky (eds), *Young people in post-communist Russia and Eastern Europe*, Dartmouth, Aldershot 1995, pp. 29–50.
15. Eurobarometer survey, *Young Europeans*, DG XXII Report, 29 July 1997.
16. On this see C. Williams, V. Chuprov and J. Zubok, 'The voting behaviour of Russian youth', *Journal of Communist Studies and Transition Politics*, Vol. 13 (1), March 1997, pp. 145–59.
17. See J. Riordan, C. Williams and I. Illynsky (ed.), *Young people in post-communist Russia and Eastern Europe*, Dartmouth, Aldershot 1995, pp. 1–3, 180–183.
18. See V.I. Chuprov, *Sotsial'noe razvitie molodezhi: teoreticheskie i prikladnye problemy*, Moscow, Sotsium, 1994, pp. 21–47.
19. E.G. Gimpelson and D. Lippoldt, *The Russian labour market: Between transition and turmoil*, Rowman and Littlefield, Lanham, Maryland, 2001, Table 1.1, p. 14.
20. See K. Nikolov, *Russia: The 1998 Crisis and beyond*, Social Market Foundation, Centre for Collectivist Studies, London, 1999.
21. On the background to this see Bobo Lo, *Soviet labour ideology and the collapse of the state*, Macmillan, Houndmills Basingstoke, 2000, chapter 4.
22. *Molodezh' RSFSR. Statisticheskii sbornik*, Moscow, Goskomstat, 1990, p. 151.
23. Gimpelson and Lippoldt, *Russian labour market*, 2001, p. 82.

24 Ibid.
25 Ibid, p. 83. Our emphasis.
26 Ibid.
27 Goskomstat data cited by J.D. Braithwaite, 'The old and new poor in Russia', in J. Klugman (ed.), *Poverty in Russia: Public policy and Private Responses*, EDI Development Studies, World Bank, Washington D.C., 1997, table 2.8, p. 58.
28 H. Domanski, *On the verge of convergence: Social stratification in Eastern Europe*, CEU Press, Budapest/New York, 2000, pp. 34, 43.
29 Ibid, p. 55.

Chapter 4
Youth Conflict in a Risk Society

As young people become integrated into a society with firmly established social and role structures, they strive to achieve a better status. Furthermore greater awareness of their present status, increases the desire for further mobility in future. However this basic need cannot be easily satisfied, as young people face many insurmountable obstacles. It is not surprising that in contemporary Russia different contradictions between youth and society are being created.

In a risk society, the probability of an increase in the level of these contradictions and the spread of social conflict rises sharply. At the same time, the growth of risk intensifies the crisis and begins to produce new risks which affect younger people. These risks are inter-linked and accumulate as a result of the various conditions of risks, the sources and consequences of which are difficult to define.

In parallel with the increase in social conflicts in a risk society, the chance of reaching a positive solution are noticeably decreasing. In all likelihood, a risk society will be faced with the escalation of social conflicts when they mutate into their extreme form (i.e. confrontation). Thus there is a close link between conflict and risk. Conflicts arise and continue to develop until they are resolved, but this process is taking place in conditions of uncertainty in Russia. As soon as a conflict situation occurs there is a risk of exacerbating contradictions and conflicts and of escalating social tensions right up to the point of mutual rejection. In this case risk plays the role of the original catalyst of social conflict.

At the same time if risk is a type of activity directed at overcoming uncertainty, it can help to resolve conflict. Thus the start of the process of resolving conflict can be seen as the first stage of certainty. On the other hand, the existence of conflict means it needs to be resolved but choice always involves the risk of making a mistake or failing. Consequently, conflict serves as an area for the reproduction of risk.

It is possible to identify three basic types of conflicts which particularly affect young people. Firstly, conflicts occur due to the *unequal status of young people* in society. This arises when young people attempt to achieve a higher social status, often in competition with members of other age groups. This frequently leads to *social inequality*. As a rule, when participating in the reproduction of different structures, young people occupy the lowest and middle levels of the social hierarchy, positions which are characterised by unequal power and less material rewards, fewer rights, responsibilities and privileges, and by less prestige. Access to the top of the hierarchical ladder requires social maturity. Consequently age plays a significant role in determining the basis for youth stratification today. Realising their wish to establish their own position in the status-role hierarchy brings young people up against resistance from other social groups, and this has to be overcome before they can succeed. Unfortunately, young people experience opposition from these groups who feel that their interests are being encroached upon. As a result, relations between the groups and young people become tense and in certain circumstances result in conflict. In other words, social interaction in modern society causes conflict insofar as the social activity of young people impinges upon the interests of other groups. Thus the cause of the majority of conflicts between young people as a social group and society can be linked to the obstacles hindering the reproduction of status.

Secondly, social conflicts arise as a result of *youth innovations* in society. The interests of young people and those of the socialisation agencies, which protect social stability, clash at this point. However, the dominant methods of dealing with and organising young people, which are typical of older generations, have not been retained and are susceptible to change. These changes also lead to conflict. Institutional norms of conflict with young people tend to act as a stimulant to activity which sometimes results in the resolution of conflict generated by risk conditions, but in certain circumstances, the opposite occurs and it generates further conflict and risk.

Thirdly, there is the conflict arising from the presence of *different types of youth subculture*. These subcultures inevitably lead to contradictions with the traditional ways and forms of social organisation. Thus conflicts between young people and society are not only social, but also cultural in nature.

Most of these conflicts between young people as a social group and society exist in every country. However all social conflicts have a specific nature as a result of the conditions of instability and uncertainty existing in a particular risk society. We will now examine these conflicts in more detail, using Russia as a case study.

Conflicts arising from inequality of social status

During their integration into society, young people are conscious of their low social status. In all societies the notion of age is characterised by some notion of status, young people suffer from inequality of social position in comparison with adults. Adults occupy the leading positions in the social hierarchy and hence are able to protect their interests and see off any unwanted competition from the younger generation.

Age discrimination is the groundless oppression of young people, as shown by the limits on their salaries. Age, whether directly or indirectly, is the basis of this phenomena. As a consequence, young people have less access to different types of activity. As Young and Shuller argue 'age plays a role in oppressing young people by keeping them within a fixed framework of roles'.[1] This has a direct effect upon the status reproduction of young people and is particularly noticeable in the economic and labour sphere.

One of the most acute social conflicts between youth and Russian society is connected with the denial of young people's labour rights, which is one cause of the risk of downward mobility. Incidents, such as illegal dismissals, fines and penalties, imposed working hours, employers using unpaid younger workers and denying young people professional training, are all widespread in contemporary Russia. It is clear that such discrimination does nothing to facilitate the self-determination and promotion of young people.

The level of youth integration into the economic sphere is closely linked to young people's ability to resolve material problems through professional work. Under present conditions, individuals can achieve a high professional status only once they have left their 'youth' behind. Therefore, the majority of youth are disadvantaged in practical terms and deprived of any chance of improving their living standards, as well as their professional experience. Our Russian data shows that most young Russians do not achieve professional self-realisation and economic independence until they are well over 30.

However age is only one reason for social inequality and youth vulnerability. The latter also arises from Russia's poorly developed system of social protection and guarantees. This hopeless situation is one of the main factors behind the risk of downward mobility facing the younger generation in Russia today.

This situation could be changed if young people were encouraged and given the necessary education, skills and experience which would stimulate their own desire for professional training. This could help them to reduce the gap, on the one hand, and the level of inequality of status between young people and adults, on the other, as well as aid youth in overcoming the barriers limiting upward mobility. However, according to one Slovak researcher, Ladislav Machachek, if young people with poor competence do not have access to the resources required for their development, then their transition will not be successful and their social status will fall even further. This also applies to those sections of youth with higher qualifications, who want to improve their qualifications and skills, but are unable to do so. This is, in Machachek's opinion, a fundamental risk.[2] This is certainty true of Russia today.

An analysis of the social position of young Russians and their life chances proves that many groups face unequal access to various types of resources, with a consequent fall in social status. As we mentioned above, a deterioration in the material background of young people has led to sharp intra-group differentiation and increased risk of inequality of life amongst different sections of young people. As is well known, if there is an unjust distribution of social wealth, power and prestige which encroaches upon the group interests, this automatically creates the preconditions for open social conflict.

Thus the first type of specific youth conflict is determined by the inequality in the status of young people and the accompanying contradictions when they try to integrate into the different spheres of social life, leading to the risk of making a false start. The risk of such conflicts erupting will grow in magnitude and danger as youth social mobility becomes more and more difficult. But conflict is not simply limited to localised risk and false live starts, it can also occur among those young people who have already achieved a certain status and become integrated into society, but who subsequently find their position threatened. This produces conflict and tends to generate new forms of risk.

Conflict with socialisation agencies

The successful transition of young people is still largely defined by class positions and class procedures. As long as modern societies remain stratified and Russian society experiences unprecedented social polarisation, differences in youth life-chances will occur. The question is how big are these differences and to what extent are they regulated by the socialisation agencies? Socialisation agencies play a socialisation and integrational role, establishing social norms, regulating youth behaviour and redistributing social welfare and regulating the social mobility of young people. They are responsible for the success or failure of this process as a whole (depending upon whether they help or hinder youth integration into society), as well as for the mobility and integration of separate youth groups. Young people occupy a special place in society, which is why their relations with socialisation agencies (the family, education, employment) are crucial.

Changes in the established socialisation agencies are a source of a number of risk situations for the younger generation in Russia. Rapid social differentiation, the breakdown of links with industry, hidden and open unemployment and the rise of new patterns of economic activity have all affected the position of the family and relations within it. The sharp decline in living standards experienced by most Russian families was also accompanied by a decline in the status of young people. The number of families who can provide their younger members with all they need during Russia's transition is decreasing from year to year. As a consequence, there is a sharply increased risk of *inequality of opportunity* for young people to achieve upward mobility.

In a risk society relations within the family, from the point of view of mutual co-operation between different generations, are subject to crisis. The source of this crisis is a developing conflict of social values within society which is simplified by the politicians and mass-media into a simple dichotomy between communist dictatorship versus democracy, or conservatism versus progressivism. Correspondingly, society is also divided. Adults, of course, face more severe difficulties of adaptation, and at the same time are more aware and critical of the repressive nature of Russian transformation. They are also stigmatised for clinging onto obsolete values and ideas. The criticisms they make of changes in policies are looked upon by the younger generation as nothing more than nostalgia for the old patterns of economic, social and cultural life (i.e. the golden age of communism). On the other hand, it is impossible to ignore the fact that in reality adults experience the same uncertainty as young people. They have lost all the basic foundations on which they based their lives. Parents often realise that the social situation and behaviour patterns have changed radically and that they are unable to support and help their children as much as they had done in the past. In this situation, young people have to make their own choices and build their own lives, which many find difficult to do. Where parents try to give advice, which is not always based on adequate experience, young people feel challenged and react with anger and negativity. They misunderstand each other and the motives behind such responses. In reality, the younger and older generations are just seeking help to reorient each other. The older generation realises that the social system and patterns of behaviour have changed, but parents find it extremely difficult to abandon their children and not offer them support. This generates conflict as youth see their actions as interference whilst the younger generation make life choices with which their parents disagree.

As a consequence of these opposing perceptions, the generation gap and alienation of young people from their families is widening. In addition, the transformation of the system is accompanied by instability of the social and economic status of a family and the gap in values, which is creating an additional source of risk for young people.

However, the danger of breaking up the solidarity and values of intergenerational succession is accompanied not only by deteriorating conditions, but also by social disadvantage. The main bastion of support and the initial source from which young people receive their knowledge and ideas is gradually being destroyed. The family, the last remaining buttress for young Russians, is losing its influence. In this way one of the main socialisation agencies is being eroded.

Unfortunately, as the functions and authority of other socialisation agencies are also being undermined, control over young people is very low (i.e. largely lost). The main adverse consequence of this is the intergenerational gap developing in a polarised and highly politicised society, which inevitably leads to 'open' conflict, something which has already happened several times in Russian history.

Lynne Chisholm stresses that the process of socialisation of young people can itself produce contradictions which are the consequence of the self-determination of young people and their distribution by the system.[3] Similarly, Johanna Wyn and Rob White argue that class is involved in the process of interrelations between individuals and groups and the socialisation agencies.[4] This is why different types of social inequality are still going strong.

In so far as access to resources for development is, from the outset, socially determined, and socialisation agencies are apt to perpetuate this, then the risk situation (which is linked to the inequality of life start chances offered to young people) will become even more serious as a result of young people's interaction with the socialisation agencies. Consequently, prescriptive privileges and deprivations have inevitable risks for young people. We will look at these below.

The education system is the most significant socialisation agency for young people, providing them with the means for social mobility. However, Russia's educational reform has produced a number of contradictions which has affected this process. For instance, the Education Act of 1992 and Article 45 of the 1993 Constitution of the Russian Federation only provides for compulsory education until class nine and no further. This has sown the seeds of serious conflict and risks in this field because this measure has put severe limits on the chance of young people receiving an education. Different groups of young people in Russia have suffered from this.[5]

The low level of teachers' wages and the fact that most schools are in a serious state of disrepair partly accounts for the above situation. Unfortunately schools no longer have any responsibility for the success of education and this has quickly given rise to the mass exclusion of young people from schools. In fact around two million teenagers found themselves excluded from school in the first two years after the Education Act was passed (i.e. between 1992/3–1994/5). Those in this category not only consisted of deviants and those not interested in learning, it also included young people from distant towns and villages who could not get to the school or college on their own (too far and no transport) as well as children living in areas where teachers were on strike. Thus recent educational reforms have increased the risks facing young people.

The widespread breakdown in the universal state education system, the development of 'elitist education' and various types of fee-paying educational institutions at the expense of state schools, have been an additional factor in the increase in the level of conflict between educational institutions and young people. As a consequence the risk situation arising from *inequality of possibilities for youth self-realisation* has become more acute in recent years.

Two factors play a decisive role here. The first is *socio-material stratification in Russia* which, although subject to periodical shifts, is essentially stable in character. The rapid impoverishment of the majority of Russian families can lead to divisions in the new education system and the formation of two separate 'upper' and 'lower' categories. It is not difficult to foresee that the education of the vast majority of young Russians will finish after the first level, as access to the second level will be restricted to the privileged young people from rich families. The second factor is a *regional* one and is connected with *the unequal development of the various regions* of the Russian Federation. One of the most significant risks here is connected with the major differences in life chances offered to young people living in the small number of large cities and those living in other regions. This is particularly important in areas where social factors of stratification are supplemented by ethnic ones. In this situation, the risk of social exclusion of these young people becomes inevitable.

As a result of these two factors, a new system of *social selection* in the sphere of education is emerging via the introduction of a unified examination test. This test will severely affect the chances of millions of teenagers living in remote regions, towns and villagers, because they will receive a *second class* education in comparison to those who live in Moscow, St. Petersburg and other big cities. But the reverse might also be true, namely that access to VUZy will be through some form of voucher-system (*vaucherizatsii*) by which entrants will be forced to pay for a voucher in order to enter university or higher education.

However, even if young people can cope with risk at the initial, first stage, they are not guaranteed against future failure. In a risk society, transition is expressed as a series of risk situations which young individuals have to overcome stage by stage. As a consequence, conflict between youth and educational institutions continues onto the next stage (i.e. vocational or higher education, training and entry onto the labour market).

The reproduction of a qualified work force in different specialist areas is another important function of the Russian educational system. Many researchers have demonstrated that the system of occupational training is essential to any country's development. Nevertheless, the system of professional socialisation in Russia remains less effective than other forms of education as it does not correspond to actual labour market needs.[6] Students in both vocational educational establishments (PTUs) as well as those in higher educational establishments (VUZy) learn specialities which do not allow them to compete in the modern labour market.

The paradox is that this problem is faced not only by those young people who have received a traditional vocational education, but also by those who have graduated from the popular faculties of fee-paying higher educational establishments. The latter are victims of the *overproduction of certain professions*. After graduation, they are unable to find suitable employment. That is why, these graduates are either not employed in their specialist areas, end up without a job and/or are forced to work in posts which require no or low level qualifications.

The lack of co-ordinated action on the education and employment front, which arises as a consequence of a lack of planning in the training of cadres, has, on the one hand, led to greater unpredictability in youth transition, and on the other, increased the level of risk they face now and in the future. The fact that at present Russia does not fully utilise the potential of qualified young cadres increases the *risk of de-professionalisation* and *downward social mobility* of the most highly qualified young people.

Other Western countries have experience of addressing the problem of youth unemployment by flexible, all-round professional training and extending the professional portfolio. With regard to the Russian system of vocational training, despite a regimented distribution of graduates, it is not quite as flexible, especially since the market transition. As a result, this has led to a deterioration in the position of young people in the labour market and to an increase in the degree of conflict between young people, economic institutions and society as a whole.

Economic institutions play a significant role in the development and level of social mobility among various social groups. This link is very noticeable in the reproduction of labour resources.

Conflicts arise over the increase in youth unemployment, discrimination against young people in the employment sphere, limits on their opportunities to improve their living standards and social promotion via employment. Imbalances between the choices offered to young people and the possibilities of realising these choices, between the needs of youth and the limited possibilities for satisfying these needs via employment are an important precondition in generating *the risk of economic and social marginalisation*.

Young people's achievement of full adult status, which is defined by professional self-determination, the creation of a family and owning one's own house, is being increasingly delayed, lets hope not indefinitely. Conversely, there is increased youth dependency on parents, the state and society and therefore a prolongation of their dependent status.

In these circumstances, the unsuccessful attempts by young people to integrate into society means that young people have to search for alternative channels of integration and as a result they need to make the difficult choice between self-realisation via work and self-realisation via youth sub-culture, which is sometimes linked with crime. This model for the integration of youth in the social structure is practically embodied in the Russian variant of reforms, in which upward mobility is the most preferred outcome, but it is difficult to achieve legally, so many opt for the illegal route instead.

In analysing the economic status of western youth, Clare Wallace and Ulrich Nagel note that young people become socialised in accordance with the 'achievement' type of orientation (fulfilling the 'American way' for instance), but nevertheless many are excluded from taking full part in market relations. This partly explains the high level of social deviance, including the growth in the level of deprivation and violence in society, and the falling ranges of offenders.[7] We concur with the view that the main reason for this phenomenon is the socio-economic institutions failure to take action against the escalation of social problems and conflicts which are linked to the integration of the younger generation in the socio-economic system (i.e. in the retreatism of the state itself).

The conflict between the interests of young people and the socialisation agencies which are caused by the limitations placed on the former's rights and opportunities is becoming an insurmountable obstacle at a crucial stage in young people's lives. This is creating further uncertainty and unpredictability among Russian youth. In view of the acute social polarisation of Russian society and the ineffectiveness of the mechanisms of social protection, the risk of social exclusion of some sections of youth is becoming inevitable and the low status of this socio-demographic group is therefore not the cause, but rather the symptom of this exclusion. In a wider social perspective, this leads to the *minimisation of youth participation* in the social reproduction of society.

Thus conflicts arise when the socialisation agencies stop providing for the goals and interests of young people as a whole or for different groups. These conflicts (which are linked to inequalities in life starts and chances for future self-realisation) also give rise to the risk of downward mobility and a *widening of the social basis for exclusion*.

The next extremely important function of the socialisation agencies is inclusion of individuals in social relations during the process of their socialisation, by means of the introduction of social norms and values. Socialisation agencies give encouragement to young people if their actions correspond to certain behaviour patterns and if they lead to social cohesion. Social norms act as measures of the social regulation of youth behaviour and unite young people into communities, providing for the creation of social structures and supporting the processes which help society to function as an interactive group system. The inter-linking of the economic, political and ideological crises has produced a state of chaos in values and standards. This crisis is affecting Russia's entire social structure, and meanwhile the socialisation agencies have not as yet produced any clear guidelines or models for socialising the young. Everything which once seemed so important and significant now needs rethinking.

As they are in a state of permanent change and reform, the socialisation agencies, starting with the family, are now unable to guide young people or to give the younger generation any idea of the rules and norms of behaviour for living in Russia's risk society. The new norms, which are being developed in conditions of uncertainty, are themselves arbitrary. This is proof that the institutions of socialisation themselves are in fact themselves experiencing anomie. This exclusion increases the de-socialisation of individuals, the loss of guidelines for young people and produces an increase in anti-social actions among young people.

This uncertainty about social norms increases the risk of conflict with socialisation agencies and creates the conditions for a rise in disorientation and alienation amongst a growing number of young Russians. The resulting social and psychological tension is evident in the increase in irrational youth behaviour, such as hostility and aggression or escapism, as well as by attempts to resolve all social problems on an individual basis or within a subculture. This can be seen, on the one hand, in the social and political passivity of young people, and on the other, in the growth of youth crime.[8]

Other institutions, such as the church, have also experienced significant change. The influence which the church has over young people is now complex. On the one hand, as a result of de-ideologisation (especially the decline of Marxism-Leninism), the religious factor plays a growing role in the socialisation of young people. This includes both the traditional Russian religions and the various newer religious sects (Krishna Consciousness, Aum Senrike, Moonie Society, White Brotherhood etc.).

Our research shows that the church is one of the socialisation agencies which is most trusted by young people. However, the majority of young people, see religion as a stereotype, which is replacing the old socialist stereotype, which is largely being rejected by the new Russian establishment. As religion does not affect youth consciousness at a deeper level, religious norms do not really have any major influence on young people's value system or their everyday behaviour. This increases the risk of a spiritual vacuum being created among youth and might leave many young people adrift without support or spiritual guidance.

As a result of the information boom outlined in chapter 1, which has spread right across the world, the mass media have become a leading factor in the socialisation of young people. The growing diversification, cultural pluralism and the many youth sub-cultures, which exist alongside the trend towards globalisation, are able to regulate the process of socialisation, thanks to the improved information technology, and in particular the growth of the mass media.

At the same time, however, the development of new information technology creates the risk of dehumanisation. Society is rightly concerned about who is manipulating social consciousness in Russia today and with what aim in mind. That is why the absence of an independent press or politically engaged radio and television stations strips the process of Russian modernisation of any real democratic content.

On the pretext of devaluing socialist views the Russian mass media is really breaking down the historical consciousness of the younger generation, depriving young people of the chance to form their own opinions, and turning them into compliant subjects for testing out new information technologies. The consequences of this are the *risk of social disorientation, alienation and an identity crisis* among Russian youth. The socialisation agencies, as a rule, try to reduce the level of youth conflict, but the fact that they are largely dysfunctional, increases the likelihood of further risk and greater conflict between youth and society.

The sub-cultural basis of youth conflicts

The successful integration of young people into society is the product of both internal and external factors based on self-determination and on feelings of unity and a sense of belonging to the community. Social identity is an important regulator of young people's consciousness and behaviour.

Values are an original 'cultural code' which in turn is an indicator, allowing us to assess the success of the process of cultural identification of groups. This means that identification with cultural values during the process of integrating young people into social groups creates a cultural basis for their social integration. This shows the degree of correlation between the cultural patterns, norms and forms of behaviour, and illustrates whether the cultural patterns of social and group consciousness are adequately reflected in individual consciousness. The combined action of people to reproduce cultural values helps to turn these values into standards and norms which are then consolidated in the consciousness and form a lasting self-identity for young people.

The recent significant changes in the field of cultural orientation, both within society as a whole and among different groups, has created an identity crisis among young people. This can lead to differentiation amongst young people, give rise to new forms of youth communities and organisations and engender new youth sub-cultures.

As is well known, the rise of youth subcultures as an alternative life-style occurs on the basis of age and social background. The structural changes accompanying the evolution of society significantly affect the standard of living and experience of the various generations. The new generation has acquired a specific set of values and behaviour patterns which are different to those accepted by adults, which can lead to tension between the generations and even generate a gap between different age groups. Consequently, Eisenstadt argues that the 'development of youth culture is replacing the broken inter-generational links which neither the family nor the school can repair'.[9]

Youth culture is the main form of organisation of young people, linking them into a relatively independent group within the dominant culture. By determining youth life styles and young people's thinking, norms, values, interests and activities, youth subcultures play a two-fold role. On the one hand, they de-stabilise the socio-cultural unity of society as a whole, but, on the other hand, they can also increase the level of youth intra-group integration and unite youth interests.

However, social position is increasingly determining the range of life chances and the different life-styles which young people can adopt. This is preventing youth consolidation.

Our analysis shows that the intra-group cohesion of Russian youth reflects the general disintegration of society. Nowadays, the only basis for consolidation is wealth (capital, income, property). Thus there is an active process of *erosion of generational identity* going on in Russia. Today youth is the most disintegrated group in the population, within which new identities are being established. Therefore integration depends upon the wealth and income of young people, whether they are linked to the power structure, and so on. As a result, there is continual differentiation of the youth culture, within which various forms of subculture are springing up. Individual groups of young people have created their own particular type of sub-culture, mass-cultures, countercultures, rock-cultures, alternative-cultures, etc.[10] In a risk society the appearance of these subcultures, with the threat of confrontation between them increases the level of social tension. However, it must be said that the areas in which modern youth subculture is developing mainly relate to music and fashion.

The position of young people in general is one of survival in an extraordinary social situation, with the accompanying feelings of alienation and devaluation which increases the risk of marginalisation. Being marginalised, both individuals and groups as a whole find themselves on the edge of society. This situation is expressed in the form of a loss of social links between the individual, group and society and the loss of any link with events around them. Eventually this leads to the alienation of young people from society and the appearance of so-called risk groups and different forms of youth countercultures.

The destruction of the socially significant basis of youth identity leads to a crisis in their identity. On the one hand, young people who are affected by rapid socio-cultural changes and unable to construct a stable social identity, show signs of what might be termed an 'identity moratorium'.[11] On the other hand, this leads to the creation of all the required conditions for establishing a delinquent youth identity.

One phenomena which has arisen as a positive reaction to social needs (and as a negative reaction to the dominant culture) is youth social innovation which can, to a certain degree, facilitate the integration of the younger generation into the renewed society. However, this innovation is not always, or not fully supported by, society. In this case there is differentiation between some groups of young people. As a consequence, they become weaker and feel the adverse effects of exclusion.

A brief historical overview will highlight the contradictions in the development of youth subculture in Russia, which have come into conflict with the official culture at all stages of its development and brought the risk of marginalisation and isolation of the younger generation.

In Russia, youth culture became an independent phenomenon at the end of the nineteenth century and beginning of the twentieth century. Until this time, the definition of youth referred to a very narrow social group of a determined age, mainly resident in urban areas. In pre-Revolutionary Russia the majority of the population lived in the countryside and the period between physiological maturity and the start of adult life was very short. This is why the notion of youth culture did not arise.

This socio-cultural phenomenon can be divided into three stages of development.[12] The first occurred at the beginning of the 1920s, when a whole myriad of young writers, artists and film-makers (Malevich, Filonov, Mel'nikov, Meierkhol'd, Mayakovsky etc.) burst onto the Russian cultural scene and brought with them their own views of the world, developing new aesthetic ways of life which differed from the traditional ways. Their ideas were taken up by young people, mainly students, and the creative intelligentsia.[13] However, youth culture could not establish a firm hold and was destroyed in the 1930s and 1940s when unitarism became the defining principle not only of the political, but also the cultural life, of Russian society.[14]

The *second birth* of youth culture occurred in the 1960s, when a kind of spiritual renaissance of society took place following the 1956 twentieth Party Congress. During this period, young people proclaimed their rejection of official propaganda by means of the so-called 'authors songs' (protest songs) under the influence of the work of young poets and writers, such as Evgenii Yevtushchenko, Robert Rozgdestvenskii, Bella Akhmadulina, Bulat Okudzgava and Vladimir Vysotsky. But very soon the new struggle to introduce ideological principles into the culture cut short the youth movements of the late 1960s and 1970s.[15]

The third stage in the development of youth culture is connected with *the impact of perestroika* at the end of the 1980s – start of the 1990s, when young people actively supported the idea of reforming Soviet society. This was mainly expressed in the development of Russian rock culture, unofficial youth movements, with young people coming forward en masse to support the democratic changes.[16] However the expectations of Russian youth were very quickly disappointed; the new politicians betrayed young people's trust, and deceived them during various elections and now the majority of young people trust no one.[17]

Faced with rejection, youth culture gradually disintegrates. Some sections of youth were able to adapt to the new conditions; whereas others fell into drugs and alcohol abuse or escaped into the underground. For the latter category, youth subculture has failed as a method of integration into the renewed society and has been transformed into a cause of marginalisation and social exclusion. As a whole, the current younger generation is content with musical subcultures and its outward expression.[18]

Modern youth culture in Russia has two main characteristics. It continues to exist as a negative reaction to the social situation. Although it acts as a way of resolving social problems, when these cannot be resolved by official methods, modern youth culture also shows signs of delinquency. Thus, firstly, subculture, by its very nature, generates conflict and it is one of the important factors in generating the risk of an identity crisis. Secondly, intra-group contradictions, which are linked to the heterogeneity of youth subcultures, are one of the factors leading to social tension and the risk of confrontation. The most widespread expression of social tension in this context is inter-generational conflict.

The causes of the risk situations threatening young people are not limited to the contradictions arising from the actions of socialisation agencies, but also arise from the decline in other structures. Risks arise because the younger generation are experiencing a lack of support from the state in those areas where they cannot reach a solution on their own, without state protectionism. For instance, this frequently involves the provision of health care for young people, where no help is received from the state.

The aforementioned factors in Russian youth sub-culture provoke conflict between young people and society and create various risk situations for young people.

Typology of risk amongst young people in Russia

By examining the reasons for conflict between young people and society and the link between them and risk in Russia, we can highlight the typical risk situations for young people (see Table 4.1).

Our typology contains at least five types of risk, which reflect the main stages of the process of the social development of youth. This typology covers the main situations in which risk can appear. These situations have been divided according to the cycles of development of young people as subjects of social reproduction.

First of all there is the reproduction of human life forces, that is humans themselves. Thus a situation arises where the *life and health of young people are under threat*. If society does not create the necessary conditions for the physical development of young people, for protecting their health and safety, then this in turn creates a real basis for risk. In this situation, young people are constantly put at risk of lagging behind their counterparts in such areas as physical and social development, more likely to suffer from chronic diseases, and hence they are at risk of seeing their health status decline culminating perhaps in the loss of life. In a social context, there is an increased risk of negative demographic reproduction.

Table 4.1 Types of risk experienced by young people living in various risk societies

Risk situation connected with:	Types of risk
1. Threats to life and health	• Risk of negative demographic reproduction
2. Uncertainty of life start	• Risk connected with unequal starting positions • Risk of false starts
3. Uncertainty of chance of self-realisation	• Social-stratification risk, limiting mobility • Risk of downward mobility • Risk of social exclusion
4 Uncertainty of values and norms	• Risk of social disorientation and alienation • Risk of rifts with socialising Agencies
5. Uncertainty of identity	• Risk of identity crisis • Risk of development of a delinquent identity

The second type of situation is linked to the *uncertainty of life start*. The lower the status given to young people, which is inherited from their parents, the greater the level of uncertainty in the choices they can make in their life. If, for young people from families with high status social backgrounds, the starting position in education, work, marriage are provided by their parents, then all others from lower status social backgrounds have an unequal life start which can either be compensated for by their own abilities and enterprise, or offset by the state. In the absence of an adequate youth and social policy, the required guarantees and other measures of social protection of these categories of young people, there is an increased risk connected with the inequality of starting positions, the risk of a false start, the consequences of which will affect young people's futures.

The third type of risk situation is linked to *the uncertainty of achievement of self-realisation for young people*. Integration into social life is a process full of drama, accompanied by unrealised ambitions, unfulfilled hopes and destroyed plans. The reason often lies not in the apathy of the young people themselves, but rather in a number of social factors. Any attempt to define one's own social status and role and to strengthen these positions is socially determined. This is why young people need state support. If this state support is not forthcoming, there is a growing stratificational risk linked to limits on the upward mobility of young people, the likelihood of increased risk of downward mobility and the risk of social exclusion.

The fourth type of risk situation is linked to *uncertainty of values and norms*. Values and norms play a decisive role in the integration of any society, making social links sustainable and irreversible. From an individual point of view, they form the solid basis for the whole personal inner world. In a risk society, which is characterised by uncertainty and unpredictability, this mechanism undergoes significant distortion and has an adverse impact on norms and values. Traditional social values are devalued and replaced by group values, the system of institutional norms is gradually destroyed and new values and norms are either ignored or cannot be enforced, even if young people concur with them. Under these conditions there arises a multitude of situations where the old norms no longer apply, in which young people have lost any guidance or feeling of support from society. This increases the risk of social disorientation, alienation and finally the likelihood of a break with the socialisation agencies and society as a whole.

The fifth type of risk situation is linked to *uncertainty of identity*. The process of integration of young people in society does not merely involve the need to include them into the social structure, but also requires them to personally identify with these structures. This will give stability to the process. Therefore, as it is concerned with stability and protecting its values, society provides for the reproduction of a certain basis of identity. However, in a risk society faced with conditions of instability, or during periods of social transition, traditional identification is destroyed and new identities spring up, which are often destructive in nature.

Societies are often unable to decide what kind of basic identity young people should be reproducing. This uncertainty is even greater in a risk society. A situation is created in which the risk of an identity crisis amongst young people becomes inevitable.

Conclusion

As we saw above, the process of reproduction of the social structure by young people is not without its conflicts. By carrying out their reproductive, innovative and transmission functions, each younger generation must overcome many obstacles put in its way by society. It is the responsibility of government to give young people something to believe in as well as youth to be more decisive. If this happens, the possibility of reducing the level of conflict and risk will occur.

Notes

1 M. Young and T. Shuller, *Life after work: The arrival of the age-less society*, London, HarperCollins, 1991, p. 37.
2 L. Machachek, *Youth in the process of transition and modernisation in Slovakia*, Bratislava, Institute for Sociology, Slovak Academy of Sciences, 1998, p. 54.

3   L. Chisholm, 'Contribution des approches de la transition vers l'age adulte', in L. Tanguy (ed.), *Les relations entre education et travail en France, Grande-Bretagne, Allemagne et Italie*, Armand Colin, Paris, 1994.
4   J. Wyn and R. White, *Rethinking Youth*, Sage Publications London, 1997, p. 28.
5   Previously education was compulsory up to tenth class, but this is no longer the case. On these issues see V. Chuprov, 'Labour Relations and Youth Employment in the Post-Soviet Period', in Helena Helve (ed.) *Unification and Marginalisation of Young People*, Youth Research 2000 Programme, The Finnish Youth Research Society, Helsinki, 1998, pp. 13–26. For more on these conflicts in education see V.I. Chuprov and J.A. Zubok, 'Sotsialisatsiya molodezhi v post-kommunisticheskoi Rossii', *Sotsial'no-Politicheskii zhirnal*, No. 12, 1996, p. 150 as well as their 'Obrazovaniie molodezhi: reformy i konflikty', in *Rossiia u kriticheskoi cherty: vozrozhdenie ili katastrofa*, Moscow, Republika, 1997 and 'Sotsial'nye konflikty v sfere obrazovaniia molodezhi', in V.T. Lisovskii (ed.), *Chelovek i Obrazovanie v sovremennoi Rossii: Sotsiologicheskie ocherki*, St. Petersburg University Press, 1998. See also Yu. A. Zubok, *Sotsial'naia integratsiia molodezhi v usloviyakh nestabil'nogo obshchestva*, Moscow Sotsium, 1998. On recent trends in Russian education see J. Sutherland, *Schooling in the New Russia: Innovation and Change, 1984–95*, London, SSEES/Macmillan, 1999 and S.L. Webber, *School, reform and society in the New Russia*, London, CREES/Macmillan, 2000.
6   For a more detailed discussion see for example, M.N. Rutkevich and V.P. Pomanov, *Posle shkoly. Opyt sotsiologicheskogo issledovaniia*, Moscow, 1995; V.I. Chuprov and J.A. Zubok, 'Sotsialisatsiya molodezhi v post-kommunisticheskoi Rossii', *Sotsial'no-Politicheskii zhirnal*, No. 12, 1996; V.I. Chuprov and J.A. Zubok, *Molodezh' v obshchestvennom vosproizvodstve: problemy i perspektivy*, Moscow RiTs, ISPR, RAN 2000; D.L. Konstantinovskii, *Molodezh' 90-kh: samoopredelenie v novoi real'nosti*, Moscow, 2000 and A.A. Shegortsov, *Molodezh' i obshchestvo: oypt sotsiologicheskii analiza*, Moscow, 1997.
7   U. Nagel and C. Wallace, 'Participation and Identification in Risk Societies: European Perspectives', in John Bynner, Lynne Chisholm and Andy Furlong, *Youth, Citizenship and Social Change in a European Context*, Ashgate, 1997, p. 45.
8   On this see J. Zubok and C. Williams, 'Youth and crime in Russia', unpublished paper delivered at the German Youth Studies Institute, Leipzig, 25 August 1999.
9   S. Eisenstadt, *From Generation to Generation*, New York, Free Press 1956, p. 37.
10 On this group see J. Riordan (ed.), *Soviet youth culture*, Macmillan, London, 1989, and H. Pilkington, *Russia's youth and its culture*, Routledge, London 1994. On more recent trends see V.V. Kostiusheva, *Molodezhnye dvizheniia i subkul'tury Sankt-Petersburga*, Norma, St. Petersburg, 1999 and J.A. Zubok, 'Subkul'turnoe povedenie molodezhi', in V.T. Lisovskii (ed.), *Molodezh': Tendentsii sotsial'nykh izmenenii*, Izd. St. Petersburgskogo universiteta, 2000, pp. 166–177.
11 J.E. Cote and A.L. Allahar, *Generation and Hold. Coming of Age in the Late Twentieth Century*, New York, New York University Press 1996, p. 74; see also A. Melucci 'Youth Silence and Voice. Selfhood and Commitment in the Everyday Experiences of Adolescents', in J. Fornas and G. Bolin (eds) *Moves in Modernity*, Stockholm, Almavist and Wiskell, 1992 and A.I. Kovaleva and L.V. Lukov, *Sotsiologiia molodezhi: teoreticheskie voprosy*, Moscow, Sotsium, 1999, pp. 279–299.
12 The following discussion is based upon A.I. Shchendrik, *Dukhovnaya kultura sovetskoi molodezhi: sushchnost, sostoianie, puti razvitiya*, Moscow, Molodaya Gvardiya, 1990, pp. 161–163.
13 For more on the impact of these trends on early Soviet youth see A.E. Gorsuch, 'Soviet Youth and the Politics of Popular Culture during NEP', *Social History*, Vol. 17 (2), May 1992, pp. 189–201; 'Flappers and Foxtrotters in Soviet Russia: Soviet Youth in the Roaring Twenties', *The Carl Beck Papers in Russian and East European Studies*, No.

1102, March 1994, pp. 1–33; 'NEP Be Damned!: Young militants in the 1920s and the culture of civil war', *The Russian Review*, Vol. 56 (4), 1997; *Youth in Revolutionary Russia: Enthusiasts, bohemians, delinquents*, Bloomington: Indiana University Press, 2000 and finally her chapter 'Smashing Chairs at the Local Club: Discipline, Disorder and Soviet Youth', in C. Kuhr-Korolev, S. Plaggenborg and M. Wellman (eds), *Sowjetjugend 1917–1941. Generation zwischen Revolution und Resignation*, Essen, Klartext Verlag, 2001.
14 On the Stalinist era see Y. Matsui, 'Youth attitudes towards Stalin's revolution and the Stalinist regime, 1929-41', *Acta Slavica Iaponica*, Vol. 18, 2001, pp. 64–78 and J. Furst, 'Prisoners of the Soviet self? – Political youth oppositionism in late Stalinism', *Europe-Asia Studies*, Vol. 54 (3), 2002, pp. 353–375.
15 See P. Vail' and A. Genis, *60-e mir sovetskogo cheloveka*, Moscow, Novoe literaturnoe obozrenie, 2nd ed., 1998.
16 J. Riordan, C. Williams and I. Illynsky (eds), *Young people in post-communist Russia and Eastern Europe*, Dartmouth, Aldershot, 1995, pp. 1–3, 180–183.
17 On this see C. Williams, V. Chuprov and J. Zubok, 'The voting behaviour of Russian youth', *Journal of Communist Studies and Transition Politics*, Vol. 13 (1), March 1997, pp. 145–59.
18 See H. Pilkington, *Russia's youth and its culture*, Routledge, London, 1994. The impact of the West has been particularly important here, although not all sections of Russian youth totally embrace global trends. On this aspect see H. Pilkington et al (eds), *Looking West? Cultural globalisation and Russian youth cultures*, Penn State University Press, Pennsylvannia, 2002.

Chapter 5

Resolving Youth Conflict: The Localisation and Globalisation of Risk

The types of social conflicts described in the previous chapter are specifically youth related (i.e. the background to the conflicts is based on the peculiar characteristics of youth as a socio-democratic group). This does not mean that young people do not participate in other types of social conflicts, as they also form a constituent part of the different structures within society (professional, political, ethnic, etc.). Although the form may vary, conflicts between young people and society are a common characteristic of every social system with a developed social structure. However, in order for the social system to maintain unity, it is important to ensure that unresolved and uncontrolled contradictions and conflicts are not allowed to continue over long periods of time. More importantly, the classical sociological theory of conflict highlights the co-functional significance of social conflicts (i.e. that they are positive as well as negative).[1] In turn, the localisation of conflict reduces the probability of risk escalation amongst young people. The way out of a conflict situation via two alternative models is shown in Figure 5.1.

The result of *implementation of the first model is the activation of integrational processes to achieve consensus.* Integration may be achieved *via youth conformity* (i.e. finding common grounds for consolidation), which is a positive way of eliminating conflict, as this leads to the minimisation of risk. On the downside, *it does not allow any possibility for social innovation by young people.* The latter can also be used as a means of integration; in this case, young people express their agreement with social and cultural goals, but reject the established ways of achieving these goals. Nevertheless, integration is still possible. Under these circumstances, the possibility of local risk in increased, but its escalation is avoided.

It is important to point out here that youth integration via innovative activity is largely dependent upon the prevailing patterns and mechanisms for resolving conflicts. Society often rejects youth innovation and tries to limit conflict. This can be seen in the attempts to smooth over or repress the most serious contradictions, none of which reduce the risk of increasing social tensions. Finally, under these conditions, this innovation itself becomes delinquent in nature and creates new risk situations.

In addition, society can chose to institutionalise and standardise these new processes and create favourable conditions for the integration of young people into the social structure on a new basis. In the latter case, innovation, which is defined by Merton as one of the forms of social deviation, simultaneously becomes both a precondition for and a means of resolving conflict and minimising risk. An example here would be the Russian government creating favourable conditions so that the majority of young people could enter the labour market. In reality, however, this has

Figure 5.1 Models of youth conflict resolution under conditions of the reproduction of risk

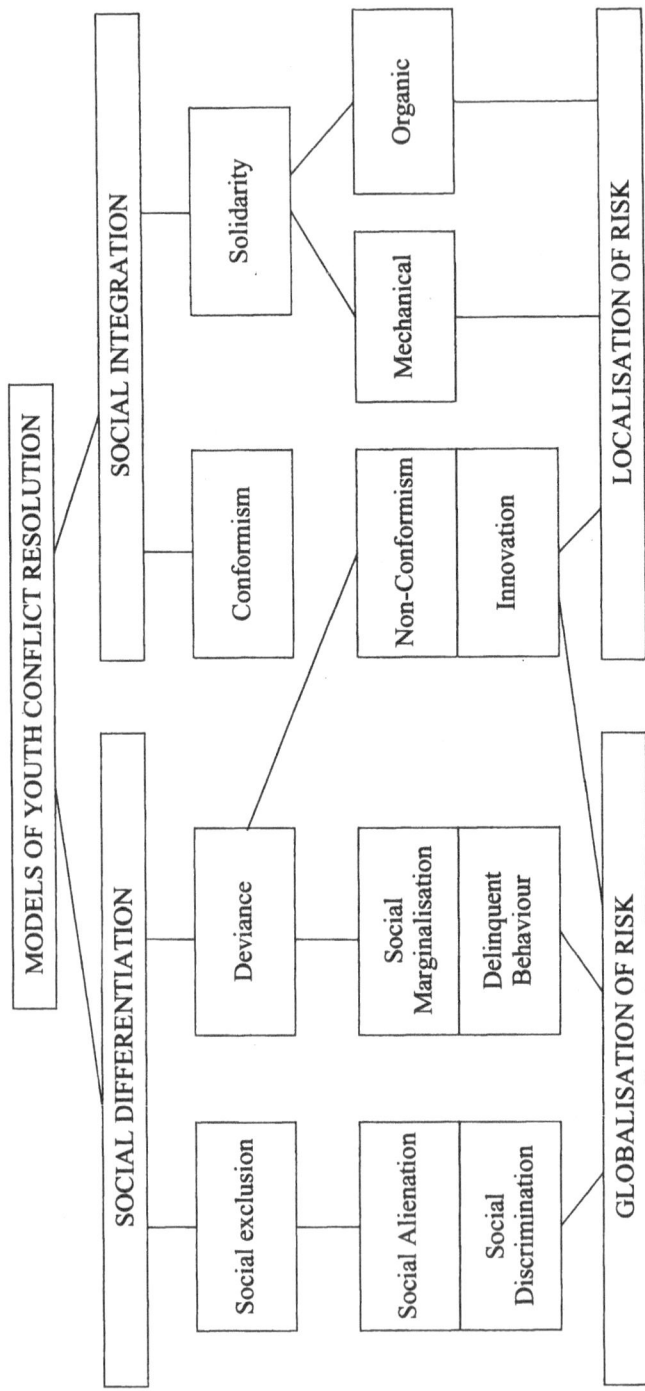

Source: Based on findings from Authors' 'Social Development of Youth' surveys, Russian Federation, 1990–1999.

not occurred despite the fact that Yeltsin approved a Presidential Programme entitled *Youth of Russia* on 25 November 1994. This Presidential decree theoretically guarantees young people the legal, economic and organisational conditions enabling youth personal development and the right to create youth organisations, movements and initiatives.

The *second model for overcoming conflict is by social differentiation among young people which also allows social innovation, leading to the stabilisation of society*. However, in the case of differentiation, this may be accompanied by increased social tension, aggravation of conflict, and the extension of social stratification with intensified disintegrational processes and increased risk.

All in all, differentiation is seen as a possible model for resolving conflict in society. It is important to acknowledge that differentiation is not always negative in character. It can have a positive effect when it creates new structures and new social relations and encourages social innovation and progress. All of these variables eventually lead to integration and gradually ensure stability in society.

As the original mechanism of society's transition from one stage to another, social conflict can play an integrational role but only if it is driven towards constructive channels. In this instance risk is at a tolerable level. However, when the differentiation is driven towards destructive channels, the conflict loses its constructive, positive elements and this leads to social discrimination, alienation and marginalisation (i.e. the exclusion of certain groups of young people from social relations).

The social ties between society as a whole and young people are being broken down. Social relations are losing their sustainability and fragmentation, rather than unity, is being reproduced. In these circumstances, the risk zone is expanding and becoming global. According to the model developed by Ulrich Nagel and Clare Wallace, there are *two scenarios in this modernisation strategy. The first is that this approach will improve the level of social mobility and individualisation of life course*. This will be facilitated by greater social participation and identification with society and its social structure. The result might be a more flexible, robust social structure and an open pluralistic society. *In the second scenario, the exercise of individual choice leads to limited social mobility, isolation from traditional resources, less security and no future guarantees*. The likelihood in this case is that young people will become disoriented, more reflexive and in the end probably doomed to failure. The result of the second scenario at a micro level is disintegration.[2] If this scenario proves accurate, then we will end up with Ulrich Beck's 'anti-modernity'.

Economic and socio-political transformation in Russia is creating a real risk of upsetting the balance between the integrational and disintegrational processes, in favour of the latter. Due to the absence of effective mechanisms for managing social relations in a risk society, the interaction between youth and society becomes, to a large extent, conflictual. Furthermore, conflicts are not localised and resolved at the micro-level, but instead are growing and becoming global, affecting the whole of society. At the same time, integrational tendencies cannot counterbalance the differential processes as integration is localised in this situation.

When applied to young people, this means an extension of the risk zone, growing marginalisation, social discrimination and alienation among more and more young Russians. Thus Russia's risk society is dominated by processes which oppose integration. Hence some groups of young people are rejected by society and made into 'outcasts', and so they suffer from social exclusion.

In this type of society, risk tends to accumulate; the loser wants to win back what s/he has lost and the winner wants to take risks again, hoping to win. The uncertainty of social life, which is typical of a risk society, gives this process a fundamental fatality, come what may. The absence of strict norms is perceived as a licence allowing people to do what they want. Anything which is not specifically prohibited is allowed. Self-control has given way to self-indulgence. The existence of risk conditions is becoming the norm and risk itself is changing from a local to a global phenomenon.

Contradictions and conflict in the social integration of youth in a risk society

In this section we shall examine how the model for resolving conflicts between young people and society is changing under the conditions of a risk society and how risk is transforming the process of youth integration.

As a fundamental factor in the process of expanded social reproduction, young people do not only inherit social experience and transform it under the new conditions, they also pass it onto the next generation. This process is somewhat contradictory. *On the one hand, expanded social reproduction can only take place in a relatively stable society. On the other hand, the degree of stability largely depends on how successfully each new generation is integrated into society.*

The social integration of young people is understood to mean the nature of the relationship between society as a whole, on the one hand, and young people as one of its constituent parts, on the other. These relationships arise as a result of the process of integrating young people into the social structure, and are aimed at supporting and reproducing stable social ties and goals. It is the totality of the processes which define intra-group youth unity.[3] Integration is not simply limited by the mechanical processes of inclusion into a community, it also requires young people to be aware that they are an integral part of that community.

Empirically, the level of youth integration into society is defined as the degree of youth involvement in various social structures (professional, political, marital, and so on) and the degree of self-identification with these structures. Self-identification in its turn refers not only to the association of young people with a particular social group, but to internalisation of all the values and norms of the community.

As a rule, the more diverse an individual's inclusion into the social structure is, the stronger the social ties are between that individual and society. In other words, the more actively an individual enters into the system of social norms, roles, obligations and social expectations, the stronger the degree of identification is with these structures. One of the main goals of youth social integration is to help young people to become fully involved in social ties, to empower them and help them become fully committed citizens. However, this situation only applies to relatively stable societies in which there is a continual process of youth inclusion and identification, due to the existence of well co-ordinated integrational mechanisms. Where there is social uncertainty and instability, this process has a number of peculiarities. First of all, this process is faced with both subjective and objective obstacles, created by society itself and its structures in response to destabilisation, which are challenged, according to Parsons, by youth activity.[4] In a stable society, the process of youth integration and the integrational processes which accompany it are not only maintained but even encouraged, whereas in a risk society these mechanisms are virtually non-existent.

Table 5.1 Comparison of youth integration characteristics in different types of societies

Stable Western risk Societies	Risk Societies in transition
1. Strengthening of integrational processes.	1. Strengthening of differentiation.
2. Existence of clear social goals and criteria for their development.	2. Absence of social goals and criteria for their development. Individualisation of identity.
3. Integration of one's possibilities and experience. Pre-determined life course and social status.	3. Fragmentation of possibilities and experience. Uncertainty of life course and social status.
4. Lessening of the influence of unpredictable factors. Increase in self-regulation.	4. Increase in the influence of unpredictable factors. Destruction of mechanisms of self-regulation.
5. Increasing dependency on family and state.	5. Reduced dependency on family and state.

As a result, the tendency towards differentiation is increased. This is the first peculiarity of youth integration in a risk society (see Table 5.2).

In reality, societies undergoing risk, just like any other social system, are in danger of collapse, if no integrative mechanisms exist. According to Z. Golenkova, certain types of integration are coming into existence because of the growth in specialisation and the differentiation of labour, an increase in bureaucratic power, universalism of market and money, the formation of contemporary political parties, systems (parliamentarianism) and electoral mechanisms, an open social stratification system, widespread rapid mobility (of all types), the weakening of traditional values (for family, religion, morals) and the growth of individualism.[5]

The *first peculiarity of youth integration* expresses itself in the breakdown of the entire mechanism of integration, whereby youth inclusion into social structure is not accompanied by self-identification with these structures. The whole process of integration becomes asymmetric in nature. Such a breakdown is evident in the labour sphere. Our previous analysis of the state sector of the Russian economy indicated that it still remains the main channel of integration of young Russians into the labour market. Almost one in two employed young people (46 percent) work in different state enterprises. In some regions of the Russian Federation this proportion is higher than for those employed in the non-state sector. However, as shown earlier young people's employment in the state sector of the economy can best be described as 'forced inclusion' for two reasons: The first is *limited labour market opportunities* and so individuals do not have any other choice (for example, because they live in places far away from economically advanced districts or because of the decline in industry) and the second relates to *the search for stability* which is more pronounced in the state rather than commercial sector. Generally youth identification with state economic structures is very weak or totally absent altogether, so that they only work in the state sector 'on paper', with most working in the private sector for the 'real money'.

Such *forced integration* is associated with Durkheim's *mechanic solidarity*. The only difference is that it is not the power of strict norms or law or collective consciousness which is important here, but the lack of choice faced by youth instead. Similar in form but different in the content is the trend observed in the non-state sector. Since the beginning of 1990 a large proportion of Russian youth wanted to work in non-state enterprises and accepted its norms and values. But their integration into private structures could not be sustained. Sharing values typical for the market young people have failed to reach a more or less sustainable status and are always in danger of losing it. Such integration is also asymmetric as soon as self-identification is compulsory, but not sufficient for complete integration. The position of young people in the non-state sector of the economy is totally dependent upon their employer. In many cases, young people, as we demonstrated in Chapters 2 and 3, are several times more likely to suffer from disfranchised status, lawlessness and vulnerability than those working in the state enterprises. Our surveys throughout the 1990s show that 42.7 percent of young people constantly experience direct violation of their rights by employers. By comparison, in the state sector this figure stands at 25.8 percent and in jointly owned enterprises at 26.6 percent.[6] Such breaches of one of the constituent parts of social integration (inclusion into structures and self-identification with them) has meant that the whole process is unstable. The risk of disintegration and social exclusion increases as a result.

Nevertheless, lack of choice and dependency on external risk conditions may become a good basis for integration. This is one of the paradoxes of a risk society. Many young people in fact conform and adapt to the new reality in order to save what they have, because changes do not always bring anything good. That is why in taking into consideration the objectivity of social integration it is wrong to reject the existence of integration mechanisms in a risk society. It is instead better to talk about the *specific foundation and functions of integration.*

In conditions which prevent their self-determination, young people are at risk of becoming under privileged and low-status groups. They might therefore have to search for alternative channels of social integration. In this case, the risk of confronting the law and becoming a outcast is likely. Obviously in both cases, youth is not free of risk. The latter is an unavoidable component of social becoming and self-assertion. The search for the self, a place in society and the transition to better positions are all linked to risk. Meanwhile the risk that accompanies choice manifests itself in a different way in relatively stable and crisis-ridden societies. Certainly, in the presence of a number of options, the risk of making the wrong choice is common. This wrong choice makes social promotion less successful than it might have been. Recently, in the former USSR, this problem has been resolved largely by propaganda that encouraged youth solidarity with societal goals. Such a policy, though, limited young people's choices, but at the same time made it easier for them. In relatively stable industrial societies life trajectories and the problem of choice also were calculable due to the social predictability and predetermination.[7] By contrast to their western counterparts young Russians more often face risk that is determined not by plurality of variants but by simple 'black and white' alternatives which can have adverse consequences. In Russia, risk is mainly dual in character and brings about opposed results: wonderful social dividends or cruel failure.

Thus, a combination of limitations on Russian youth opportunities for self-realisation, on the one hand, and absence of social goals and criteria, on the other hand, gives the process of social integration its *second peculiarity*, namely its duality based on simplified choice between *conformism* (i.e. one's self-realisation in an institutionalised but not advantageous way) and complete identification with youth subculture and *delinquent innovations*. It should be pointed out here that as soon as integration models and patterns of social reproduction are determined by prevailing social relations, then it is much easier to be integrated into society using criminal elements and activity. And if, for example, incomes earned by illegal activity are higher and lead to better status in comparison with legal, hard work then youth integration strategies need more attention and careful handling.

The situation then is even more dramatic because of the fact that young people mainly conform in today's 'dead-end' Russian society. In such circumstances there is always the risk that they will reproduce an entire range of negative trends and phenomena. Hence, in a situation where the younger generation is deprived of this essential help and only faces obstacles, the development of different patterns of identity leads to the individualisation of goals for young people. When the younger generation receives relatively stable support from the values and norms system, then this type of experimental behaviour is no threat either to society or other individual groups.

But this has not occurred in Russia. It follows on from this that the risk of negative integration of youth in Russia has therefore changed from a potential threat to a real one. Sociological data confirms that in addition to the crisis of collectivist tendencies, we are also seeing increased levels of anti-social and illegal activities being carried out by young people. It is also important to point out that individualistic tendencies have taken a firm hold in youth consciousness. Furthermore many young people are willing to embark upon different kinds of deviation, especially criminal activities. When the balance between social control and self control is upset, a shift from social neutrality to inter-group confrontation takes place. This can frequently be seen in the process of the criminalisation of Russian businesses. The removal of the state monopoly on trade, for instance, which was accompanied by the discrediting of socialist and collectivist values on the one hand, and the promotion of the new values of individualism and enrichment by any available means, on the other, has led to the rise of a powerful stratum of shady businesses in the commercial sphere. Thus, instead of integration, we have a system within which there are various parts which are not interconnected, but which, on the contrary, are divided by clearly defined lines. According to Durkheim, these relations do not correspond to any positive social ties.[8]

The unity of society is largely based upon the integration of possibilities and actual experience, whereby young people's individual abilities are taken to their logical conclusion and correspond to the possibilities and guarantees provided by society. Under these circumstances, self-control and cohesive behaviour are possible. However, in the case of negative integration, mutual obstacles and struggles destroy the possibility of young people achieving social unity. The clash between youth interests and those of the state as well as conflicts between different groups of young people are inevitable and they are sometimes resolved at the expense of the interests of others. This can be seen in the case of Russia's risk society where integration may have an opposite effect, namely to multiply the level of destructive processes. Thus, not all types of integration are positive.

The *third* peculiarity of integration of youth in a risk society is connected with *contradictory identity formation and with a new base for identification.* This peculiarity needs to be analysed alongside individualisation in risk society. Individualisation is a phenomenon which is linked to the development of post-industrial societies. Thus one recent sociological report on youth concluded that:

> the process of socialisation is replaced in post-modern society by a process of individualisation, while the politically designed project for social progress is replaced by an individual's life project. But how to achieve social cohesion? Social cohesion they continue, becomes therefore crucially dependent not on a shared belief in an ideal model of society, but on the ability to help everybody acquire those cognitive, emotional and psychological resources they need to become a successful economic actor and realise their personal project.[9]

Evans and Furlong explain this phenomenon by pointing to a range of factors: firstly, the high level of differentiation within youth as a group which is the result of the growing range of routes into adulthood. Secondly, the transformation of socialisation agencies which have lost their effectiveness as agencies of social reproduction in a risk society. They no longer encourage individuals towards specific niches. This means that young people have to define their own values in education, work, family life, consumption, political participation, and other aspects of life.[10] In this sense, as Ken Roberts argues, individualisation reduces the number of those whose biographies are close or similar.[11] Partly because of this, any social and class ties become weaker, at least on a subjective level, and the individualisation of youth life styles increases. Despite the fact that young people's life chances remain socially determined, they nevertheless still try to resolve their common problems on an individual rather than group level. This is the conclusion reached by sociologists analysing modern western societies.

A similar phenomenon is being seen in Russian society today. However, in Russia it is being expressed in a rather unique way. As the normal way of life is being destroyed, young people are feeling a greater need to define their own place within the system of social ties. They are searching for niches not only in the economic sphere, but also in other spheres. They have to decide which social groups and strata they wish to identify with. The individualisation of Russian youth therefore leads to the transformation of the basis of identity. The disorganisation of the socialisation agencies, as we saw in the previous chapter, together with the absence of past predictability, allows young Russians the total freedom to experiment with their identity. This also helps to overcome ideologically unified patterns of socialisation and identification in post-Soviet Russia. This is another aspect of individualisation in Russia.

At the same time, reflexivity is a necessary pre-condition for individualisation. This is based upon individual ability to critically evaluate their own actions in accordance with shared values. As Ken Roberts argues virtually everything which individuals do and experience is still shared with others – the only difference being individual combinations and different consequences.[12] However, as our research data shows, class and group identity, which were cultivated in youth consciousness and behaviour over several decades of communist rule, have gradually been replaced by individual and corporate identities in the last decade or so. As a result, young people nowadays do not always consider society-oriented values. Hence individualisation among Russia's younger generation reflects the breakdown in essential links between action and constraints. In this situation, motives for action largely relate to personal interests, goals, tastes and desires. With the loss of a sense of identity, due to rapid changes in the social environment, which in itself is an important regulator of youth self-awareness and behaviour, then young people might realise individual goals without taking into account the interests of society. This increases the risk of centrifugal tendencies within society, as young people do what they want even if this threatens other sections of youth or society as a whole. This is largely the product of the lack of social or self-control. As a consequence, collectively oriented values gave way to self-oriented individual identities in 1990s Russia.

As noted in chapter 1, according to Giddens, sustainable identities, maintained by feelings of continuity and constancy of one's social world, form the basis for ontological security in modern societies. In Russia's risk society, the opposite trend of psychological tension among youth occurs because of feelings of instability and a lack of confidence, which consequently leads to a narrowing of identities. This crisis of trust affects the whole system, and is also spreading among youth, as a constituent part of society. As one of the main factors in the transformation of youth identities, this crisis of trust indicates the degree of internalisation of norms, typical in a risk society, by young people. This situation frequently turns into a personal struggle with reality and unwarranted self-reproach for failures which cannot be avoided at a personal level. Such fragmentation and 'individualised identity' does not, according to Roberts, help either the intra- or inter-group integration of young people. In turn this leads to the individualisation of risk for young people.[13] The individualisation of the life pathways of Russian youth is linked to distortion of identity. As Patricia Allat argues:

> even during the safest periods, all young people live in a marginal space which threatens both themselves and society as a whole. A period of social change intensifies this danger.[14]

The most extreme forms of the gap between young people and their social surrounding is the so-called 'identity moratorium' whereby young people do not identify with anything or anyone, or possess a 'delinquent identity' characterised by the internalisation of criminal norms.[15] Our research findings in the 1990s suggest that more than half (57.8 percent) of young Russians are convinced that nobody can be trusted and of this group, over a third (36 percent) prefer to rely on themselves instead.

Individualisation and growing differentiation of young people's interests gradually change the main patterns of integration. In a risk society, it is founded on different grounds than it was in the past. These foundations have become fragmented, so that the whole process of youth integration is also characterised by a certain degree of fragmentation. Social fragmentation has lead to the emergence of many micro associations among youth, and this process symbolises the absence of a universal scenario of integration in a risk society. However, present scenarios do not always provide for social cohesion and solidarity among large social groups. All in all, this determines the *fourth peculiarity of social integration, namely that it is becoming local in character*. Such integration, however, only affects some groups and does not envelop the whole system. Nevertheless, these micro-social worlds are highly integrated themselves because they are predominantly built upon communal relations.

Relations with partners, family and other close relatives play a leading role in youth identity formation in contemporary Russia. Such relations are based on the possibility to share problems, seek advice and on the opportunity to resolve all problems jointly. Inside of these groups, integration processes are based on mutual support, trust and genuine co-operation. This kind of integration, in sociological terms, is an example of *positive solidarity* which means that friendship and love is developing more intensively. As Abrams and McCulloch note friendship embodies the most positive image of social relations that do not have a place anywhere in capitalist society.[16] Hence, friendship contains particular potential in terms of integration. Friends, accordingly to Pahl, are an anchor in an individual's life and act as a source of emotional support and stability at times of uncertainty and risk situations.[17] Thus, a risk environment itself calls this type of integration, which is linked with the necessity to resist and cope with the adverse affects of a risk society.

The need to survive uncertainty and unpredictability leads to the accumulation of an inner energy of consolidation in the face of total risk. In a society where risk is growing and neither employment, nor other formal relations are able to provide a sense of safety and security, certain types of friendship become a vital source of happiness and personal identity. Through these relations young people *can organically integrate into modern society*. Thus, risk stimulates a synergetic effect and paradoxically becomes one of the factors encouraging social integration. The latter is based on personal interaction. Hence, the *fifth peculiarity of social integration in a risk society is linked to the integrational function of risk itself.*

Under conditions of Russian uncertainty risks become an essential part of young people's everyday life. On the one hand, problems such as uncertainty of opportunities in education, labour market, promotion, living standards and so on expand the sphere of risk. On the other hand, however, the desire to escape this uncertainty pushes young people to be more active (i.e. to take new risks). Thus, a risk society as an objective environment presented to the younger generation, in reality turns into a subjective risk coming from youth activity. Being closely interwoven objective and subjective risks together reflect the essence of a risk society.

Such inevitable risk situations demand the necessary response and actions from young people. In fact, adequacy under risk, means constant risk-taking. The risk environment, outlined in chapters 1–3, penetrates young people's lives and activity and becomes a distinctive model of youth integration into a risk society. In this context *risk is seen as young individuals activity undertaken in order to achieve certainty*. However, the total risk environment does not assist them in reducing uncertainty, but instead brings unpredictable results for individuals and groups alike. Consequently, chaotic and spontaneous processes differ during the process of social integration in a risk society.

Thus, our analysis of youth integration in contemporary Russian society proves our initial hypothesis that a risk society is able to reproduce integrational mechanisms providing a basis for its integrity and way of development. All in all, the peculiarities of such mechanisms in a risk society are as follows:

- Asymmetric character of integration because of the imbalance of mechanical and organic elements.
- Simplified duality of integration.
- New non-traditional bases for identification.
- Local character of integration.
- Presence of integrational function of risk.
- Spontaneous nature of integration processes.

Although the aforementioned peculiarities of youth integration in a risk society have been discovered using Russia as the case study, we believe that our model may be universal and can therefore be applied to other risk societies.

Localisation of Risk

The problem of the localisation of risk amongst youth is closely linked to the possibility of resolving specific youth conflicts. In resolving conflict by means of integration, society stabilises the situation, reduces risk and manages to localise it. In turn the localisation of risk means that the field for new social conflicts is narrowed (see Figure 5.1).

As we saw above and in the previous chapter, the integrational processes occurring in Russia's risk society has peculiarities which distinguish it from the normal integrational processes experienced in more stable West European and American societies. However, despite these 'negative' features, in general, youth integration under risk conditions still has a positive influence on society. As the mechanisms of social reproduction are somewhat self-regulating (as we emphasised in chapter 1) and integration is carrying on as before, risk is gradually localised. Thus integration helps to limit the zone of risk as well as to reduce the number of people subjected to it. This in turn increases the probability of a positive outcome. Moreover growing social differentiation in the social status of young people in a risk society, which has reached extreme proportions in the sense that it borders on the dissolution of the social system, increases the need for social integration. This can be achieved by means of expanded social reproduction which involves the integration of all constructive elements which are contained in a separate differentiated structure.

Thus the rapid development of youth subculture in Russia at the beginning of the 1990s, which we described briefly in chapter 4, has led to the appearance of many groups and associations with various interests. On the whole this was a positive process, although not all the newly developing youth structures complied with established norms. Over time some groups disappeared or merged and others changed the nature of their activities. In the circumstances of widespread social change which takes place in a risk society, the existence of all of these organisations was threatened. The only ones to survive were those which could integrate into the prevailing process, a difficult task amidst on-going change. As a result of their integration, the risk (for them at least) was localised and reduced to a minimum. Thus one can conclude from this that in circumstances of uncertainty, integration can localise risk within separate structures, hence the borders of risk might be narrowed in the process.

The absence of a severe reduction in the number of social goals and criteria for development, which is a characteristic of a risk society, is inevitably reflected in youth identity. As we saw earlier, the individualisation of identity is largely accompanied by individualisation of goals and lifestyles which also have both positive and negative consequences. This theme was discussed in great detail above, so suffice it to say here that individualisation itself can lead to the spreading of risk, which in turn increases the probability of more adverse outcomes. This was seen during the time when liberal reforms were introduced in Russia and when the devalued socialist social patterns ceased to provide the basis for individual and group norms. This is why, in the absence of a comprehensive new system of norms and values and the declaration of individualism as an alternative to collectivism, it was perceived to be a justification for the reproduction of the basest forms of human behaviour. Thus nowadays young people can get away with acts of a severe nature which would not have been tolerated in the communist era. As a consequence of this distorted version of individualisation, Russian society is being rocked by endless disorder. This is not only an internal problem, but also a threat to other countries (as in the case of young people's involvement in organised crime).

This would not have occurred if the separate patterns of individual youth identity had been gradually integrated into the existing gap in norms. In this instance, the risk connected with different types of individual phenomena of personal subjectivity would have been minimal. Thus it can be seen that integration helps to ensure the individualisation of risk, localising it within the boundaries of separate groups or individuals.

In a risk society the consequences of individualisation are linked to the fragmentation of opportunity and experience, which significantly increases the uncertainty of the life courses and social status of young people. In turn, this uncertainty is linked to the risks which lie in wait for young people at every stage of the transition process.

By removing predetermination and predictability and accompanying this with firm guarantees and constant ideological pressure from the state, which were typical of Soviet society, the new post-Soviet risk society has provided greater freedom of choice for young people's life trajectory. However, the resulting fragmentation of the established ties between individual experience and the opportunities for realising this goal, previously granted by the state, has significantly increased the risk of the wrong choices being made. This upsets the balance between the subjective and objective components of risk. For instance, the introduction of reforms ushering in new education systems as an alternative to the old state system was supposed to provide greater opportunities and wider choices for young people. However, if we take into account the fact that fee-paying alternative education is gradually replacing free state education, and that only a minority can afford to pay, it is clear that there is a wide gap between promises and reality. Instead, such reforms increase the likelihood that many young people will not gain a higher education.

The process of social integration of youth into a risk society presupposes a reduction of uncertainty in their activities (the objective component of risk) and an increase in young people's readiness to take decisions, taking into account the nature, scale and dynamics of this uncertainty (the subjective component of risk). This in itself helps to localise the risk by reducing the threshold of uncertainty. The programme *Youth* was one attempt to co-ordinate youth policy in the Republics of Tatarstan, Stravropol and Khabarovsk krai, Tver and Novgorod oblasts and the city of St. Petersburg. This programme marks the first step towards trying local approaches to address risk among young people in certain parts of the Russian Federation.

In a risk society, the role of chaotic factors increases and gradually becomes a large scale phenomenon. To some extent the chaotic, spontaneous processes which occur during the course of youth social development can have a decisive impact. Without these, youth innovations, which are required for expanded social reproduction, cannot be fully realised. However, these chaotic processes are accompanied by a great deal of risk, the consequences of which are unpredictable. This was frequently seen during the transition to a market economy in Russia since 1985. Whilst the market has helped some enterprises and initiatives, it has ruined others and robbed some young and older people of their livelihoods. The fact that the majority of the population are living below the poverty line is an additional argument for the opponents of a totally uncontrolled market, who favour the idea of a more regulated market. The experience of the many regions who have chosen this path of development shows that by economically and socially regulating youth integration into market relations, risk can at least be localised and controlled, although not eliminated altogether.

Youth integration into a risk society takes place under conditions of a decreased dependence of young people on the socialisation agencies. This loss of family and state influence on young people on the one hand gives them more independence, but on the other hand, it also increases the probability of risk and offers fewer guarantees of help in the case of failure. The *localisation of risk* in the process of youth integration *can only be achieved as a result of a reduction in the level of uncertainty in youth activities by means of social protection against risk.*

On the basis of the aforementioned analysis, the following ways of localising risk in the process of youth integration are proposed:

- Narrowing the boundaries of risk.
- Individualisation of risk.

- Reducing the threshold of uncertainty.
- Regulating the direction of risk; and
- Social protection in the event of failure.

The conflicts between young people and society can be realised not by integration, but conversely by differentiation of the conflicting structures (see Figure 5.1). The appearance of new structures may also contribute to the localisation of risk within specific boundaries, but under certain conditions it might veer out of control, like an avalanche (or to use Gidden's term, produce an uncontrollable juggernaut). During the process of separation of the systems, uncertainty is intensified and more and more new risks appear which affect more people. The outcome is not simply localisation but the globalisation of risk.

Social determinants of the globalisation of risk

The large majority of social scientists would concur that most modern societies are experiencing globalisation. In this context, however, we are talking about the globalisation of risk. In this final section we would like to examine the origins and importance of this phenonmena for post-Soviet Russia.

For more than a decade Russian society has been experiencing the second round of destruction of its normative consciousness, namely the eradication of social norms. The deliberate devaluation of the old norms and values of socialist society is still on-going, but a sufficient period of time has now passed to allow us to make a tentative assessment of the impact of the reform process on young people. Two types of difficulties have appeared. Firstly internal ones, which are connected to the Russian establishment's inability to overcome its long-term crisis, and secondly external ones, which are defined by Russia's changed position in the world. In the end both of these factors have had an effect on the globalisation of risk in Russia.

The impact of different internal factors has become concentrated in young people's value orientations. This means that the globalisation of risk is largely determined by the appearance of a so-called 'contrasting purpose' in the system of social values, when there are changes not only in the structure and the constituent parts of the old system of values, but also a more profound change, namely the transformation of these values into their diametrical opposites (thus white becomes black and vice versa). For example, the idea of free compulsory education for all young people, which is acknowledged as one of the main socialist values, is now being replaced by a totally different value system – elitist education, which in essence reflects the risk society tendency of turning education into a privilege for the minority. This not only contradicts former thinking concerning the prestige of education, its value and importance of qualifications, in which learning was viewed as a value in itself, it also comes into conflict with the real economic needs of Russia's crisis-ridden society. In avoiding its responsibility for guaranteeing to provide all its young citizens with an education, the Russian state has virtually created the conditions for widening the zone of risk faced by young Russians.

Following Ulrich Beck we acknowledge that risk is unequally distributed amongst the different social strata and groups. Thus the risk of failing to obtain an education is much higher amongst those from low-income families than among young people from well-off (New Russian) families. However, for the latter category, the threat of being thrown out of their educational institutions can be higher, as they are often more dependent upon their parent's financial input than on their own academic proficiency. Therefore the globalisation of risk means that young people from all social strata are now being affected by it and most face common problems. Freedom of self-determination, which is typical of a risk society, brings young people face to face with these problems. They cannot count on any help and have to rely on their own ability to cope. As this situation plays a key role in the formation of social maturity, *youth self-determination in a risk society is a significant factor in the globalisation of risk.*

A number of contradictions arise from this, which increase the level of risk. Firstly, *there is the contradiction between the widening spectrum of individual choice in social, professional and political spheres on the one hand and the narrowing of opportunities to find and occupy one's own place in society on the other.* Secondly, self-determination is one of the most basic of human needs and therefore is a key factor for successful youth participation in social reproduction. Furthermore, as a result of just this reproductive function, youth is defined as a specific social group. This is why *the failure to ensure full self-determination on a generation-wide scale has global consequences, as it affects the social character of young people.* Not only in Russia, but in other risk societies, young people are being transformed from a social group into a demographic group, (i.e. the social group characteristics of youth are being replaced by age differences). Another aspect of this problem is caused by the definition of independent or free self-determination in Russian society. This process is hardly linked to 'diversification' of young people's pathways into adulthood or the opportunity to try different areas in order to gain the best outcome. Instead, nowadays this doctrine is understood to be a young person's right to chose between learning and non-learning, or work and non-work, which is being taken to its most extreme form in Russia. For instance, because of the collapse of compulsory education, high fees in private educational institutions, and the growing pressure of unemployment, most young Russians have no alternative but to make a choice in favour of idleness. It is not surprising that with no possibility of earning a livelihood, the risk of increased dependency among youth becomes global.

As for the external factors of globalisation of risk, these are currently predominantly defined by contradictions which are typical of young people's attitude towards the West. These contradictions which have *deep historical roots*, are connected with youth awareness of Russia's geopolitical interests, the theoretical and philosophical heritage of the Slavophile-Westerner debate, the long-term class struggle, the Cold War and finally by the new attempts by NATO countries to re-divide the world. A major role in this process is played by a *perceived Western economic superiority.* The events in Yugoslavia (the Kosovo crisis of 1999) clearly demonstrated the significance of the external factor in Russia's globalisation of risk. *The idealisation of western democracy which was evident in youth consciousness during the mid-1990s, went a long way towards destroying the values of the former Soviet period. However, recent military aggression against a sovereign state (Serbia) has seriously shaken this idealised image of the West.* Although declaring their own interests in furthering the development of democracy in Russia, by becoming involved in the Balkans war, NATO countries have not provided the best example of democracy. Despite good intentions, Western policies were not clear cut and young Russians witnessed a policy of double standards in which the powerful dictated to the weak. This in turn gave the former the 'right' to ignore international law, to manipulate public opinion (via the mass media) and to destroy towns and annihilate populations in the name of private economic and political interests.[18] This is exactly what the West criticised the previous totalitarian Soviet regime for.

In this new climate, it is not surprising that the western threat has again taken a leading place in different risk factors in the consciousness of young people. In fact many rank this as the most important risk factor in recent times. As a result, the younger generation in Russia has found itself at the cross-roads between a discredited past, an unacceptable present and an uncertain future.

Conclusion

In the past many Soviet youngsters identified with the state. It in turn was an integration mechanism which encouraged solidarity. This role was, of course, largely propaganda, but it also contained an element of truth. The decline of the state has been accompanied by the fall of collectivism. As a consequence, in the 1990s, the younger generation in Russia has tended to identify with the non-state sector and to integrate into these structures. So what we have today in Russia's risk society is an old form of integration (the state, identification with it and its structures) which has now disintegrated and gradually been replaced by an imperfect private sector, which is as yet not sufficiently developed enough to act as an integration mechanism. The consequence is that young people risk social exclusion and marginalisation. Youth wanted to be integrated into society, but the specific conditions do not exist and the integration mechanisms are largely dysfunctional.

In stable risk societies, life trajectories and choices are made by young people with fewer barriers in their way than in unstable risk societies where conditions on the whole tend to be more extreme. In the latter case, the choice seems to be between win (gain a social dividend) or lose (ruin). Therefore the system choice, and the means of integration, which young people choose, lies between conformism and non-conformism, namely obey the rules of society on an instrumental basis and be seen to identify with it or decide to participate in youth sub-cultures and risk becoming involved in delinquent behaviour and actions. Some young people have opted for a third way, which integrates them into society after a fashion, namely by becoming involved in criminal activity and using that as a route into society. The irony of this situation is that those who tend to conform have little to gain and will probably only experience negative outcomes. Under these circumstances it is hardly surprising that young people tend to distance themselves from society or take destructive action.

One means of integration is a strong sense of identification with society. But the process of individualisation in Russia makes this extremely difficult. Nevertheless, Russia has gone some way towards unifying its education system which might generate some sort of relationship between youth and society. Young people themselves must also reflect on this and decide whether or not their interests, choice and preferences coincide with those of society, because as Evans and Furlong point out, *it is very important for young people not only to define their own goals, but also to be sure that their choices and aspirations correpond.*[19] If they do, then integration might follow; if not, and there is a clash between individual and corporate identity, then integration is unlikely. Working against this strong sense of identification with society is the highly unstable nature of things in Russia. In a country were over half of its young people (57.8 percent) are runaways and a third (36 percent) cannot look after themselves, it is not surprising that youth tend to be egoistic and individualistic in outlook. This tendency towards individualism means that the integration process is rather fragmented.

Another means of integration is on an individual rather than group basis. For this local route to be possible, young people would need to identify closely with their peers, family and friends and slowly build up solidarity in this way. As a result, if they become more co-operative in nature and less instinctively individual in focus, then over time they may associate more with society and its values. This gradual approach certainly seems to apply to capitalist societies[20] and even at times of risk, young people tend to have a strong emotional attachment to their society and a strong desire to be integrated into it.[21] Here the psychological make-up of individuals is decisive.

In order for integration to take place, there needs to be some form of interactive relationship between young people and the societies in which they live. If young people perceive that they have a good education, nice job, interesting work and are relatively financially secure, then this will encourage their integration into society and reduce the sense of risk. But at the same time, this degree of comfort may encourage them to take new risks. Whether or not individuals do this will depend upon their own subjective judgements. Finally, young people may in this context embark upon spontaneous integration.

Summarising our findings on youth conflict and its relationship to the localisation and globalisation of risk, the above analysis argues that there are several ways in which young people may become part of integrated (that is identify closer with) society. These are: strengthen the mechanical and organisational mechanisms (i.e. socialisation agencies); develop alternative means of managing the integration process; develop new non-traditional ways of identifying with society; encourage integration on a local basis; facilitate the integration function of risk and finally, encourage integration of young people with society in a spontaneous fashion.

Notes

1 See L. Coser, *The Functions of Social Conflict*, Free Press, New York, 1964.
2 U. Nagel and C. Wallace, 'Participation and Identification in Risk Societies; European Perspectives', in J. Bynner, L. Chisholm and A. Furlong (ed.), *Youth, Citizenship and Social Change in a European Context*, Aldershot, Ashgate, 1997, p. 43.
3 See Yu. A. Zubok, *Sotsial'naia integratsiia molodezhi v usloviakh nestabil'nogo obshchestva*, Moscow, Sotsium 1998, pp. 18–20; 'Iskliuchenie v issledovanii problem molodezhi', *Sotsiologicheskie Issledovaniiia*, 1998, No. 8; 'Exclusion in the study of the problems of young people', *Russian Education and Society*, September 1999, pp. 39–53; Social Integration and the Exclusion of the Youth in an Unstable Society', in V. Puuronen

(ed.) *Youth in Everyday Life Contexts*, Joensuu, University of Joensuu, 1999, pp. 297-304; 'Molodezh' mezhdu integratsieu i isluicheniem: sotsial'no-ekonomicheskii aspekt', *Sotsial'no-gumanitarnoe Znanie*, 2000, No. 2.; 'Social Integration of Russian Youth – Trends in the Risk Society', in V. Puuronen (ed.), *Youth on the Threshold of 3rd Millennium*, Joensuu, University of Joensuu, 2001, pp. 103–117 and her 'Integration versus exclusion: youth and the labour market', *International Social Science Journal*, Vol. LII, No. 2, June 2000, pp. 171–183.

4   T. Parsons, *The Social System*, Simon and Schuster, N.Y. 1965, p. 204.
5   Z.T. Golenkova, 'Teoriia modernizatsii', in G.V. Osipov (ed.), *Rossiskaia sotsiologicheskaia entsiklopediia*, Moscow, 'gruppa NORMA-IFRA', 1998, pp. 552–553.
6   The term 'jointly owned enterprises' refers to enterprises which are partly state and partly private owned.
7   See, for example, K. Roberts, *Youth and employment in Modern Britain*, Oxford University Press, 1995 and A. Furlong and F. Cartmel, *Young people and social change: Individualisation and Risk in Late Modernity*, Open University Press, 1997.
8   E. Durkheim, *Division of Labor in Society*, Simon and Schuster, New York, reprint, 1997.
9   *European Youth Trends 1998*, Council of Europe experts in youth research cited at www.ca.fr/youth/research/trends.htm
10 K. Evans and A. Furlong, 'Metaphors of Youth Transitions; niches, pathways, trajectories or navigations', in J. Bynner, L. Chisholm and A. Furlong (eds), *Youth, Citizenship and Social Change in a European Context*, Aldershot, Ashgate, 1997, p. 33.
11 K. Roberts, *Youth and Employment in Modern Britain*, Oxford University Press, 1995, p. 113.
12 Ibid.
13 Ibid, p. 118.
14 P. Allat, 'Young People and Families. En/Countering Social Exclusion', in H. Helve (ed.), *Unification and Marginalisation of Young People*, Youth Research 2000 Programme, The Finnish Youth Research Society, Helsinki, 1998, p. 79.
15 J.E. Cote and A.L. Allahar, *Generation in Hold. Coming of Age in the Late Twentieth Century*, New York, New University Press, 1996, p.74.
16 P. Abrams and A. McCulloch, *Sociology and Society*, Cambridge, Cambridge University Press, 1976, p. 44.
17 R. Pahl, 'Friendship: the social glue of contemporary society', in J. Franklin (ed.), *The Politics of Risk Society*, London, Polity Press, 1988, p. 103.
18 On Russia's predicament here see C. Williams, 'The New Russia: From Cold War strength to post-communist weakness and beyond', in P.J. Anderson, G. Wiessala and C. Williams (eds), *New Europe in Transition*, London and New York, Continuum 2000, pp. 248–266. For a critique of NATO see C. Williams, 'Kosovo: A fuse for the lighting', in A. Weymouth and S. Henig (eds), *The Kosovo Crisis: America's last war in Europe?*, Pearson Education, London, 2001, pp. 15–38, 288–290 and for an assessment of Russian views of the Kosovo crisis see C. Williams with Z.T. Golenkova, 'Russia: Walking the tightrope', in A. Weymouth and S. Henig (eds), *The Kosovo Crisis: America's last war in Europe?*, Pearson Education, London, 2001, pp. 204–225, 298–300.
19 K. Evans and A. Furlong, 'Youth Transitions; niches, pathways, trajectories or navigations', in J. Bynner, L. Chisholm and A. Furlong (ed.), *Youth, Citizenship and Social Change in a European Context*, Aldershot, Ashgate 1997, p. 34.
20 C.M. Young, *Young People Leaving Home in Australia; The Trend Towards Independence*, Australian Family Formation Project Monograph, No.9, Canberra, 1987 and P. Ainley, *Young People Leaving Home*, London, Cassell, 1991.
21 P. Abrams and A. McCulloch, *Sociology and Society*, Cambridge, Cambridge University Press, 1976, p. 44 and R. Pahl, 'Friendship: the social glue of contemporary society', in J. Franklin (ed.), *The Politics of Risk Society*, London, Polity Press, 1988, p. 103.

Chapter 6

Risk Trends in the Life Situation of Young People

We explored the localisation or globalisation of risk in the previous chapter. Here it is important to point out that risks at an individual level, increase or decrease, according to life situations. Thus risk expresses itself as a series of situations.

In a risk society, spontaneous factors or uncontrollable processes assume particular significance according to either the social situation or the degree of uncertainty which individuals face on a daily basis. Thus an individual's desire to make things more certain and predictable is closely connected with risk. This is comparable to someone going from a dark tunnel into the light. However, if s/he remains inside the tunnel, there is a high risk of an accident occurring. But the quicker one comes into the light, the less chance there is of a collision. In the aforementioned example, we were referring to going from uncertainty to certainty but the opposite can also occur. Sometimes an unexpected event occurs and disrupts the routine and predictability of our lives. In this case, an individual would go from a room full of light to one that is in complete darkness. S/he would lose their orientation and the risk of collision or an accident would increase again. As a consequence, risk is not simply a state of uncertainty, but a process of transition from uncertainty to certainty or vice versa. In both cases, individuals have to reach a decision and act without knowing the full consequences of their actions. We shall refer to this as *non-motivated risk*. By contrast, individuals often taken voluntary decisions. In this instance, individuals are not forced to react but to make a comparison of the possible positive and negative outcomes of a particular course of action. We shall use the term *motivated risk* to describe this situation. Any individual estimates their chances of success based on their own ability and experience as well as on the likelihood of failure. In this case, we are really talking about *reasonable* or *unreasonable risk*.

Acknowledging that there may be different types of risk situations, in Chapter 4 we devised a typology of risk (see Table 4.1). Using sociological and survey data, we shall now present our empirical findings on the risk tendencies in the life situations of Russian youth, comparing the latter to that of youth in other global risk societies.

Socio-demographic situation

Demographic reproduction is a significant aspect of societal reproduction. Birth and death rates, health status and life expectancy are all useful indicators of the wealth of a society. In Russia today, there is an extremely unfavourable demographic situation and this is one of the most acute difficulties facing Russian youth. Creating a family of distinction, having children, providing for the health and welfare of your family and ensuring that they are safe, are among the greatest uncertainties in Russia today. Growing uncertainty in all these areas is generating increased risk. Russia's demographic situation is affected by numerous factors, the key ones of which are economic, social, social-psychological, political and ecological. An analysis of the demographic situation should therefore be the starting point in any attempt to identity the initial stage and development of Russia as a risk society.

The data presented in Table 2.3 together with that in Table 6.1 below shows that Russia's demographic decline has coincided with a new systemic crisis which has accelerated since 1992. Russia's constant de-population is strong evidence of the escalation of risk in Russian society. The declining birth-rate is another indicator of Russia as a risk society (see Table 2.3).

Table 6.1 Population trends in Russia, 1990–2001

Year	Changes over the year (000s people)			
	Population size as of 01.01 (in millions)	Natural increase or Decrease (-)	Due to migration	General level of growth or decline (-)
1990	148.0	338,000	164,000	502,000
1991	148.5	110,000	51,000	161,600
1992	148.7	-207,000	176,100	-30,900
1993	148.7	-737,000	430,100	-307,600
1994	148.4	-869,000	810,000	-59,700
1995	148.3	-831,000	502,000	-329,700
1996	147.9	-817,600	343,600	-474,000
1997	147.5	-737,300	349,000	-388,300
1998	146.7	-800,000	213,000	-630,000
1999	146.3	-400,000	196,000	-660,000
2000	145.6	-700,000	n.a.	n.a.
2001	144.8	-800,000	n.a.	n.a.

Key: n.a. = data not available

Sources: *Rossiya: Vyzvodyi vremeni i puti reformirovaniya*, Moscow, 1998, p. 93; *Zhenshchiny i muzhchiny Rossii 1999: Kratkii statisticheskii sbornik*, Goskomstat, Moscow, 1999, p. 34; *Zhenshchiny i muzhchiny Rossii 2000*, Goskomstat, Moscow, 2000, p. 30 and V. Osipov and V.V. Lokosov, *Sotsial'naia tsena neoliber'nogo reformirovaniia*, Moscow, 2001, p. 58.

The birth coefficient rate by 1997 had fallen to 1.23, which is 0.91 less than the level required for simple reproduction.[1] The difference between the death rate and birth rate is 2.3 million between 1991–2000. Even if we take into account, the influx of migrants, this still leaves a 1.6 million deficit compared to 1990. All in all, the crude death rate has been 2.8 times higher than the crude birth rate since 1991. The escalation of risk has affected marital trends in Russia too. As a rule, when conditions are uncertain, people refrain from getting married or starting a family. Together with the decline of the birth rate, especially in large cities, such as Moscow, as well as in the Russian Federation as a whole, the rate of marriage is also falling while the number of divorces is on the increase (see Table 6.2).

Table 6.2 Marriage and divorce trends in the Russian Federation, 1991–2000

Year	Marriages		Divorces	
	Number in '000s	per 1,000 population	Number in '000s	per 1,000 population
1991	598	8.6	1,277	4.0
1992	639	7.1	1,053	4.3
1993	663	7.5	1,106	4.5
1994	681	7.4	1,080	4.6
1995	681	7.2	1,066	4.6
1996	502	5.6	824	3.8
1997	555	6.3	929	3.8
1998	501	3.8	849	3.4
1999	n.a.	6.3	n.a.	3.7
2000	n.a.	6.2	n.a.	4.3

Key: n.a. = data not available

Source: G.V. Osipov and V.V. Lokosov, *Sotsial'naia tsena neoliber'nogo reformirovaniia*, Moscow, 2001, p. 58 and Goskomstat data cited at www.gks.ru.

The number of registered marriages fell every year by 97,000 or by 16 percent in the period 1991–1998 alone. Furthermore, in 1991, nearly 1 in 2 marriages ended in divorce, but by the late 1990s, there was a 60 percent chance that your marriage would end in divorce. As a consequence, in the last 5 years, 2,800,000 children in Russia live in single-parent families.[2]

Table 6.3 Changes in the size of the youth cohort in Russia according to age (in percent), 1989–2000

Year	Age-group			
	15–19	*20–24*	*25–29*	*30–34*
1989	6.8	6.6	8.5	8.8
1993	7.1	6.6	6.8	8.6
1994	7.2	6.7	6.5	8.4
1995	7.8	6.9	6.4	8.1
1996	7.4	7.0	6.5	7.7
1997	7.4	7.1	6.5	7.3
1998	7.6	7.2	6.6	7.1
1999	8.0	7.6	6.4	6.7
2000	8.1	7.4	7.2	6.4

Source: V.I. Chuprov, Yu. A. Zubok, R.A. Mamededov and I.N. Staroverova, 'Sotsial'nyi potentsial molodezhii', in *Rossiya: predolenie natsional'noi katastrofy*, Moscow, RiTs, ISPI, RAN, 1998, p. 78; *Zhenshchiny i muzhchiny Rossii 1999: Kratkii statisticheskii sbornik*, Goskomstat, Moscow, 1999, p. 17 and *Zhenshchiny i muzhchiny Rossii 2000*, Goskomstat, Moscow, 2000, p. 16.

Moving on to discuss the demographic situation among Russian youth, the available data indicates that they share many of the above difficulties (see Table 6.3). Thus, the size of the age group 15–24 years increased from 13.4 percent to 14.8 percent between 1989–1998 whereas the reverse is true of those aged over 25 years, which fell from 17.3 percent to 13.7 percent over the same period. The main reason for these trends is a dramatic change in the health status of the younger generation, which becomes progressively worse with each passing year. Since 1991, the number of young Russians suffering from various diseases of the endocrinal system, the digestive system, blood etc. has increased and many have ended up with very low immunity levels. New diseases of the nervous system and of the sensory organs, which have risen from 7 to 10 percent, are now being discovered for the first time among youth. Another area of concern is the rise in serious diseases, such as cancer among children (up by 18 percent), oligophrenia (mental sub-normality) (up 24 percent) and tuberculosis up by 170 percent. The number of cases of syphilis among children has also increased from 38 in 1991 to 2,626 in 1997 or by 1,447 percent which is due to rising paedophilia and the unbridled sexual revolution during the last decade.

Teenagers health status shows similar tendencies. Table 6.4 shows the morbidity level among Russian teenagers between 1991–1996, the last year for which data is currently available. Most of this increase is the product of rising drug and toxin addiction, alcoholism as well as the spread of venereal and other diseases.

Table 6.4   Morbidity trends among Russian teenagers (cases per 100,000), 1991–1996

Year	Rate per 100,000 teenagers
1991	57.8
1992	60.9
1993	67.0
1994	66.8
1995	71.0
1996	70.0
Change between 1991–1996	121 percent

Source: *Sotsial'noe polozhenie i uroven' zhizni naseleniya Rossii: Ofitsial'noe izdanie 1997g*, Moscow, 1997, p. 282.

As we can see from table 6.4 for the first few years of the post-communist period, the general disease level among Russia's teenagers rose by 21 percent. At the same time, the number of young drug addicts has increased 9 times from 1,618 to 14,600 cases. Today, the proportion of healthy teenagers in the Russian population only constitutes around 25 percent (i.e. one in four). In addition, the neglect of the health of youth, its physical condition and the collapse of mass sport facilities, has also contributed to the aforementioned trends. For example, the number of beds in children's hospitals has been reduced from 1,826 in 1991 to only 109 per 10,000 by 1997; the number of beds in maternity homes fell from 748 to 194; the number of visits each day to children's polyclinics declined from 7,235 to 2,426 and finally, the number of visits per day to women's consultation clinics fell from 2,295 to 900 between 1991–1997. These trends resulted in a more than 2-fold increase in the number of adolescents born with abnormalities and it is probable that this will also reduce their long term life expectancy.

The aforementioned increases in child and adolescent morbidity, coupled with the mortality trends shown in Table 6.5, are unprecedented for peacetime. As a consequence, nowadays in Russia, the proportion of healthy young people is relatively small. The most meaningful indicator of this fact is the crude death rate amongst youth in comparison to other population groups. The other noticeable trend is murder, accidents and other illness as a source of death among young people. This was not the case in the past.

The socio-demographic situation remains difficult for most of the Russian population, but especially for those who live in the regions (*oblasti*), as they have experienced massive de-population and there is also a gross imbalance between youth and the elderly. Thus the proportion of the population who are OAPs is 1.3–1.6 times higher than the number of young people living in towns such as Pskov, Tver, Tula, Ivanovo, Ryazan and Kursk. This fact, among other things, is eroding the social system in many of Russia's regions.

Under the present social and economic conditions prevailing in Russia, young people are starting to reconsider their *reproductive orientations* (i.e. their desire whether or not to have children). One 1992 official Goskomstat survey found, for example, that only two percent of the young couples did not intend to have children. Two years later, however, one in four young women did not want to have any children and one in two intended to have just one child. Among those couples who already had one child, 76 percent said they did not want any more and the corresponding figure for couples with two children was 36 percent.[3]

Table 6.5 Mortality trends among Russian youth by age-group (in percent), 1990–1996

Age-group	Crude Death Rate (in percent)			Growth rate (in percent)
	1990	1995	1996	
15–19	1.1	1.5	1.6	145
20–24	1.7	2.7	2.6	153
25–29	2.1	3.4	3.2	153
30–34	2.7	4.6	4.1	152

Source: *Sotsial'noe polozhenie i uroven' zhizni naseleniya Rossii: Ofitsial'noe izdanie 1997g*, Moscow, 1997, p. 261.

Many new-born children are in poor health. The proportion of children born with an illness has increased throughout the 1990s. In 1990, every seventh baby was born ill but by 1992, this figure had increased to 1 in 5. By 1995 it had risen to 1 in 4 and finally by 1996, 1 in 3 new-born babies were ill. Abnormalities amongst Russia's new-born increased 1.6 fold between 1990–1996.[4] Today, Russia is ranked 117 out of 189 countries in terms of the life expectancy predictions for its new-born.

The desire to get married among youth and their marital behaviour has also dramatically changed. More and more young people are rejecting marriage and children, preferring instead to simply live together. Thus one micro-census of 1994 discovered that nearly 15 percent of young men and 12 percent of young women aged 18–19 years were living with their partners, but were not married.[5]

Our analysis of Russia's demographic situation among youth shows an unfavourable situation. Hence, the probability of risk of the negative demographic reproduction is on the increase. After the year 2004 Russia's labour force will be under pressure due to the declining birth rate in the second half of the 1980s.

Furthermore, by the year 2010, Russia will need to implement special measures in order to resolve many problems accompanying this declining birth rate. All in all, this negative trend was caused by both objective demographic processes as well as by the negative impact made by social-economic factors, a rapid decline in the living standards and the absence of a sensible social and youth policy at the macro-political level.

Life start situation

Young people's life start situation can be considered as their initial potential in terms of social reproduction. Of course every younger generation does not start with a 'blank sheet' because they inherit some material conditions and life experience from the previous generation. From a sociological point of view youth life start refers to the legacy of cultural traditions and material conditions that young people gain from their parents and which society wants them to reproduce as continuity provides simple reproduction in society. Nowadays, however, the tempo of social development is becoming so rapid that it renders past experience useless. This is the reason why youth life start could be potentially innovative which is the basis for expanded social reproduction. Youth life start can de defined in many ways, for example, in terms of biological cycles of development, so it is probably best to talk in terms of *social start*, which refers to the bottom age limit of youth, namely to those between the ages of 15 to 18–20 years when young people come of age. This phase is determined by one's health status, level of physical and cultural development, material well-being and so forth. All these factors in turn impact upon young people's education, qualifications, employment, the ability to start a family and on the prospects for promotion. Lots of problems which young people cannot cope with occur at this stage. In accordance with the well-known concept developed by Erickson, this age period is linked with the search for identities when young people have to answer the questions 'Who am I?' and 'To what extent am I independent?' Everything happens *for the first time*, many things are therefore uncertain but nevertheless decisions still have to be taken. The risk of making mistakes is therefore extremely high.

The majority of the *problems arising are closely connected with inequalities of life start* which occur because of one's social background. The extent to which young people face various life starts reflects differences in gender, class, ethnicity and age-group, region and the urban/rural divide. As Karen Evans and Andy Furlong point out young people's ascribed characteristics are *important as differential resources* and provide them with a *set of advantages or disadvantages which affect their transition outcome*.[6] In addition, Roberts and Jung argue that young people's situations and future prospects continue to be governed by their *family origins, school records, gender and places of residence*.[7] Thus social origins, gender and class in our view still produce unequal starting points and perhaps even false starts for certain sections of European youth. In this regard, Evans and Furlong aptly note that:

pockets of relatively high youth unemployment within cities are the product, less of the local employment opportunities than of the low qualifications, disadvantaged family background and other characteristics of the young people who lived there.[8]

Developing Beck's ideas on specific features of risk society, Ken Roberts argues that Western Europe is facing a process which he terms 'structured individualisation', namely a situation in which various determinants of life chances continue to operate *but in a much greater variety of configurations.*[9] He then goes on to suggest that young people derive competencies for dealing with risk and uncertainty from *their backgrounds and socio-economic environments* which enable them to be *more or less effective negotiators or navigators* in the process of transition.[10]

However, the extent to which that *structured individualisation* takes place would undoubtedly vary according to the degree of economic, political and social in/stability prevailing in any society and on the balance of the forces detailed earlier in chapter 2. In Western Europe, this process will probably almost certainly be *more structured* than it is in Russia and other countries in transition. Our research suggests that young people in all societies face the risks outlined in chapters 3–5, but young people's ability to resolve these risks varies according to whether or not young people live in stable rather than unstable risk societies.

Whilst the degree to which this is true varies according to which section of youth we are referring and to what society they are living in, we would concur with Roberts' conclusion that in Western Europe social patterns are reproduced. Hence young peoples' families advantages and disadvantages in both continents are *transmitted to their children.*[11] Thus, in the case of young people from a new Russian family background the choice might be one of where to study – at home or abroad; whereas for those young persons from white-collar families the choice is likely to be study or work. Finally, for those sections of youth coming from poor families, the choice may be even more stark, namely live a pitiful existence or a life of crime.

Of course, no society can provide totally equal life start situations among all sections of youth for obvious reasons, but the democratisation process assumes some levelling of rights among different categories of young people, so that they can be fully integrated into society. In this way, the goal is that initial life start inequalities will be minimised.

In today's world, the transmission of knowledge and experience, for reasons outlined in chapters 1–2, is constantly changing. Previously the latter took place from parents to children but nowadays it involves the transmission of knowledge and experience from the education system, the mass media (and latterly parents) to young people. This is, as Margaret Mead recognised, a particular type of pre-figurative consciousness whereby young people emphasise not the past or even present, but keep an eye on the future. As the famous Bulgarian sociologist, Petar-Emil Mitev points out, a so-called 'juvenialisation' is occurring. In other words, not only do young people accept the attitudes and opinions of adults, adults also accept the necessity for youth innovation. At the same time, young people still wish to be self-reliant and do not want to depend upon others, such as their parents. Nevertheless trying to 'go it alone', does carry risks.

The level of uncertainty in the social start situation becomes greater in a risk society. Different life start positions and other factors mean that not all young people have equal chances of succeeding, for example, in the education system (school through to university) or in the labour market. But the uncertainties and insecurities do not stop here. In the past, social networks and other ties might have helped young people find a job or integrate faster into the labour market, with the inevitable variations according to class, ethnicity and gender. The difficulty in the 1990s and into the twenty-first century is that these old social networks have been under strain and in some cases under threat. Because of the latter situation, current social networks have not proved adequate for integrating youth into society. Thus a crucial role belongs to the family, as it becomes almost a single 'island of integration' of youth into society, even if it is in crisis itself.[12] Research on social exclusion amongst youth in Finland undertaken by Heikinen and Puuronen suggests that some social networks (communities and associations), such as those consisting of young unemployed people, can help them develop a more positive attitude, prevent loneliness and isolation and ensure that they maintain strong social ties.[13]

Alongside this, a young person's responsibility for making decisions also increases. The latter can be useful in so far as it aids the development of social maturity and encourages young people to make an adult adjustment to their environment. A series of factors – educational attainment, position in the labour market, the breadth and depth of one's interests and the direction of an individual's value orientations – are all indicators of the degree of success (or failure) to which individuals have secured a firm place in the social structure and identify with it (or not). Of course, the degree of success (or failure) varies according to the socio-economic and political changes in any given risk society. As a result, models of youth life start are different.

We have already seen that the shift from a modern to a risk society has a number of implications for young people. It is evident that the life-start, life-chances and life-course of youth in numerous countries is more fragmented that it was several decades ago. One of the biggest consequences of this situation is that old reference points and identities held by young people (and in the past transmitted to them by their parents) have either become distorted and transformed, or disappeared altogether. This has led to uncertainties of identity and growing risks of social exclusion and marginalisation.

OECD reports show that youth integration in the 1970s when there was optimism about youth labour market prospects was easier. But since the end of the 1980s and into the 1990s, as many researchers suggest, changes of the model of life start occurred among western youth and this resulted in *major difficulties in successfully integrating young people into the European labour market*. As a consequence, one of the most striking changes in recent years has been a *growth in the proportion of young people remaining in full-time education*. Hence OECD statistics show that the average number of 22 years olds staying on in education has increased from 19 percent in 1984 to 34 percent in 1997. This has also meant a declining number of early school leavers, the proportion of which fell from 50 percent to 33 percent over the same period.[14] In addition, the number of youths aged 16–24 years neither in education nor work in the OECD fell from 22 percent in 1984 to 14 percent in 1997. The extent to which full time education is preferred to temporary or no work, on the one hand, or to a combination of education and work, on the other, varies according to country. On the positive side, in more recent years, we have witnessed the quasi-stabilisation of those combining education with employment. On average within the EU, 17 percent of 16–19 year olds were studying and working in 1997 whilst 61 percent were studying only.[15] This approach is favoured in countries where apprenticeship schemes still operate or where part-time employment is common. In the former case, research shows that young people have a better chance of gaining a foothold in the labour market.

Some indication of the fate of various European, American, Canadian and Australian secondary school students after they finished their compulsory education in 1996 is shown in Table 6.6.

Table 6.6 Learning to work in various OECD countries, 1996

	Type of training scheme		
Country	Apprenticeship	School based vocational	General education
Australia	3	2	94
Austria	41	37	22
Canada	1	5	94
Czech Republic	–	82	18
Denmark	44	14	42
Finland	5	47	48
Hungary	–	70	30
Japan	–	26	74
Norway	25	27	48
Portugal	4	32	64
Sweden	–	60	40
Switzerland	60	9	31
United Kingdom	24	33	43
United States	–	12	88

Source: OECD Labour Statistics and EUROSTAT data, 1996.

The aforementioned table indicates that in some countries, students preferred general education (Australia, Canada, Japan and the USA), whereas in others, apprenticeships were more common (Switzerland) or else school based vocational training was used (Czech Republic, Hungary and Sweden). The rest preferred a mix of two or all three. Unfortunately, the availability of apprenticeship type training in the late 1990s was well down on what it had been in the 1960s and 1970s.

On the question of part-time work trends, EU-wide surveys show that a third of women work part-time compared to only 6 percent of men. Female part-time work is especially high in Sweden (41 percent), the UK (45 percent) and Holland (68 percent). In 1997, 20 percent of those working part-time stated that this was because they couldn't find full-time employment. In overall terms, this figure has risen by 10 percent since 1990.[16]

A major difficulty has been in retaining school pupils so that they can complete their compulsory education. OECD data demonstrates that on average, one in five teenagers do not attend school. In some countries, such as the UK and Holland, the figures are particularly high – 44 percent and 35 percent respectively.[17] Governments tend to view those who truant from school or drop out as 'deviants' and hence as a cause of great anxiety. As Julian Tanner points out:

> ... dropouts are viewed as rejectors of the goals and values of education. They are also a visible reminder of the failings of an allegedly meritocratic educational system.[18]

Whilst most youth research in the 1970s and 1980s highlighted 'the persisting connections between social origins [and] educational achievements' as the main reason for poor or under-achievement amongst certain groups in Western societies, Tanner argues that these sections of youth are best seen as 'reluctant rebels' for several reasons: first, although they don't like school, these young people do recognise the importance of education as a training for work; second, they don't necessarily hate education, just the authoritarian atmosphere and lack of freedom and autonomy in the particular educational establishments at which they studied, and finally, Tanner believes that even if they have dropped out now, this does not mean that these young people have 'cut their ties to the dominant economic and normative order' altogether.[19] We do not deny the existence of high dropout rates in many countries, as shown in Table 6.7 below, but advocate instead that there is an urgent need to reconceptualise the issue of young drop-outs.

Nowadays greater significance is attached to individual achievement in school, jobs and throughout life. Thus because the number of young people completing secondary school is high – 75 percent in the OECD as a whole – *those who fail to gain qualifications tend therefore to be heavily penalised in the labour market.* Research shows that young people 'leaving school without any qualifications' face a greater 'risk of [social] exclusion and poor labour market prospects'. John Bynner et al. argue that young people fall into three broad categories: those getting on, getting by or getting nowhere.[20] Those who fall into the 'getting nowhere' category tend to be those youngsters who leave school without qualifications and/or who fail to gain a foothold in the labour market. In this context, OECD researchers found that on average in 1996, young men with low educational attainment had an unemployment rate of 16 percent whilst those with tertiary/university education had better chances and a lower unemployment rate of 8 percent. For young women, the figures were 20 percent and 9 percent respectively.[21] As a consequence, this group constitute:

a 'hard core' of disaffected young people, a stigmatised minority with cumulative disadvantages, often related to intergenerational factors, such as poverty, unstable family backgrounds and life in communities with high overall unemployment.[22]

But it is also true that those young people who leave education with qualifications and skills not demanded by the labour market, might, of course, also find it difficult to get jobs.[23] A combination of all these factors means that some young people fail to acquire the skills necessary to negotiate the transition to adulthood successfully.

Table 6.7 Proportion of youth giving up school, 1996

Country	End age of compulsory education	Percent not in education one year after end of compulsory education
Australia	15	3
Austria	15	9
Canada	16	20
Czech Republic	15	1
Denmark	16	18
Finland	16	8
Hungary	16	26
Japan	15	2
Norway	16	7
Portugal	14	10
Sweden	16	4
Switzerland	15	13
United Kingdom	16	26
United States	17	18

Source: OECD Labour Statistics and EUROSTAT data, 1996.

The relationship between study and work, on the one hand, and work and society, on the other, is also rapidly changing. The emergence of a risk society has meant that finding employment was more problematic in the 1990s than it was in the previous two decades. As a result, the transition from education to the labour market now takes longer than it used to. On average, school level education is completed at the age of 18 years and tertiary/university education at 22 years in most European countries.

Numerous reasons can be cited for the delay in entry to the labour market, including: staying longer in education, the fact that reforms in teaching methods and curriculum have made education more attractive, poor job prospects and a preference for being in education rather than face unemployment. All of these factors point to increased insecurities and uncertainty among today's youth. Fear of lack of opportunities – the availability of only casual, temporary or part-time jobs – and unfulfilled potential – marginalisation, underemployment, being stuck in a dead-end job, coupled with the difficulty a young person faces in trying to find their niche in a recession labour market – means that young peoples life course is no longer as orderly and linear as it was in the past.

As a consequence, in 1997, on average 56 percent of 18 years olds were still in full-time education; whilst only 44 percent of 22 years olds were in employment.[24] Of course, it is sometimes possible, depending upon national characteristics and policies, to combine education and work. In the UK this is highly common, but elsewhere it is rarely the case. Part of the reason for this is that it is harder to find jobs nowadays. Thus, whereas 52 percent of 15–24 year olds were in employment in 1979, this figure had fallen to 44 percent by 1997.

Although the structures and values of different types of European societies will determine youth life-course and life-chance patterns, what all these countries have in common is that they are risk societies. This minimises differences and maximises similarities. In this respect, it is possible to outline the concerns which all countries have regarding the impact of the emergence of a European risk society on youth. These concerns are as follows: firstly, youth labour market prospects have not improved; secondly, the employment gap between adults and young people has widened, and thirdly, young people tend to be more disadvantaged and therefore to swell the ranks of the unemployed.[25]

In overall terms, OECD surveys show that in the 1980s and 1990s, despite increases in the level of educational attainment, youth labour market participation and employment rates fell. Two key trends have emerged since the 1970s: higher youth unemployment and falling relative wages in relation to older workers. The disadvantageous social position of youth is connected with the fact that young people are more often than not engaged into low-paid work which is usually attributed to inadequate work experience. In general, the salary of young people is 40–80 percent lower than that of the older generation. Up to 20 percent of young people in Austria and Sweden rising to up to 63 percent of youth in the USA find themselves in this situation. To resolve this conflict in a risk society young people often choose to stay on in education, which delays their entry into the labour market.

The emergence of a risk society has extended youth as a life phase and made the period of life start longer. This occurs, firstly, because young people struggle to achieve their personal goals, and secondly, because of many risk factors which turn failure into reality and therefore young people experience a shortage of time to overcome such failures.

Thus, our analysis of the main characteristics of western youth transition leads to the conclusion that problems arising at the period of life start are determined by risk which has increased in different societies over the last decade. It expresses itself in growing difficulties in achieving economic independence and sustaining one's occupational status, starting a family and purchasing housing (see later). In a risk society these processes differ by difficulty and prolongation in comparison to previous periods. Young people stay on longer in the education system, have difficulties finding their labour market niches, are concentrated in low qualified and low-paid work, delay starting a family and remain dependent on their parents and family. At the same time, all the aforementioned processes are very contradictory, just like a risk society itself, because phenomena such as long-term education as well as secondary employment, are not always negative.

These changes are also reflected in young people's life start patterns in Russia. For example, when there was widespread optimism in *the mid-1950s, education was given high priority*. Thus if young people failed their entrance examinations, this was considered a 'tragedy'. By the time of Khrushchev's reign (1955–1964), *greater emphasis was placed upon gaining the necessary work experience*. This if university entrants had two years work experience in industry then they didn't need to sit the entrance examination and could avoid any competition for VUZy places. In the 1970s, during the *Brezhnev era* (1965–1982), due to the impact of the scientific and technical revolution, the *acquisition of a technical secondary education was virtually made compulsory*. Gorbachev's policy of *perestroika* and the introduction of the market *also affected young people's life start. Thus from the mid 1980s to the early 1990s, an exclusively instrumental approach dominated young people's motivation and behaviour.*

As for the current post-Soviet younger generation, their life start has occurred at a very difficult time, one of crisis. Thus young people's life starts in the 1990s were full of contradictions. Nevertheless, by most statistical measures, the life start of most young Russians today is reasonable. Table 6.8 below which uses the example of start positions in education, demonstrates this fact.

Table 6.8 Level of education of young people in Russia aged 15–18 years according to gender (as percent of gender group), 1999

Young people aged 15–18 years	*Level of education*		
	Incomplete secondary	*Complete secondary*	*Vocational training*
Men	49.0	43.6	7.4
Women	39.9	53.3	6.8
Group as a whole	43.8	49.2	7.0

Source: Authors' 'Social development of Russian youth' survey data, 1999.

It is clear that nearly half of our sample of young people (49.2 percent) have already completed their secondary education, whilst 7 percent have finished their vocational training. Although young men demonstrate clear potential at the start they gradually fall behind their female counterparts, with 10 percent more girls gaining full comprehensive schooling.

Using start positions in education as an indicator, the situation in 1999 was much better than it was at the end of the Soviet period (1990), as a comparison of Table 6.9 and 6.10 demonstrates.

Table 6.9 Type of activity undertaken by young people in Russia aged 15–18 years according to gender (as percent of group), 1999

Young people aged 15–18 years	a	b	c	d	e	f	g	h
Men	4.4	49.0	35.6	12.6	4.1	0.1	4.1	1.7
Women	3.2	59.3	23.3	14.2	3.9	0.7	5.6	1.8
Group as a whole	3.8	54.2	29.4	13.4	4.0	0.4	4.9	1.7

Key: *a* Work *b* Study at school
c Study at PTU/technical college *d* Study at H.E.I
e Work and study *f* Street trader
g Neither work nor study *h* unemployed

Source: Authors' 'Social development of Russian youth' survey data, 1999.

The main reason for this is the low value attached to education during Gorbachev's perestroika. The falling prestige attached to education was particularly strong as early as 1992, when pupils left schools in droves preferring instead to be involved in petty-commerce and street trade. As a result, the proportion of young people leaving comprehensive schools with complete secondary education (11 years) was as low as 24.4 percent according to official statistics. It took until 1997 for the number of pupils leaving comprehensive schools with complete secondary education to reach its mid-1980s level.

Table 6.10 Type of activity undertaken by young people in Russia aged 15–18 years according to gender (as percent of group), 1990

Young people aged 15–18 years	a	b	c	d	e	f	g	h
Men	6.0	36.9	51.5	4.6	0.5	0.0	0.5	0.0
Women	9.0	47.1	32.8	7.6	2.5	0.0	1.0	0.0
Group as a whole	7.7	42.5	41.1	6.3	1.6	0.0	0.8	0.0

Key: *a* Work *b* Study at school
c Study at PTU/technical college *d* Study at H.E.I
e Work and study *f* Street trader
g Neither work nor study *h* unemployed

Source: Authors' 'Social development of Russian youth' survey data, 1990.

One of the most encouraging trends is the fact that the majority of young people in Russia aged 15–18 years are still studying: 54.2 percent at school; 29.4 percent in PTUs or technical colleges and 13.4 percent at an higher educational establishment (VUZ). Approximately one in ten young people in Russia aged 15–18 years work or manage to combine study and work. Only 4.9 percent of young people in Russia aged 15–18 years do no work or study. These trends are shown in Tables 6.9–6.10 which also indicates that the social start indicator for females is higher than that for males.

A slightly different picture was noticeable in the West. One recent UN Report on youth trends pointed out that young women constitute two-thirds of those who have never worked or studied or who have not completed school education.[26] At the same time, those girls that do study tend to be ahead of their male counterparts in terms of their higher educational qualifications.

In Russia, meanwhile, our research demonstrates that more women study at VUZ and combine study with work than men. It is also the case that more men than women are in temporary jobs or study part-time. If young people in Russia aged 15–18 years favoured vocational training in 1990, then nearly a decade later (by 1999), the same group now wished to study social science and humanities subjects. Once again girls were more advanced than boys.

Our research also demonstrates that relatively few of the post-Soviet younger generation make any connection between life start and commercial activity. Less than one percent of our sample in 1999 devoted themselves to petty-business or trading, down from 7 percent in 1994. However, this generally good picture does not highlight the difficult and dramatic changes in the personal life situations of young Russians since the mid-1990s. Young people in Russia now have a number of difficult choices: study and/or work; which university and in which city/region; which job and profession; commerce or conscription. Many of these choices are delayed for want of money. This problem is becoming particularly acute because neither parents or young people are able to earn enough money to enable a decision to be reached on the aforementioned dichotomies. Thus choice is accompanied by uncertainty. As some of these decisions, such as which university to go to and in which city/region, often have to be made in relatively short time periods, this accentuates matters and increases the degree of uncertainty and risk. Thus in making a choice, and escaping the dilemma or delay, the level of risk rises.

Over the past decade, the proportion of young people in Russia who neither study nor work has increased 3-fold. Although the number of young people involved in percentage terms is relatively small, in absolute terms, it constitutes around 350,000. This category includes the disabled, infirm and a small group who prefer leisure time to study or work. This section of youth can easily be termed 'a group at risk' as they are faced by total uncertainty and no better prospects. The term which applies in such cases is a *suspended start*, because for reasons largely beyond their control, these categories of young people are being deprived of the opportunity to be integrated into society.

Youth unemployment is one of the main aspects of contemporary models of life start. This phenomenon is quite common in Western countries. Since the mid-1990s there has been a steady increase in youth unemployment from 16.3 percent up to nearly 1 in 4 at 21.5 percent by the end of the 1990s. Unemployment causes delays in starting a family for two-thirds of young Europeans and 45 percent of the young unemployed receive financial support from their parents. It is not surprising that unemployment was estimated as a more acute problem than environmental issues (60.2 percent) and the development of advanced technologies (54.4 percent) by young people. For instance, 75.7 percent of young people in the 1997 Eurobarometer survey thought that youth unemployment should receive top priority among social measures in the European Union.[27]

As regard the question, 'What skills are most useful for finding employment', the following answers were given by West European youth: good general training (42.8 percent); language ability (40.4 percent); good communication skills (37.6 percent) and familiarity with information technologies (32.3 percent). These skills were viewed as more important than good presentation, ability to work in a team, apprenticeships, knowledge of the business world, and scientific qualifications (put in last place with 8.6 percent). In terms of linguistic skills, young Europeans are progressing well. In a previous survey carried out in 1990, Eurobarometer observed that, in addition to their mother tongue, 60 percent of young people were able to speak another language well enough to have a conversation. By 1997, 71.3 percent of young Europeans (almost three out of four) stated that they could converse in a second language, so much progress has clearly been made since 1990. The three most widely spoken languages (not including native speakers) were: English (53.7 percent), French (19.9 percent) and German (11 percent). Spanish is the number one language that young people would like to learn (23.1 percent), closely followed by French (21.7 percent) and English (19.8 percent).[28] This proves that young people are concerned about future employment opportunities and it also demonstrates their readiness to do their best to improve things. Finally, it is very important to note that although only 1.1 percent of young respondents in the West would consider working in the 'black economy', 24.6 percent of their Russian counterparts, according to our surveys, do not exclude such a possibility, no matter what the consequences are.

Young people's desire for independence from their parents also faces insurmountable obstacles. Instead of achieving their life goals and in particular autonomy, young people are often forced to rely on others for help and are experiencing a prolonged dependency on adults and the state. Lets take the example of housing. Housing provision is adversely affected by the availability and price of housing provided by the state and the private sector. Given that few young people have jobs and even those in jobs traditionally earn less than adults, young people find it increasingly difficult to find housing they can afford to rent, let alone buy. Shortages of low cost housing applies especially to cities, but even in rural areas the situation is by no means easy because in Green's words 'wealthy urbanites have purchased second homes'.[29] So far, few EU countries provide young people with adequate housing benefits to overcome these problems.

EU surveys show that some Europeans live alone with the number increasing from 8 percent in 1981 to 11 percent today and it is forecast that this figure will rise to 13 percent by 2010.[30] General trends in 1995 according to EU member state are shown in Table 6.11.

Table 6.11 Young people in Europe living alone (in percent), 1995

Country	Percent of those aged 20–24 years living alone
Austria	9
Belgium	6
Denmark	n.a.
Finland	24
France	15
Germany	18 (excluding new lander)
Greece	8
Ireland	4
Italy	2
Luxembourg	5
Netherlands	19
Portugal	2
Spain	0
Sweden	n.a.
UK	8

Key: n.a.= data not available

Source: Eurostat data, 1997.

Thus the number of young people living alone ranges from none in Spain to as low as 2 percent in Italy before rising to 15 percent in France and a peak of 24 percent in Finland. This situation reflects many things, including differences in housing policies throughout Western Europe. Green points out in this regard that a housing policy geared towards youth is strongest in Scandinavia (Denmark) and Germany, barely exists in Southern Europe and in the UK and Ireland, the stress is on welfare not housing provisions.[31] In the UK this benefit was removed in 1988, and even in certain parts of Scandinavia (such as Sweden) which tends, as we have seen earlier to be more progressive, municipal housing subsidies for young people were eliminated in 1993 due to pressures on governments to reduce expenditure on social welfare.[32] Finally, the desire to leave home might also be influenced by relationships within and outside the family.[33] All of these factors will determine the ability of young people to achieve independence.

Not surprisingly in this context, youth homelessness has become more and more common in recent years. Green estimates that the number of homeless young people under 25 years was somewhere between 1.25–2.5 million in EU in the mid-late

1990s.[34] A large majority of the young homeless have suffered abuse at home or else previously been in state care – in the UK and Ireland, the figure is as high as 40 percent.[35] All in all, Green concludes that many young people have often borne the brunt of these changes and consequently form a growing proportion of the homeless in European cities.[36] In any event they have enormous problems in moving towards independent living, so not surprisingly many fall along the route.[37]

Lynne Chisholm on the basis of French experience talks of a three-fold typology of 'social risk'. In the *first category* are those young people with stable jobs and good social networks who have managed to become successfully integrated into society; the *second category* includes young people who still live with their parents and have not yet entered the 'adult world' and finally, those in the *third category* tend to be older sections of youth who, through no fault of their own (for instance, redundancy), have been rejected by the labour market and subsequently have become poor and fallen on hard times.[38]

Clearly, many of the young people discussed in this chapter fall into one of these three categories. The consequences for young people, on the one hand, and for their relationship to society, state and its agencies, on the other, differ markedly in each case. Those in the first category are less likely to be in conflict with the state and society whereas those in the second and third categories are more likely to be alienated and to suffer from social exclusion. Thus, these sections of youth are highly likely to be in conflict with both the state and society.

In Russia, the dependency problem is much more acute than it is in the West. More than 80 percent of young Russians under the age of 29 years are financially dependent on their parents. About half a million of young people start off after compulsory education as unemployed. In addition, 25,000 young people go straight to labour exchanges directly upon leaving educational establishments. The risk of a false start among this category of youth is an unpleasant reality and may play a crucial role in their future lives.

How successful young people's life start is, largely depends upon the opportunities provided by society for the realisation of their interests. Interests are one of the main factors that unite young people into groups. Moreover, due to common interests, individual life start situations tend to turn into social phenomenon.

As we can see from Table 6.12, a successful life start is closely connected with gender. It is evident that the interests of young females tend to be slightly wider than their male counterparts. Nearly one-third of our sample (31.9 percent) has been or still is studying on different courses that allow young people to acquire extra skills (such as foreign languages, computing, needle-work, etc.). Almost half (47.9 percent) attend so-called 'extra-curricula clubs'[39] and more than half of youth (54.2 percent) have been or are still attending sporting schools. Finally, nearly one in five (18.8 percent) attend music schools. In comparison with 1990, youth interests have changed for the better. However, the proportion of young people attending such clubs has decreased by 30 percent because the clubs themselves are in crisis. Taking into account the mounting costs of such types of courses, young people are doing their best to sustain such activity.

Table 6.12 Changes in interests of young people in Russia (as percent of group aged 15–18 years), 1990–1999

Sphere of interest	1990						1999					
	Studied previously			Continue studying			Studied previously			Continue studying		
	M	F	Both	M	F	Both	M	F	Both	M	F	Both
Courses	4.3	2.9	3.4	3.6	2.9	3.2	16.7	21.1	19.6	13.0	11.6	10.3
Coaching	5.2	6.7	6.1	2.9	5.1	4.2	15.2	14.1	14.6	4.8	6.3	5.6
Extra-curricula	32.2	49.2	42.2	20.6	18.7	19.5	35.9	42.3	39.2	5.9	11.3	8.7
Music	13.9	25.7	21.0	2.6	2.5	2.6	13.3	18.3	15.9	1.9	3.9	2.9
Sport	27.1	24.3	25.4	21.0	7.2	12.8	42.2	27.1	34.5	27.8	12.0	19.7

Key: M = Male   F = Female

Source: Authors' 'Social development of Russian youth' survey data, 1990–1999.

Another noticeable feature is the difference between the percentage of young people who were involved in this type of activity and those who still are. This has grown over the last decade. Although certain changes in youth interests have taken place during the 1990s, such changes largely reflect the limited opportunities available, which are heavily constrained by financial considerations. Most families are simply not able to pay for such activity, as they are desperately saving money for their children's possible future entry into higher education. Thus, the risk of unrealised possibilities in physical and cultural development is increasing at an early stage in the life start of youth.

Youth orientation toward acquiring more education varies. Our research data suggests that 5.9 percent of school leavers are not going to continue in education. At the same time, a quarter of our sample said they were definitely going onto the next educational establishment. This indicates that a considerable proportion of Russian youth is thinking about their long-term prospects, especially with regard to vocational or higher education. Secondary education is seen only as a spring-board by 25 percent of youth in Russia. Our surveys discovered that three-quarters of young people have no intention of continuing with their education and that 63.5 percent were generally satisfied with the level of education they had acquired. The reason for this trend is society's poor attitude towards education in contemporary Russia. Our research shows that if a young person feels comfortable with the knowledge s/he has acquired (especially if this knowledge is not valued and used by society) then there is no incentive to improve it. Uncertainty of needs, instability of cognitive interests and the absence of societal encouragement, increases the risk that 70 percent of youth will remain only 'half-educated' in Russia.

The transition to a market economy has changed youth values. This can be seen at the very beginning of their lives. Instrumental attitudes towards education dominate among 36.7 percent of youth. They see education as a means of achieving other goals. Often they only want a degree. Similar attitudes are expressed by young pragmatics towards work. Of school leavers 59.8 percent see work as an 'unpleasant obligation' or source of income. A minimal income defines youth preferences and choice of job whereas their parents will only settle for a much higher wage. If they were sufficiently well off 10 percent of young Russians would not work at all. Such an orientation has nothing in common with the labour ethic of western youth living in societies with developed market economies. Hence, the risk of reproduction of poor labour ethic patterns among Russian youth is likely.

Our findings show that there is no universal model of life start among youth in post-Soviet Russia. This is caused by youth social differentiation. At least, three clear models exist. The *first model* applies to 25–30 percent of youth whose life plans and contemporary activity are inclined towards higher education. However, there is no reason to think that they are simply motivated by a desire to gain knowledge. One third of this category is driven by instrumental motives only, namely a desire to avoid conscription or to have a 'qualification' (in theory, rather than practice) in order to enter a prestigious occupation. The *second model* of life start is also connected with education but without any clear idea of its type and form. Youth orientation very much depends on circumstances, such as the presence of education establishments in the area, the level of knowledge provided by compulsory school, the costs of education, family financial opportunities etc. About

60–70 percent of young people fall into this category. Most try to enter any specialised educational establishment, even college or technical school. In making their choice, young people don't care about their professional profile and are simply happy to have been offered a place. Many young people are happy to become students, but will not regret it if they subsequently fail. What is common for this model is that work is considered as an undesirable consequence of bad luck in education. The *third model*, which applies to about 10 percent of young people, includes those who are not oriented towards education but instead desperately search for a job. A large proportion of this category (67 percent) are forced to do so simply because of money worries. This is why the size of their salary is the leading criterion for this group. The nature of the job and working conditions do not matter to them. Young people with a delayed start and those who choose leisure instead of work or study are also among this group. Most of the latter rely on occasional earnings and parental support in order to survive. All three models contain great risk. This stems from the social and youth policy of the Russian state which is based on a desire to keep a firm distance from the social problems of youth.

What then do the start positions of young people and their strategies depend upon? Youth life start models are certainly dependent on the educational status of their parents, living standards, region and many other factors. However the degree of influence of each varies.

Table 6.13 Correlation between the main indicators of youth life start and social differences (by rank), Russia, 1990–1999

Factors	*Importance of Integral coefficient*	*Rank*
Mother's education	0.39	1
Father's education	0.32	2
Residing region	0.24	3
Material position	0.21	4
Gender	0.15	5

Source: Based on findings from Authors' 'Social Development of Youth' surveys, Russian Federation, 1990–1999.

Our analysis of the connection, if any, between the main indicators of youth life start and social differences is presented in Table 6.13. First place is occupied by such socio-cultural factors as parental education with the greatest influence exercised by a mother's education. The latter is largely determined by the distribution of sex roles in Russian families, where traditionally *the mother is always closer to children and her influence is therefore stronger*. Region is more influential than material factors. The enormous social differentiation among regions in the Russian Federation is crucial here. In addition, traditional differences between urban and rural ways of life have polarised during a decade or more of crisis. All of this impacts upon youth start positions. Thus *socio-cultural differentiation becomes a leading factor in stratification among Russian youth in terms of life start.*

Table 6.14 Impact of mother and father's education, material well-being and area of residence on young people's activity (as percent of group)

Factors	Education	Type of activity						
		a	b	c	d	e	f	g
MOTHER'S EDUCATION	Incomplete education	12.8	35.5	35.5	6.5	0.7	4.8	3.2
	Complete education	5.5	39.3	34.3	10.0	5.2	3.6	2.1
	Higher education	2.2	52.0	16.0	23.6	2.9	2.2	1.1
FATHER'S EDUCATION	Incomplete education	8.0	40.2	36.8	5.7	4.6	2.3	1.4
	Complete education	3.9	43.3	33.1	11.5	3.0	2.6	2.6
	Higher education	3.3	46.7	15.2	25.4	4.1	3.7	1.6
REGIONAL RESIDENCE	Moscow/St. Petersburg	5.1	39.1	25.7	20.6	5.9	2.4	1.2
	Large city	3.2	46.9	30.9	13.6	2.1	1.1	2.2
	Small town	3.9	43.7	32.0	10.6	3.9	3.9	2.0
	Village, rural area	15.9	37.9	28.2	8.4	2.1	4.7	2.8
MATERIAL POSITION	Low income	5.5	40.5	32.4	10.7	3.4	4.4	1.7
	High income	2.5	52.7	24.3	15.7	1.6	3.2	0.0

Key: a Work b Study at school
 c Study at PTU/technical college d Study at H.E.I
 e Work and study f Neither work nor study
 g Unemployed

Source: Based on findings from Authors' 'Social Development of Youth' surveys, Russian Federation, 1999.

This is natural under conditions of total impoverishment and given the socio-economic polarisation of the population (see Table 2.2). Hence living standards are not so different as the majority of families find themselves drifting towards the poverty-line. Being in need is a common practice and this characteristic of the group does not in any way reflect their social position (i.e. stratification). *However material well-being starts playing a notable role when we compare the position of the rich minority with the poor majority.* As for gender, different male and female roles are evident at an early stage of life start. In Russia's case gender is important, but not as significant as the other factors previously mentioned.

In order to examine the influence of various socio-economic and cultural factors on young people's life start we analysed the relationship between the aforementioned factors and youth employment. It is clear from Table 6.14 that youth activity is being affected by all these factors in a particularly strong way. This table suggests that parental education, and that of a mother in particular, remains very influential in youth life start strategies. The higher the level of their education, the larger the proportion of young people studying at schools and universities tends to be, and vice versa. In families where parents have a low educational status, the proportion of working youth and young people studying at vocational educational establishments is also increasing. This trend tends to determine the level of inequality of youth life start and biographies.

Possibilities for young peoples' self-realisation

Young people's first achievements are the initial stage of their further self-realisation in later life. Achieving their personal potential in line with their abilities and interests, young people integrate themselves into social life, attain and then become more aware of their new social status. This is why the search for a place in society and self-affirmation in different spheres (education, labour, policy), is difficult to achieve. This also explains why self-realisation and expression is a complex process.

On the road to youth self-determination individuals inevitably face many obstacles and difficulties. Their ability to overcome these challenges depends not only on the young themselves, but also on the opportunities provided by society. In a risk society such opportunities undergo changes. On an individual basis, risk in the sphere of one's self-realisation involves uncertainty in putting into practice youth goals and life plans in accordance with their inclinations and gifts. This also affects young people's ability to gain individuality and independence. The main societal consequences of uncertainty of young peoples' self-realisation are becoming more and more obvious and starting to impact upon young people's social position, social mobility and social differentiation.

Our research data shows that uncertainty of youth self-realization in different risk societies is the product of the relationship between individual conditions and successes. Young people need to choose occupational goals and pathways which meet society's requirements, on the one hand, as well as their own self interests, on the other. However, in reality, sociological findings suggest that youth self-realisation is actually beyond their control and influence.[40] In this respect, there are several different transition strategies which young people can adopt, as shown in Table 6.15.

Table 6.15 Risk coping strategies among youth

Category	Strategy
Strategic	Young people carefully plan their lives by making a *clear cut vocational choice* related to *definite occupational goals*
step-by step	approach relates to *unclear occupational choices* by young people, who still nevertheless *search for interesting occupations but without definite occupational end goals*
take chances	involves the realisation by young people that occupational and other trends are *unpredictable* but they still try to *determine their self-interest* and so *seek training and educational improvements* in order to try and achieve their ambitions; and
wait and see	category includes those young people who have a *past history of failure and of being victims* of a risk society and so they tend to rely more *on luck*.[41]

Source: Adapted from K. Evans et al., *Learning and work in the risk society: Lessons for the Labour Markets of Europe from Eastern Germany*, Macmillan/Anglo-German Foundation for the study of industrial society, Basingstoke and New York, 2000, p. 125.

Of course, self-realisation does not simply refer to gaining a job, it could also mean getting married, starting a family, buying a house, leaving home and so forth. Besides occupational achievements, it also involves family of destination, independence from parents, housing, and so on. The problem is, as Nagel and Wallace highlight, that an extended transformation is taking place in all these aspects of youth transition. Thus they note:

> The transition from single person to marriage, establishment of an independent couple household and then children, paralleling the transition from school to work is *now replaced by* a variety of transitions into parenthood, marriage, a partnership without marriage, establishing a household with or without a partner or living with a variety of other people and so on.[42]

In this regard, Bob Coles makes the important point that different aspects of transition are closely related to one another. Thus it is not a question of one transition, for example from school to work, but of numerous transitions. Thus the school to work transition strongly interfaces with changes in the family and housing situation.[43] A prolonged phase from school to work or delayed entry into the labour market can therefore strongly influence young people's ability to realise their life's ambitions. Such difficulties might be the product of different families of origin/ destination and/or the failure to realise one's goals. This might in turn produce tensions within the family, for instance between different generations, or between young people and their parents.

All in all, self-realisation remains as much an acute social problem for western youth as it does for their Russian counterparts. At the same time, according to Western researchers, individualisation of risk takes place. Individualisation refers to the priority given to individual interests, ambitions and commitments over class ties and collective solidarities.[44] While individual achievements are considered very important by sociologists, the emergence of a risk society makes the realisation of one's personal goals difficult and even impossible. This can be linked to class, socio-demographic and socio-cultural differences among youth. In some countries (for example, in Britain) class origins play a crucial role in one's self-realisation. In other countries, however, such as Germany, the influence of one's class position is not as obvious. Whilst gender and age are important in both these countries, they are shaped by the particular social context.[45] All in all, although class continues shaping our lives in risk societies, inequalities in such a society might also transcend class, gender and race. Hence Evans and Furlong point out that:

> Class, gender and ethnicity become *important as differential resources in life course but not as determinants of outcomes...*[46]

The reason for this is the weakening of collectivist traditions and the growing power of individualised values.

All in all, a *pluralisation of the patterns of youth self-realisation in Europe* has now occurred. If in the 1970s, youth opportunities were dominated by the old patterns (class, gender, etc.) then during the 1980s and 1990s youth self-realisation became considerably more individualised. The necessity for greater geographical mobility and prolongation of education meant that young people increasingly found themselves detached from their families, friends or partners. As a result, they had to search for individual ways of integration. Risk is therefore increasing but a variety of youth self-realisation models exists.

The aforementioned changes are not just taking place in the labour sphere, but also occurring in other spheres of life. For young Europeans different patterns of political participation, leisure and integration into communities exist. However, this does not necessarily mean that all ties with traditional institutions are broken, even if such links are under serious threat in a risk society.

On the basis of the aforementioned analysis the following *components of risk affecting youth self-realisation* in Europe's risk societies can be outlined. *Firstly*, a delay in achieving socio-professional status by youth is due to uncertainty in the labour market and the limited prospects for employment connected with this uncertainty. *Secondly*, an increasing gap between younger and older generations in terms of patterns and success of self-realisation and *thirdly*, changes in the influence of institutions as determinants of one's self-realisation and life-chances is occurring alongside the strengthening of individualisation.

In Russia's risk society, uncertainty of youth self-realisation has a particular influence on young peoples' position in the social structure. As we saw in chapter 2, the redistribution of youth employment between the state and non-state sectors of Russian economy has already taken place. Since 1991, the number of young people remaining in state enterprises has fallen dramatically. Forced idle time, poor wages, and the state sector's systematic delay, together with the risk of bankruptcy, have shaken young people's hope and faith in the state sphere of the economy as a guarantee of stability. This channel of youth occupational self-realisation has now become extremely limited.

However, this is only one of the ways to earn money in the many regions of Russian Federation. The number of young people leaving the sphere of material production is still ongoing. Furthermore, the proportion of youth in the entire Russian workforce has decreased 2–6 fold since the mid-1980s, depending upon branch of industry. Many young people only work in the state sector 'on paper', with most working in the private sector. In the latter case, young people know that if they fail or lose their jobs, they will always have the state sector to 'fall back on'. The collapse of collective farms (*kolkhozy*) and the difficulty of becoming an individual farmer have, in turn, determined the process of marginalisation of a considerable proportion of rural youth. Migration to a town or a city is the only solution in such cases. Since 1991, the proportion of young villagers moving to an urban area has increased 2.5 times. Unfortunately nobody, except criminal groups, is waiting for them when they arrive in the city. Difficulties connected with limitations on geographical mobility and possibilities for re-location often prove to be insurmountable obstacles for the majority of Russian youth. Existing administrative measures (gaining permission or temporary registration) together with a lack of funds necessary for this kind of mobility across Russia, put youth chances of gaining an education and finding a job under serious pressure.

A totally different situation can be observed in EU countries. The three notions gaining most support among young West Europeans were being able to work (62.4 percent), live (51.5 percent) or study (45.7 percent) anywhere in the Union. For European youth, freedom of movement was viewed as very important. More than half of young Europeans (57 percent) had visited another European Union country in the two years preceding the 1997 survey. Whether for leisure, studies, or employment, young people like the opportunity to move freely between one country and another. When asked about the foreseeable future benefits of the Union, their number one concern was to travel, study, work and live anywhere in Europe (47.7 percent).[47]

As pointed out earlier in chapter 2, during the course of reform in Russia, young people were the least protected part of the labour force and have suffered from all sorts of social discrimination. Unlawful dismissals, sanctions, arbitrary regulation of working time by employers, engaging a young person in unpaid work for a lengthy 'probationary period' without any guarantee of a permanent job, are all being practised on a large scale. Whether or not young people are successful in their jobs largely depends upon their relations with their boss and colleagues. As a result, in our 1990s surveys, amicable colleagues and friendly bosses were ranked in second and third place of importance after salary by Russian youth. This situation strongly influences the occupational mobility of youth, which is determined by subjective factors and not just based on ability.

The introduction of a market economy and modernisation of labour relations have not brought about freedom in youth occupational self-determination. Young people rarely succeed in getting rid of the former total administrative control. Hence young people have again become dependent, this time on employers and shareholders, whose activity is unconstrained due to the undeveloped social protection system in contemporary Russia (see chapter 2). All this is part of the social discrimination against youth according to age. In some instances, there are laws to prevent such violations of youth rights, but they are not enforced; whilst in other cases, no such laws exist because no new laws have been implemented due to the rapid pace of change. In our sample, more about two thirds of young people felt unsafe and unprotected, only 9 percent of respondents believed that their legal rights in the labour market were protected and no more than 12 percent thought that the law protects everyone against discrimination.

Unemployment becomes a considerable factor that limits youth self-realisation in the labour sphere in Western and Russian risk societies. It is viewed by experts as one of the fundamental consequences both of the socio-economic transformation in post-socialist countries and the changes that occurred in Western economies at the end of the twentieth century.[48] Those under the age of 25 years are hardest hit by unemployment. One in five of those aged between 16–25 years is jobless. The average OECD youth unemployment rate increased by 4 percent between 1979–1997, reaching 16 percent overall. By the mid-1990s, unemployment rates in the EU had reached around 20 million. There are wide differences between countries. For instance in 1997, participation and employment rates ranged from under 10 percent in France, Belgium and Korea to as high as nearly 70 percent in Denmark.[49] Teenage and young adult unemployment was higher in 1997 than it was in 1979 and is now in double figures.

Unemployment rates throughout the OECD are shown in Table 6.16. In considering this data, we need to bear in mind, as Eluned Morgan points out, that there is no uniform method of calculating or defining youth unemployment.[50] Therefore the OECD and Eurostat data are used here as a means of illustrating general youth unemployment trends. These figures reflect the shift from economic boom in the 1960s and 1970s, which was halted by the oil crisis of 1973, to economic recession in the 1980s and 1990s brought on by a series of monetary crises. Although youth unemployment is high, it is evident that young male unemployment tends to be lower than young female unemployment in many countries. Thus in 1997, only Austria (men), Denmark, Germany and Japan (women) had teenage unemployment rates under 10 percent whilst rates of 35 percent and over for women were recorded in Belgium, France, Greece, Italy, Poland and Spain (men only).

Risk Trends in the Life Situation of Young People 155

Table 6.16 Youth unemployment among 15–24 year olds according to country (in percent), 1979–1997

Country	1979 15–19 M	1979 15–19 F	1979 20–24 M	1979 20–24 F	1989 15–19 M	1989 15–19 F	1989 20–24 M	1989 20–24 F	1997 15–19 M	1997 15–19 F	1997 20–24 M	1997 20–24 F
Australia	14.6	20.4	8.4	8.0	12.9	14.6	8.0	7.9	20.2	18.4	15.3	12.1
Austria	n.a.	n.a.	n.a.	n.a.	n.a.	n.a.	n.a.	n.a.	6.0	14.5	5.3	4.7
Belgium*	n.a.	n.a.	n.a.	n.a.	16.3	29.5	10.7	19.0	27.2	39.3	16.4	24.4
Canada	16.3	15.8	10.9	10.3	14.5	11.4	10.9	9.0	22.8	20.7	14.4	12.6
Czech Republic	n.a.	n.a.	n.a.	n.a.	n.a.	n.a.	n.a.	n.a.	13.3	19.4	5.6	7.4
Denmark*	n.a.	n.a.	n.a.	n.a.	7.9	9.5	12.7	14.4	7.3	9.0	6.1	10.6
Finland	16.7	16.2	8.0	7.6	14.1	13.8	4.6	6.4	26.3	34.0	19.8	20.2
France	13.8	32.6	7.8	14.4	25.2	4.7	24.0	6.5	38.9	8.3	32.2	11.2
Germany	2.4	4.7	3.2	5.6	4.7	6.2	6.5	7.1	8.3	8.8	11.2	9.9
Greece*	n.a.	n.a.	n.a.	n.a.	14.0	39.3	18.1	32.1	27.0	51.6	20.8	37.7
Holland	n.a.	n.a.	n.a.	n.a.	14.1	20.5	9.2	10.5	13.6	16.0	6.3	6.2
Hungary	12.7	12.3	8.3	5.0	29.1	27.2	19.3	14.6	28.4	29.3	14.3	11.0
Ireland	26.5	39.7	17.9	24.3	34.0	48.9	25.1	36.9	20.2	23.2	15.7	12.5
Italy	5.4	2.7	3.2	3.3	8.0	6.0	3.8	3.8	30.9	42.9	28.4	38.2
Japan	n.a.	n.a.	n.a.	n.a.	7.7	7.9	9.5	4.5	10.3	7.6	6.2	6.1
Korea	n.a.	n.a.	n.a.	n.a.	15.8	15.8	13.1	9.5	11.6	8.7	8.9	6.2
New Zealand	8.8	12.0	4.9	4.3	17.7	13.8	9.4	9.5	16.3	15.8	11.0	10.7
Norway	n.a.	n.a.	n.a.	n.a.	n.a.	n.a.	n.a.	n.a.	15.4	15.6	7.8	9.1
Poland	n.a.	n.a.	n.a.	n.a.	n.a.	n.a.	n.a.	n.a.	28.6	39.1	20.5	26.2
Portugal[a]	13.3	30.0	9.8	24.1	8.1	15.8	8.6	14.4	14.2	24.0	14.6	17.9
Spain[b]	23.6	27.4	13.7	17.7	24.8	45.6	24.2	41.2	36.5	59.3	28.1	42.2
Sweden[b]	9.7	10.5	3.8	4.0	5.4	5.4	3.3	3.1	28.2	26.7	21.7	20.4
UK[b]	n.a.	n.a.	n.a.	n.a.	11.7	9.2	10.4	8.9	18.2	14.0	14.0	8.9
USA[b]	15.9	16.4	8.7	9.6	15.9	14.0	8.8	8.3	16.9	15.0	8.9	8.1
OECD average[c]	13.8	18.5	8.3	10.6	14.1	18.4	11.3	13.9	18.5	23.0	13.4	15.4

Key: M = Male F = Female * = Based on EUROSTAT data n.a. = Data not available
a = 1996 instead of 1997 b = 16–19 instead of 15–19 years c = unweighted

Source: OECD Labour Statistics and EUROSTAT data, 1979–1997.

All in all, by the late 1990s, one in ten young people in OECD countries were unemployed. OECD researchers have also discovered that young people tend to be unemployed longer. On average, one unemployed teenager in six is long-term unemployed compared to only one in three young adults.[51] Morgan argues that around half of those currently unemployed in the EU have no recognised skills and less than 10 percent receive any training. Despite, the vocational training patterns discussed earlier, almost 15 million 16–25 years olds in the EU have no formal qualifications at all and it is also thought that 20 percent of those who leave Europe's education and training systems do so without any recognised marketable qualifications.[52] This situation – a reduction in the number of apprenticeships and increasing youth unemployment – has had a negative impact on young people's working lives, family life and lifestyle because some young people are excluded from large areas of occupational life, citizenship rights and as a result have become alienated from society. Even those who are lucky enough to find jobs often face discrimination. Thus, unemployment is a constantly existing threat for youth self-realisation in a risk society.

Table 6.17 below shows how unemployment coverage varies for those under 25 years old in various EU countries in 1998. It is evident that young people receive between 40 (Greece) and 100 percent (Portugal) of their previous or the minimum wage. During unemployment, though, young people are entitled to different degrees of state support ranging from 20 ECU's a month in Italy to 1,906 ECU in Sweden. In the Italian case, high levels of family support would be required whereas the opposite might be needed in Sweden, although the cost of living is higher in the latter case. The length of time during which young people are eligible for state support ranges from as low as three months in Spain to nearly nine years for those under 21 years old in Holland. Finally, in the large majority of cases, young people can start claiming unemployment benefit as early as 16 years with the odd exception (Belgium, Finland, Germany, Portugal and Sweden).

Although unemployment in general is slowly stabilising, it still remains relatively high (see Table 2.1). Youth unemployment is a relatively new phenomena for Russia. One third of all the registered unemployed are young people under the age of 29 years (see Table 6.18). Most of this group have just graduated from various educational establishments (secondary and vocational schools, colleges and universities). The average duration of youth unemployment has risen for all age groups. By 1999, it was 7.2 months for those under 20 years, 8.3 months for those aged 20–24 and finally 9.7 months for those aged 25–29 years.[53]

Table 6.17 Youth unemployment coverage in Europe, 1998

Country	Percent of previous wage	Flat rate max. (min. ECU per month)	Duration of Entitlement (in weeks)	Min. age for claim
Austria	80		20	16
Belgium	60 (first year), 42 (thereafter)			18
Denmark	90		260	16
Finland	up to 75 percent of min. wage	596	71	17
France	60 (first year), 53 (thereafter) depending on length of contributions		20	
Germany			52	17
Greece	40		20	
Ireland		357	156 (under 18) 390 over 18	
Italy	30	26		
Luxembourg	80 percent; up to 2.5 times the min. wage			
Netherlands			441 (over 21)	
Portugal	70–100 percent of min. wage		40	17
Spain	75 percent of min. wage		12	18
Sweden	80 percent	max of 1,906	43	20 for assistance
UK		233	24	16/18

Source: Country Reports and SCAD (Plus) (1998), Practical Guide to the Free Movement of Persons cited at www.europa.eu.int/comm/sg/scadplus/scad_en.html.

Table 6.18 Youth unemployment in Russia (in percent), 1992–1999

Year	up to 20 years	20–24 years	25–29 years
1992	16.8	19.0	12.7
1993	15.0	18.8	13.1
1994	11.4	17.4	13.1
1995	11.1	18.3	14.1
1996	10.3	18.0	12.9
1997	9.2	17.4	12.7
1998	8.1	18.0	12.7
1999	7.0	16.3	13.3

Source: *Rossisskii statisticheskii ezhgodnik: Statisticheskii Sbornik*, Moscow, Goskomstat 2000, p. 118.

Several peculiarities of Russian youth unemployment can be distinguished. *Firstly* youth unemployment is caused by changes in socio-economic policy, which has led to the decline in industry because of the lack of subsidies. Jobs and workplaces that were traditionally occupied by young people are no longer available, because various enterprises have now closed down. *Secondly*, according to the Federal Employment Service, young people under 25 years of age (around 20 percent) dominate the ranks of the unemployed. Because of the fall in living standards of most of the Russian population, and the declining age of new entrants to the labour market, 45 percent of all registered unemployed are under 18. In accordance with Russian law, many are not defined as 'unemployed', but in reality they are. This category needs to be paid particular attention, as it is the main source of the so-called 'status Zer0 group' (a term coined by Howard Williamson). Having no professional qualifications and being excluded from other types of activity, except leisure, young people with a *zero status* constantly live at risk and are a source of instability for the whole of society. The question of their social backgrounds also arises. As Howard Williamson argues:

> Many did come from divided families, many did have fragmented and partial schooling histories ... Furthermore, some had been involved in criminal activity from an early age ... But on the other hand, many did not ... Some of these young people never expected that they would be experiencing Status Zer0. Some had been anticipating staying on at school or going on into further education. Some had very clear ideas about what they would like to be doing within the mainstream training and labour markets ... In their terms, something had happened, beyond their control, which had almost propelled them into Status Zer0.[54]

This situation creates a personal feeling of uncertainty and leads to a desire to live one day at a time. *Thirdly*, the cause of youth social exclusion via unemployment in a crisis-ridden society is the imbalance of the whole social system leading to a rupture of ties between all of its parts and to the ineffectiveness of its integration channels. The on-going systemic crisis outlined in chapter 2 has adversely affected the social institutions, which can hardly cope with the acceptance and distribution of new entrants. Moreover these integrational mechanisms are sometimes being transformed into insurmountable obstacles during the process of self-realisation of young people. As a result, young people cannot find their proper place in the labour market. Instead, youth integration into the labour sphere tends to be rather chaotic and unpredictable.

Similar problems occur with regard to youth self-realisation in the educational sphere. The number of young people excluded from schools, totals millions in contemporary Russia. More and more young Russians cannot continue studying at secondary and high school. As a result, there has been an increase in the number of illiterate young people of call-up age (*conscripts*), who often do not even possess a primary education.

Thus, in the process of self-realisation of young people in a risk society a 'chain' of interconnected and interdependent events emerge. The aforementioned social disadvantages of different groups of young people are the consequence of social transformation and the cause of the social exclusion of youth at the present time. This gives birth to various underprivileged, low-status groups and outcast members of society who have failed to compete in a risk society. Hence, in an unstable society, marginalisation and alienation as particular forms of exclusion impacts upon many social groups and is on the increase. Even educated and well-qualified young people find themselves in danger of discrimination, alienation and marginalisation in relation to occupational self-determination due to uncertainty.

The risk of downward social and occupational mobility, on the one hand, and of non-realisation of young people's aims, on the other, is reflected in youth consciousness, as shown by their sense of alarm (21.1 percent), indignation (3.4 percent) and indifference (13.8 percent). According to our 1999 research data, one in five of our respondents are scared and nervous and in fear of losing their job. In addition 65.9 percent of young people in 1999, as against 51.3 percent two years before, were full of these emotions, especially in relation to their financial position. The acceleration of this and other states of uncertainty among young people are signs of the transformation of Russian society into a risk society and vivid indicators of the degree of social tension within it. The alienation of the younger generation from society and an increase in the degree of social exclusion are the result of constant uncertainty and risk. Society is more and more often facing the consequences of social exclusion, such as the individual's rupture of ties with reality, the immersion of a person in a world of his/her own problems, or so called 'self-exclusion' as shown by various expressions of youth protest behaviour. Uncertainty of one's self-realisation has also led to the revival of such youth categories as the neglected, vagrants, refugees, homeless, etc, a phenomena that has not existed since the 1920s in Russia.

Of course, once a risk is taken not everybody fails. It is important to point out though that only a relatively small proportion of youth (2–3 percent) want for nothing, as they are well of. Most of this successful group of young people belong to the families of the former and present administrative and economic elite. These young businessmen are supported and protected by their powerful parents and are very often 'figureheads' in their powerful father's business. The prosperity of others in this category stems from illegal activities.

Thus, our analysis of the social changes among the younger generation in contemporary Russia shows the adverse consequences of uncertainty of youth self-realisation in a risk society. The wider the social opportunities created by society for young people then the greater the possibilities there are for their upward mobility. This means that in assisting young people in their self-realisation via occupational activity, education, political participation, family of destination, leisure, and other spheres, society is developing and improving its own social structure. However, the opposite is also true because by taking no part in the process of youth social integration, and even putting obstacles in young people's way, risk societies are increasing the likelihood of downward mobility and social exclusion. In the process, young people are doomed to failure and degradation.

This point is evident when the contradictions with regard to occupational mobility are analysed. Following de-ideologisation, the Russian state has proclaimed youth professional self-realisation as the latter's own responsibility and therefore the state has made no attempt at aid or regulation. Thus, there has been an increase in the number of young people without professional education or training. In the sphere of material production this figure has doubled since 1990. Most of this category are teenagers who either left education or entered the labour market just after they finished school. Generally they are engaged in unattractive, unqualified, low-paid jobs. Their occupational position is highly unstable. Furthermore, 27.4 percent of those who graduated from vocational schools (PTU), 33.4 percent of college graduates and 38.2 percent of those with higher education degrees were also in jobs in 1999 which differed from their professional training. This is evidence of the high quality of the resources of the Russian younger generation but also of their poor utilisation. Nevertheless the fact that two thirds of working young people (67.7 percent) possess a professional education means that certain interests and ambitions exist among youth. Unfortunately, Russian society has failed to meet these needs. In comparison with 1990, the proportion of young people with a professional education has increased in some branches of industry, such as mechanical engineering (machine-building) (by 6.6 percent), light industry (by 21.5 percent) and construction (by 5.9 percent). However, this positive trend is meaningless due to the conditions of the general collapse of the post-Soviet economy. After 1994, young people's level of professional education started to decline in many branches, especially agriculture. This large gap in youth professional training according to the sphere of the Russian economy is demonstrated in Table 6.19. It is clear that the number of young people with professional education fluctuates from 50 percent in agriculture up to 73.1 percent among those working in the transport sector.

Furthermore, the growth in the number of young people with only primary and incomplete secondary education in all branches, excluding light industry, also needs to be highlighted. This trend is supposedly determined by the number of teenagers leaving school. However this hypothesis is only partially true. Our figures suggest that the increase in the number of young people working for only one year applies largely to agriculture, trade and municipal services. Instead a growing number of young people with only the minimal level of education have come into the labour market in Russia.

Table 6.19 Changes in the educational level of young people in different occupational groups in Russia (as percent of each group), 1997–1999

Occupational group	Level of Education							
	General secondary education		Specialised secondary education		Incomplete higher or higher education		Total of those possessing professional education	
	a	b	a	b	a	b	a	b
Industrial workers	23.3	27.0	47.2	58.6	10.7	6.5	57.9	65.1
Light industry workers	23.5	22.7	70.6	68.2	3.0	4.5	73.6	72.7
Construction workers	14.5	23.1	58.2	65.4	8.9	7.7	67.1	73.1
Agricultural workers	12.5	34.1	37.3	43.2	2.0	6.8	39.3	50.0
Transport workers	21.2	30.3	60.0	52.8	3.8	5.6	63.8	65.6
Engineering/ technical workers	17.2	9.7	36.4	45.1	46.4	42.4	82.8	87.5
On average	18.7	24.4	51.6	55.5	12.4	12.2	64.0	67.7

Key: a 1997   b 1999

Source: Based on findings from Authors' 'Social Development of Youth' surveys, Russian Federation, 1997–1999.

Youth occupational self-realisation is indicated by one's qualifications, the degree of correlation between one's professional education and the actual content of labour, and finally by one's attitude towards one's profession and work. High indicators would characterise a sustainable socio-occupational position and a high level of self-realisation among youth. Table 6.20 shows that since 1997 young people's self-estimations of their level of qualifications, the degree of prestige of their job and the level of job satisfaction, have all risen. This indicates a positive attitude towards work and a high degree of professional self-realisation amongst Russian youth by the end of the 1990s. At the same time, ironically, the gap between professional education and work is increasing among all professional groups, except those in light industry. In general, a third of young people (33.3 percent) we surveyed are engaged in jobs which are totally different to their training and qualifications. Hence they are at risk of occupying a rather marginal position in their particular professions.

Changes in youth estimations of the prestige attached to work are shown in Table 6.21 which indicates that youth attitudes towards work have improved considerably since the mid-1990s. This is particularly true among those young people involved in intellectual work. The growing feelings of pride attached to their profession amongst youth positively characterises their opportunity for self-expression and self-realisation at work. It is also evident that young people's assessment of the prestige attached to different occupations is largely based on real opportunities (i.e. on whether or not youth can obtain such positions). The better the opportunities to earn money, become a good professional, make a career etc., the higher the level of youth integration is.

Table 6.20 Socio-occupational status of youth according to job in different branches of the Russian economy (according to individually specified scales and by average weighting), 1997–1999

Occupational group	Level of qualification $C = 7$		Degree of work fulfilment $C = 4$		Prestige of profession $C = 3$		Level of job satisfaction $C = 3$	
	a	b	a	b	a	b	a	b
Industrial workers	4.14	4.45	2.74	1.94	1.66	1.70	1.18	1.58
Light industry workers	4.52	4.86	2.86	3.27	1.38	1.40	1.03	1.68
Construction workers	3.84	4.61	2.60	2.57	1.40	1.96	1.50	1.84
Agricultural workers	4.04	4.68	2.71	2.63	1.37	1.86	1.36	1.75
Transport workers	4.55	5.02	2.82	2.71	1.58	1.84	1.36	1.99
Engineering/ technical workers	4.58	4.90	3.11	2.96	1.73	2.05	1.65	1.99

Key: C = Coefficient   a = 1997   b = 1999

Source: Based on findings from Authors' 'Social Development of Youth' surveys, Russian Federation, 1997–1999.

Our analysis demonstrates that these conditions, which are integrative factors, play an important role in youth occupational orientations. However, they differ according to urban and rural divide, especially by residence in regional centres and small settlements. In some cases, great differences exist but in others they do not exist at all. In the latter case, stability of youth integration into a professional group is due to the nature of their employment, an example being those working in agriculture.

Table 6.21 Changes in the degree of prestige attached to their work amongst different youth occupational groups in Russia (as percent of each group), 1994–1997

Occupational group	Attitude to your work							
	Pride		Indifference		Constraint		No answer	
	a	b	a	b	a	b	a	b
Industrial workers	21.6	24.8	35.8	48.6	6.2	3.3	36.4	23.3
Light industry workers	14.9	26.7	37.3	36.4	11.9	5.9	35.9	31.0
Construction workers	11.1	34.6	37.0	46.2	9.7	2.6	52.2	16.6
Agricultural workers	21.9	25.0	46.9	54.5	6.8	2.3	24.9	18.2
Transport workers	23.2	24.7	43.0	53.9	0.1	2.2	33.7	19.0
Trade and municipal workers	23.3	23.4	49.5	46.1	17.2	7.0	10.0	23.4
Intelligentsia	20.0	45.4	33.8	33.3	4.6	2.3	41.6	19.0

Key: a = 1997   b = 1999

Source: Based on findings from Authors' 'Social Development of Youth' surveys, Russian Federation, 1994–1999.

Notable changes have also been found in other areas of youth self-realisation (see Table 6.22). Here our findings, based on average youth self-estimations among those working in different sectors of the economy, show that the best opportunities for self-realisation exist in construction (C = 3.77).

Table 6.22 Comparison of young people's possibility to improve their salary, qualification and promotion prospects according to occupation (Mean on 7 point scale), Russia, 1994–1999

Occupational group	Improve wages		Improve qualifications		Prospects of promotion		Average by occupation	
	a	b	a	b	a	b	a	b
Industrial workers	3.50	3.30	4.13	4.24	2.74	3.81	3.45	3.58
Light industry workers	3.39	3.72	3.63	4.00	2.72	3.04	3.24	3.58
Construction workers	3.86	3.65	3.92	4.38	2.51	3.30	3.43	3.77
Agricultural workers	2.25	3.34	2.37	3.63	1.68	2.52	2.10	3.10
Transport workers	3.57	4.00	4.10	4.67	2.60	3.51	3.42	4.06
Trade and municipal workers	3.27	3.54	3.64	3.84	2.82	3.52	3.24	3.60
Intelligentsia	3.39	3.82	4.49	5.04	3.01	4.25	3.59	4.37

Key: a = 1994 b = 1999

Source: Based on findings from Authors' 'Social Development of Youth' surveys, Russian Federation, 1994–1999.

This is why this sphere is given a relatively high prestige rating by young employees. In addition, high estimations also exist with regards to jobs in transport (C = 4.06) and trade (C = 3.60) sectors. On the contrary, fewer opportunities for solving young people's problems exist among young workers living in rural areas (C = 3.10). This also correlates with youth employment in enterprises with different forms of property (state and private). As the data in Table 6.22 indicates a large section of those young people who work in the private sector of the economy or who are self-employed, include traders, builders or transport workers. This means that under current conditions youth involvement in the market economy plays a positive role in occupational self-realisation and in the expanded reproduction of professional structure.

Table 6.23 Correlation between youth life situations and their estimations of the opportunities for self-realisation (Mean on 7 point scale), Russia, 1999

Assessment of life situation	Evaluation of opportunities to					
	a	b	c	d	e	f
Stability and order	4.15	4.63	3.97	3.57	4.09	2.45
Uncertainty and risk	4.05	4.49	3.74	3.78	4.07	2.77

Key: a Find work   b Improve qualifications
      c Increase wages   d Promotion
      e Protection under the law f Do business

Source: Based on findings from Authors 'Social Development of Youth' surveys, Russian Federation, 1999.

This also proves that self-regulation of the market economy allows youth to reduce uncertainty and risk to some extent. More than this, a risk situation itself may encourage and facilitate the realisation of young people's creative abilities in a better way. Such a synergetic effect is the main characteristic of risk and becomes one of the important factors of youth self-realisation under particular conditions.

Our empirical analysis indicates that certain links exist between these two phenomena (see Table 6.23). Furthermore our findings suggest that in stable situations young people have better opportunities to find a job and to improve their qualifications and incomes than in situations of uncertainty and risk. However, risk provides young people with better chances for career promotion and business. Only the protection of one's rights does not depend on life situations.

An even stronger correlation exists between these indicators, when an analysis of youth orientations towards stability/risk is undertaken, as shown in Table 6.24. An analysis of the data presented shows that there is a strong correlation between risk and the opportunities for self-realisation among youth, especially in the socio-cultural sphere. All indicators are considerably higher among those young Russians oriented towards change and risk. In other words, young people who opt for risk-taking estimate that their chances of success are higher than those who choose the status-quo (i.e. stability). It is also evident that young people with a desire for change and risk have more chances of realising their creative potential. This section of youth are likely to carry out the innovations necessary for expanded social reproduction and so can be seen as the main force of modernisation in a risk society. However, a risk situation tends to equalise the chances for gain and loss. This is why the degree of youth integration into society largely depends on the outcomes of risk strategies.

Our research findings suggest that despite a positive trend for youth self-realisation in 1999, it is still the case that the number of losers (i.e. those unable to realise their abilities and interests) is relatively high. Thus the chances of finding a job in 1999 were lower than the average for 33.9 percent of young people in Russia.

The same also applied to those who wished to improve their skills (23 percent lower) and living-standards (44.6 percent lower), make a good career (43.8 percent lower), protect their rights (36.3 percent lower) and finally to those young people who wished to go into business (70.8 percent lower than the average).

Table 6.24 Correlation between youth orientations towards stability/risk and their estimations of the opportunities for self-realisation (Mean on 7 point scale), Russia, 1999

Direction of orientation	Evaluation of possibilities to					
	a	b	c	d	e	f
Stability and order	3.94	4.49	3.55	3.60	3.97	2.40
Uncertainty and risk	4.30	4.77	4.06	3.92	4.40	3.20

Key: a Find work b Improve qualifications
 c Increase wages d Gain promotion
 e Gain protection under the law f Do business

Source: Based on findings from Authors' 'Social Development of Youth' surveys, Russian Federation, 1999.

Our research demonstrates that changes in youth opportunities for self-realisation are closely connected with social differentiation trends in a risk society. Under conditions of rapid change in a developing society, the process of social differentiation might have positive results because it produces new opportunities for various youth interests enabling some fulfilment of self-realisation goals. But the totally opposite situation exists in Russia's risk society. In such circumstances, young people's first opportunities for self-realisation are mainly governed by chance and tend to be rather chaotic in character. But it is also true that in this situation youth life chances remain increasingly dependent on social backgrounds. Because of the destruction of key mechanisms of institutional regulation of social differentiation, the risk of further polarisation and conflicts is never ending.

Similar trends exist with regard to youth self-realisation and self-expression through social and political participation. In the late twentieth century, young people in Europe were reluctant to get involved in groups, but on the other hand, they were quite prepared to commit themselves to specific projects and show a remarkably tolerant attitude towards others. Roughly half of young people (52.4 percent) belong to an association or organisation, whether politically, socially, culturally, artistically, religiously or sporting oriented. However, only 4.4. percent belong to a trade union or a political party, 1.5 percent to human rights movements and 0.9 percent to consumers' associations. The exceptions are the Scandinavian countries, such as Sweden and Denmark, were, for example, young people's involvement in associations and organisations (82.8 percent and 77.2 percent respectively) is significantly above the EU average. Moreover, also in comparison to the European average (4.4 percent), young people in Scandinavia are five times more likely to join trade unions and political parties (25.8 percent in Sweden and 22.4 percent in Denmark respectively).

In general, although young people are unwilling to join organisations, in their leisure time, nearly three out of four (73.4 percent) like to meet friends; one in two (49.7 percent) do sport and hence 27.6 percent of young Europeans are also members of a sporting association. This activity is well-ahead of membership of youth organisations (7.4 percent) or cultural associations (5.1 percent). Meeting friends is the first priority (73.4 percent), followed by listening to music (68.7 percent). A small proportion of young people belong to an association for the protection of nature/animals or the environment (5.5 percent) and only 8.7 percent belong to a religious organisation. In addition, 42.6 percent of young people in the EU consider themselves non-practising believers, 19.4 percent are practising, 15.1 percent are atheist and 11.6 percent agnostic.[55]

Another form of European youth social participation that is directly associated with EU citizenship is the right to vote. For 19.9 percent of young people, European citizenship means the right to vote in local elections in the Member State that they live in. In this context, European survey data suggests that one in five young Europeans are active in elections at a regional level.[56] This figure reflects the relatively low level of youth self-realisation through politics. The latter depends not only on the formal opportunities given to young citizens but also on a real possibility to influence politics and decision-making processes in the region where they live through elections. This includes youth participation in political programmes, debates and voting itself. European surveys point out, however, that less than a third of contemporary youth fully exercise this right.[57]

By comparison, Russian youth constitute about 24 percent of the electorate and in theory at least, have similar opportunities in the sphere of politics to their Western counterparts. By the end of 1998, for example, the number of young voters had increased by more than a million due to new comers reaching the age of 18–19 years. Traditionally this group of young people is active as soon as they have the first chance to vote because this is associated with reaching adult status. However, young people (in line with the majority of the population) are unable to express their interests by participating in elections. Although young people were initially keen to vote in the early post-Soviet period,[58] gradually after the 1996 Presidential and parliamentary elections, a smaller proportion of young people voted, with most preferring not to participate. Thus by 1999, only 1.9 percent of youth belonged to a political party and 1.3 percent to youth organisations in Russia.

Our research data point to the fact that the younger generation in Russia is not a united political force. The young electorate in Russia is highly differentiated and its political orientations and preferences are weak and uncertain. This makes young people a very convenient object for any kind of manipulation, especially by the mass media. Youth voting patterns during the December 1999 elections to the Russian parliament are shown in Table 6.25. The most noticeable point in the table below is the fact that 38.1 percent of young voters between the ages of 18–29 years did not possess clearly defined political preferences and so voted against all candidates. This is a form of *social protest* on their part. No one political party or association was supported by the majority of youth, with *Fatherland All Russia* gaining the greatest support (14 percent), followed by Grigory Yavlinskii's *Yabloko* (with 8.6 percent) and Zhirinovsky's LDPR with 6.1 percent. Finally, Unity and the *CPRF* were equal fourth with only 4 percent of the youth vote. A significant proportion of young people in post-Soviet Russia seem to be drawn to small, unknown political parties.

Table 6.25 Voting by Russian youth in the December 1999 parliamentary elections (in percent)

Political party	Percent of youth vote
Fatherland All-Russia	14.0
Yabloko	8.6
Liberal democratic party of Russia	6.1
Unity	4.0
Communist Party of the Russian Federation	4.0
Union of Right Forces	3.9
Our Home is Russia	1.6
Russian National Republican Party	1.4
Other	17.5
None of the above	38.1

Sources: Based on exit poll data from Authors' 'Social Development of Youth' surveys, Russian Federation, 1999.

This situation reflects the high level of distrust of key political and social institutions amongst Russian youth, as shown in Table 6.26. This indicates that the trend which we outlined elsewhere in relation to the period up to the 1995 parliamentary and the 1996 Presidential elections,[59] has continued into the second half of the 1990s. Thus a declining number of young people trust various state and public institutions and an increasing proportion of youth had little faith in the then Russian President, Boris Yeltsin, or his government. In line with the trends outlined in chapter 2 and beyond, it is hardly surprising that few young people trust political parties, regional leaders, trade unions or the mass media.

In the year 2000, though, a more consolidated voting pattern started to emerge among Russian youth, especially during the March Presidential elections. This was mostly due to the fact that young people thought that the new President, Vladimir Putin's programme largely corresponded with their socio-political orientations. The main declared goal (which has since been partly achieved) was to introduce order in the country. This met with enthusiastic support among youth. By voting for Putin, the younger generation in Russia expressed its disappointment with the policy of the previous Yeltsin administration and hoped for greater stability in the future via a strengthening of the new political forces.

Table 6.26 Level of trust and distrust in different institutions and organisations among Russian youth (as percent of sample), 1997–1999

Institution/organisation	Trust	Distrust	Trust	Distrust
	1997		1999	
Russian President	14.2	50.1	3.1	81.2
Russian government	8.2	52.6	11.6	66.9
State Duma	6.8	54.4	5.6	71.9
Regional leaders	13.8	45.2	20.0	51.9
Courts	20.2	43.6	25.7	49.4
Police	13.3	56.9	17.3	61.7
Army	24.3	39.7	37.2	28.3
Political parties	3.7	57.5	5.9	70.0
Trade Unions	13.2	47.8	15.5	52.6
Mass media	21.8	37.8	32.0	41.2
Church	32.0	27.2	37.5	32.7

Source: Based on Authors' 'Social Development of Youth' surveys, Russian Federation, 1997–1999.

All in all, however, young people only have a limited opportunity to influence political trends in a risk society. There is very little space for self-realisation for large sections of youth both in Russia and the West.

Throughout the years of reform, the basis of social stratification have been considerably transformed. Some traditional means of social differentiation (occupational status, type of work, content of labour, etc.) are nowadays accompanied by new significant ones. Some of the former have lost their significant role as a result. In the 1990s and into the twenty-first century, social stratification is built on socio-cultural, ethnic, regional, financial and property grounds. Such specifically Soviet patterns, as membership in the CPSU's *nomenklatura* or access to distribution of goods in short supply, have now become things of the past. Level of education and intellectual work have also lost their former strong influence. Instead property, access to resources for life-support (job, salary, other material and financial grounds) as well as access to citizenship rights and belonging to the so-called 'power structures' (Home office, FSB, etc.) are now the main determinants of youth inequality (see Table 6.27). It is evident from Table 6.27 that differences based on property, material well being and type of settlement affect youth life-chances (qualifications, living standards, business opportunities, social and career promotion) and exist on a large scale. Our findings show that this is especially true of those working in the private rather than the state sector. *The opportunity to improve one's qualification is seen as significant for the future only if it is accompanied by a growth in wages.* Better skills do not necessarily lead to upward social mobility, but they nevertheless influence the process of self-realisation amongst young people.

Table 6.27 Youth opportunities for self-realisation depending upon social and economic backgrounds, Russia, 1999

Basis of stratification	*Symptom of stratification*	*Possibilities for self-realisation by:*			
		a	b	c	d
Place of work	State	4.21	2.89	3.02	2.26
	Private	3.97	3.70	3.31	3.09
Material position	High income	2.45	2.07	1.99	1.60
	Low income	2.28	1.51	1.59	1.33
Type of settlement	Moscow	2.36	2.02	1.90	1.45
	City	2.64	2.06	2.04	1.69
	Village	1.99	1.49	1.50	1.27

Key: a Improving qualifications   b Increasing wages
       c Gaining promotion   d Doing business

Source: Based on Authors' 'Social Development of Youth' surveys, Russian Federation, 1999.

The connection between opportunities for self-realisation and material differentiation is even closer. The 'poor' constitute the majority of the Russian population and they face a lack of opportunities in comparison to those who are 'well off'. The poor are becoming poorer while the rich are getting richer in Russia, despite the 1998 crash. This makes social stratification deeper.

The regional factor generates significant differences in youth opportunities. The most unfavourable situation exists in rural areas where youth life chances are much narrower than for those living in urban areas. However, urbanisation has only had a limited impact. Thus in our 1990s surveys we found that young people from Moscow estimated their life chances as lower in comparison to their counterparts in other regions. The explanation for this is the level of social differentiation and quality of life which is much higher in the capital and, hence it is harder for youth to achieve. Moscow has accumulated a large number of banks, different types of private firms and joint-stock enterprises with good salary and career prospects.

People working in these structures act as a 'role model' for the majority of Russian youth. Hence, young people's aspirations to enter such reference groups are driven by their strong desire to achieve a certain social status and standard of living. However, most young people are deprived of the opportunity to become integrated into their 'desired' economic and financial structures. This is consequently reflected in youth consciousness as low estimated life-chances.

A heterogeneous ethnic environment is the next important factor influencing social stratification and youth self-realisation. Our research data shows that the more sustainable the ethnic status of young people is, then the more optimistic their estimations of future prospects are. Due to obstacles in the way of youth ethnic self-determination, such as discrimination on ethnic grounds, this factor strongly affects young people's life-chances. We shall use a comparison of answers given by young Russians and their Tatar counterparts in order to illustrate this point (see Table 6.28).

Russian and Tatar youth were deliberately chosen because Russians are the numerically dominant ethnic group whereas Tatars are a smaller ethnic group possessing an autonomous state inside the Russian Federation.[60] As we can see from Table 6.28, young Russians see their opportunities as being far less favourable than those of young Tatars whose ethnic identity is stronger.[61] This correlation is more obvious when a comparison of the fate of young Tatars and Russians living in Tatarstan is undertaken. In this case, young Russians are becoming a minority and their opportunities are decreasing. This suggests the presence of certain limitations and obstacles on the grounds of ethnic origins in Russia. All in all, it is clear that a number of factors including type of property, place of work (state/private sector), income, ethnic environment and regional differences all affect life conditions and determine youth self-realisation in a risk society.

Table 6.28 Comparison of youth opportunities for self-realisation depending upon ethnic status (Mean on a 7 point scale), Russia, 1999

Opportunities to	*Young people*			
	Living in Russia		*Living in Tatarstan*	
	a	b	a	b
Improve qualifications	2.34	2.37	1.61	2.38
Increase Wages	1.79	2.10	1.05	2.22
Promotion	1.78	1.85	1.13	1.98
Do business	1.48	1.41	1.05	1.47

Key: a Russians   b Tatars

Source: Based on Authors' 'Social Development of Youth' survey, Russian Federation, 1999.

Searching for a moral foothold and social reference points

During the process of self-realisation, young people need a reliable life orientation. Without this strong support and foothold, which can be provided by society and group values, it will be very hard for young people to find a personal meaning in life, to define their immediate and future goals and to choose the right means to achieve these aims. It is important to emphasise that youth motivation requires a single minded and clear purpose, which involves an effective search for a reference point that might act as a basis for youth self-awareness. This depends, of course, upon the young person concerned and on the particular circumstances. In any case, this is a difficult and very contradictory process which becomes even more unpredictable as it is taking place under conditions of uncertainty and in a risk society.

In Western countries there has been a shift of youth values towards the so-called 'post-modern' model in which individual freedom has withstood traditional (modern) values.[62] However, the speed and direction of this shift from modern to post-modern values in various countries is determined by youth well-being. This connection was first noted by Abramson and Engelhart in their research at the start of the 1990s.[63] In other words, providing for basic needs (comfort etc.), contemporary societies tended to concentrate on idealistic and universalistic aspirations.[64] Moreover these new values are combined with traditional liberal ones in such a way that freedom of activity co-exists with tolerance.[65] In fact post-modernism challenges the values of the middle class.[66]

A question therefore arises, namely, how far has society left its traditional values behind? An apolitical youth, its passiveness and alienation from political processes is often cited as a key example of the breakdown of traditional values. However, a closer analysis shows that young people's seemingly apolitical stance is attributable to the absence of political forces which represent youth interests. Youth, in turn, feel outside the political doctrines that currently prevail. Nevertheless, the fact that young people from many countries across the globe are involved in today's anti-globalisation protests proves that the notions of an apolitical, passive youth is a myth. However, young people still feel alienated from the political process. According to its virtues, young people are well ahead of older groups and have already entered the post-modern phase. Hence, young people adhere to post-materialistic, humanist values, along with egalitarian and 'green' (environmental) attitudes. Although this shows that young people have clear value orientations, no leader has as yet emerged from inside or outside their ranks, who is capable of converting current youth concerns into concrete policies. Finally, the mass manipulation of young people's consciousness has led to a change in the meaning of political participation.

The classical forms of political participation have lost their attractiveness for youth; nowadays, cross-national programmes, such as the protection of the environment, the struggle for human rights, and aid to the developing countries, have become more central to young Europeans.[67] It is also important to emphasise that individualism is not synonymous with anomie, which reflects modern trends in the development of societies. If 20 years ago, young people actively stood for democracy and equality, then today, the right to individuality has become more important to them. Such individualism can be seen in the value which young people place on satisfaction of personal needs, which is especially strong during times of uncertainty and risk.[68] This is why it is not surprising that contemporary Western youth, whose childhood was generally comfortable in terms of economic and physical security, tends to pay more attention to post-material cultural values. Such values as the quality of life, are more important to contemporary youth than it was to the post-war generation, for instance. Values associated with higher income and material well-being are gradually giving way to a greater emphasis on human relations, self-development and quality of life.

Of course, the significance attached to various values, varies according to social status and gender. Young females, according to our research, tend to be more critical in their views on social reality and on the prospects for non-stop socio-economic growth than their male counterparts. Furthermore, females demonstrate greater flexibility in their perceptions of the world and are more pluralistic in outlook.

Besides gender differences, the regional dimension is also crucial in determining youth values. In general in Western Europe, individualism is more highly rated and young people are satisfied with their status. For example, in the Netherlands, Denmark and Germany, where young people have better living standards, the level of toleration of others is high. According to data collected by Jean Charles Lagree, racism and the environment are the issues which matter most for youth.[69] Similarly, Helena Helve's research emphasises that post-modern values totally correspond to the social criticism by youth and are reflected in alternative movements, such as Greenpeace, animal rights, feminism, new age and others.[70]

However, a different picture of youth values emerges in Southern Europe. Against the background of the fight to preserve the family, values, tolerance and unlimited freedoms are being repudiated. In these societies, young people tend to be more religious and also differ from other parts of Europe in their higher level of socio-political activity and participation. Thus the degree of satisfaction with socio-economic status is the key factor determining the dominance of materialistic or post-materialistic values among contemporary youth in these regions of Europe. The same variables also determine the political values of youth (i.e. whether or not that are 'left', 'right' or 'centre').

In Russia, the socio-economic transformation and the introduction of irrational reforms, which we described in Chapter 2, have led to distortions in values. Thus increasing individualisation in Russian youth consciousness has been accompanied by a breakdown in the level of social control and by the failure to set 'new moral limits'. Furthermore, this new relatively free normative value structure has halted the reproduction of strong life goals and norms which might have acted as reliable social reference points. This, in turn, has led to uncertainty in people's lives not just their social status but world view. This is especially true of young people.

An important issue which needs addressing is young people's perception of the situation in Russia and how they view their position in Russia's risk society. These questions are explored in Table 6.29. The answers given to the five selected questions suggest that a growing proportion of young people in post-Soviet Russia are fully aware of the uncertainty that prevails in their country today, and also acknowledge that this generates instability and risk in their own lives. 44–82 percent of young people in Russia by the end of the 1990s did not want children, had little trust in others, disliked the political uncertainty and the fact that everything in life had lost its meaning, and therefore, two out of three young Russians lived each day as if it was their last and did not worry about the future.

Table 6.29 Youth views of the situation in Russia and their place in it (answers as percent of sample), 1997–1999

Question Posed	Percent of youth agreeing with statements posed in first column	
	Year	
	1997	1999
The political situation is so uncertain, it is difficult to know what is happening	73.4	81.9
Everything in life has lost its value and meaning	73.5	73.7
Everybody lives each day as it comes and doesn't think about the future	51.4	64.8
Nowadays, it is difficult to trust others	57.0	57.8
As long as the future remains uncertain, I do not intend to have any children	40.7	43.4

Source: Based on Authors' 'Social Development of Youth' survey, Russian Federation, 1997–1999.

Given these answers, we decided to explore the issue of uncertainty and risk further. Our findings are presented in Table 6.30.

Table 6.30 Young people's value orientations according to the degree of stability or uncertainty in Russia (as percent of group), 1999

Orientation	Values									
	Education		Work		Commun.		Wealth		L-ship	
	a	b	a	b	a	b	a	b	a	b
Stability	67.2	32.8	51.2	48.8	71.5	28.5	49.3	50.7	32.7	67.3
Uncertainty	63.3	36.7	44.3	55.7	70.7	29.3	33.4	66.6	33.9	66.1

Key: commun. = Communication   L-ship = Leadership
       a = valued in itself   b = instrumental values

Source: Based on Authors' 'Social Development of Youth' survey, Russian Federation, 1999.

The answers which young people gave to the direct questions about the degree of stability and the level of uncertainty in their lives are compared in Table 6.30. The responses can be put into three categories: Calm and stability prevail in the lives of 30.6 percent of young Russians; by contrast, uncertainty and risk exists among 34.4 percent of Russian youth; and the remaining 35 percent of our sample stated that stability and risk in their lives existed in equal proportions. Obviously, in the latter case, the degree to which stability or risk prevailed varied according to the specific circumstances. Consequently, we can conclude that for the majority of young people in Russia (around two-thirds), a constant state of uncertainty and risk is a normal state of affairs. Table 6.30 suggests that education, work, communication, wealth and leadership are viewed as important in themselves when stability prevails; whereas during times of uncertainty and risk young people tend to view education, work, communication, wealth and leadership as a means to an end.

All in all, our analysis shows that there is a strong correlation between the degree of uncertainty and risk in young people's way of life and the extent to which instrumental values prevail. Uncertainty and risk tends to distort values, goals and activities which leads to a gradual shift from terminal (valued in itself) to instrumental (means to an end) value orientations, depending upon the circumstances. However, it would be wrong to conclude that value systems are being destroyed at times of uncertainty and risk. It is better instead to talk in terms of changes in the structure of value orientations at times of uncertainty and risk as well as about the appearance and reproduction of new values in a risk society. This can be seen if we analyse the cultural values of Russian youth in the late 1990s.

Thus Table 6.31 indicates that terminal values exist in equally high proportions at times of stability (70.5 percent) or uncertainty (68.2 percent). Moreover, the proportion of young people denied all cultural values is similar in both societies. These findings disprove the widely held notion concerning the existence of a 'spiritual or moral crisis' in risk societies.[71]

This table reveals two trends. Firstly, despite a noticeable conservatism in cultural values, their structure has nevertheless changed during times of uncertainty. Thus interest in sport is greater than interest in literature and poetry. Furthermore, youth interest in classical music has fallen two places. Although the number of young people going to the theatre or listening to folk music is higher, they too have declined in ranking. Secondly, uncertainty is not marked by signs of stagnation in youth values, instead the opposite is occurring. In absolute terms, the coefficient characterising the cultural values of Russian youth at times of uncertainty is slightly higher than when things were more stable. In general, though, the trends in Table 6.31 are rather contradictory, and there seems to be very little difference between youth values in stable and unstable conditions, when one might have expected the opposite to apply. Perhaps the main reason for this is the majority of our sample (60.9 percent) desired stability and calm and so held on to key cultural values at times of uncertainty. In this respect only around a third of our youth sample (29.6 percent) were willing to alter their cultural values at times of risk. This group, who are in favour of change and who embrace risk, are worthy of a more careful analysis. Of those young people inclined towards risk, 41.2 percent work, 31.9 percent study and finally, 6.4 percent of school and university students combine work and study as do 3.9 percent of adults with permanent jobs, who tend to take part-time evening courses. Only 2 percent of those young people inclined towards risk were unemployed. Our analysis of those young people inclined towards risk, also revealed that different age groups were represented in this category. Hence, this category of youth is a distinct socio-cultural group with positive attitudes towards risk. This makes them fascinating in terms of the main theme of this book.

Table 6.31 Comparison of the cultural values of young people in Russia at times of stability or uncertainty (average weighting on 7 point scale), 1999

Cultural values	Stability		Uncertainty and risk	
	a	b	a	b
Communicating with loved ones	6.29	1	6.31	1
Communicating with relatives and friends	6.28	2	6.24	2
Nature	5.28	3	5.40	3
Cinema	5.09	4	5.20	4
Variety, pop music	4.64	5	4.64	5
Literature, poetry	4.06	6	4.08	6
Sport	3.87	7	4.13	6
Antiquity	3.79	8	3.80	8
Theatre	3.70	9	3.99	9
Classical music	3.30	10	3.29	12
Art	3.26	11	3.39	11
Folk music	3.21	12	3.42	10
Rock music	3.07	13	3.25	13
Religion	2.98	14	2.98	14

Key: a Coefficient b Rank

Source: Based on Authors' 'Social Development of Youth' survey, Russian Federation, 1999.

Table 6.32 compares the value orientation of those young people inclined towards risk with those young people who prefer instead to avoid risk altogether (i.e. they desire stability and calm).

Table 6.32 Changes in the cultural values of young people in Russia at times of stability or uncertainty (average weighting on 7 point scale), 1999

Important values	Stability		Uncertainty and risk	
	a	b	a	b
Interesting job	6.19	1	6.18	2/3
Cosy family	6.16	2	5.88	6
Material success	6.15	3	6.18	2/3
Acquisition of knowledge, professionalism in work	6.09	4	6.19	1
Stability in society	6.00	5	5.92	5
Freedom of choice	5.89	6	5.95	6
Honesty, respectability	5.77	7	5.45	9
Equal opportunities for all	5.69	8	5.26	10
Sexual harmony or compatibility	5.34	9	5.62	8
Entrepreneurship, risk taking	5.02	10	5.63	7
Beauty in nature and art	4.97	11	4.98	12
Power	4.46	12	5.03	11
Belief in God	3.80	13	3.52	13

Key: a Coefficient   b Rank

Source: Based on Authors' 'Social Development of Youth' survey, Russian Federation, 1999.

The principal difference in the values held by these two groups of young people is evident in the way that those who prefer stability and calm tend to build their lives in a 'traditional way' stressing for instance, an interesting job, cosy family, material success, acquisition of knowledge and professionalism in their work. This contrasts with those who prefer change and want to take a risk. In this youth category, acquisition of knowledge and professionalism in their work rank as number one in their value orientation, an interesting job and material success share third place and freedom of choice takes fourth place. Furthermore values, such as entrepreneurship and risk taking, sexual harmony or compatibility and power, tend to be more important to those who prefer change and want to take a risk than to those young people who prefer stability and calm.

The priority attached to *social achievement* among those preferring change and risk is evident here, although it has its own Russian specifics (i.e. it is linked to the on-going crisis and extremely unstable conditions). This is why the desire for 'stability in society' is ranked in fifth place among those who prefer change and want to take a risk as well as among those young people who prefer stability and calm. *Russian youth, therefore, acknowledges that calm and reliability and change and risk can only co-exist successfully in sustainable, dynamically developing societies.*

Trends in young people's estimations of their personal characteristics, as shown in Table 6.33, are evidence of the sustainability of the aforementioned correlation. In both groups, the self-estimation given overlaps with the distribution of key values displayed in Table 6.32. This proves that, on the one hand, young people have specific traits. Thus, those young people oriented towards stability tend to fit the pre-1990 personality profile, whereas those inclined towards risk are totally modern in value orientation. The characteristics of the latter group include: individualism (57.8 percent); responsibility (54.4 percent); rationalism (37.3 percent); entrepreneurship (34.8 percent); law-abiding tendencies (34.7 percent), unselfishness (29.9 percent) and collectivism (24.8 percent).[72] Of course, we must bear in mind the fact that this is a self-portrait in so far as these qualities are based upon self-evaluations. Nevertheless, the data in Table 6.33 suggests that *new value orientations among youth have emerged which are in line with the market, individualism and the development of a risk society. The rise of non-conformism is another characteristic of Russian youth today.*

Table 6.33 Self-estimations of personal characteristics of young people in Russia at times of stability or uncertainty (average weighting on 7 point scale), 1999

Important personal quality (self-estimations)	Orientation			
	Stability		Uncertainty and risk	
	a	b	a	b
Responsible, sense of duty	2.62	1	2.45	2
Law abiding	2.51	2	2.23	5
Individuality, self-awareness	2.50	3	2.50	1
Unselfishness	2.31	4	2.21	6
Pragmatism, rationalism	2.26	5	2.27	3
Collectivism	2.24	6	2.17	7
Entrepreneurship	2.10	7	2.24	4

Key: a Coefficient b Rank

Source: Based on Authors' 'Social Development of Youth' survey, Russian Federation, 1999.

Young people's desire for autonomy in decision-making, which manifests itself in the priority given to one's own experience rather than that of the older generation, prevails among 74 percent of those young people who prefer and want to take a risk. By comparison, among those preferring stability 60 percent hold such a view. Relying on their own experience and not taking into account that of their parents, young people in Russia tend to be less cushioned against their mistakes. Nevertheless, they still have a better opportunity to realise their own innovational potential.

In quantitative terms, the group inclined towards risk is not very large, but it has the possibility of expanding and gaining greater influence, as the level of risk increases. Our analysis of youth responses to the question 'What would you prefer, if you had a choice – reliability and calm or change and risk' is given in Table 6.34.

Table 6.34 Comparison of the proportion of young people preferring reliability and calm to change and risk in Russia (as percent of sample), 1990–1999

Orientation towards	Distribution according to year			
	1990	1994	1997	1999
Reliability and calm	38.8	47.0	60.4	68.0
Change and risk	37.8	26.5	18.5	20.2

Source: Based on Authors' 'Social Development of Youth' survey, Russian Federation, 1990–1999.

The above table shows that throughout the 1990s in Russia, there was a consistent increase in the number of young people who desired stability (up from 38.8 percent in 1990 to 68 percent by 1999). This reflects young people's attempts to resist the mounting crisis in Russian society, economy and polity. In this way, young people are also making an active contribution to the stability of the society in which they live. However, it is also clear from Table 6.34, that a small proportion of young people are oriented towards change and risk (down from 37.8 percent in 1990 to 20.2 percent in 1999). The falling number of young people willing to take a risk (down to one in five) reflects the tremendous changes which occurred in the last decade of the twentieth century in Russia, ranging from the collapse of the USSR in 1991 to the severe economic crisis in August 1998. *Given the speed and pace of change, and the high level of uncertainty prevailing, it is hardly surprising that most young people prefer to 'protect' themselves against change whilst only a few are willing to try and respond to risk by embarking upon innovative activity.*

Thus in a risk society, the role of young people as a factor in social reproduction has become more widespread. The activation of this function, which is directed towards the continuity of basic values, is geared towards resisting the destructive trends occurring during periods of uncertainty and risk. Once activated this social reproduction function is aimed at assisting the stabilisation of society. As for youth innovation, which is connected to the renewal of the value system, this tends to compensate for any possible adverse consequences arising out of risk and now serves as the basis for the development of society (i.e. expanded social reproduction).

Youth identity crisis

The search for a moral foothold and social reference points is closely linked to the process of identity formation among young people. If young people identify with a particular group then they tend to accept its norms and values and are also aware of their social surroundings. They are ready to merge with this particular group and maximise their participation in it by embarking upon joint activities. In the sociological sense, due to self-identity, the social integration of the younger generation becomes more sustainable. In this respect, it is no coincidence that one of the widespread interpretations of youth as a social phenomenon is connected with the period when the identities formed are more stable.[73] The instability and changeability of youth identification models is a well-known fact. The flexibility of youth identity is natural in circumstances in which youth identity is changing due to pressure from inside and outside their particular group. The development and shift of society from traditional to modern has produced great variations in the social ties between individuals and groups, thereby determining the nature of youth social identities.

In modern sociology, there are different approaches to the empirical analysis of this process. Some theorists stress the link between identity and class, gender and ethnicity,[74] whereas others talk in terms of the crucial role played by production, consumption, education, family, leisure and changes in the labour market in determining youth identity.[75] Although, scholars are still debating what concepts and frameworks are necessary for analysing the impact of risk societies on youth identity in contemporary Europe, one thing is still clear: there is a consensus that youth identities have been transformed as a result of the existence of a risk society. Thus the perception of youth identity was that *youth was a stage*, as Ali Rattansi and Ann Phoenix point out, *when 'identity' becomes 'more established and settled.'*[76] This was the view Erikson held when he stressed that *adolescence was a crucial stage in youth development as young people headed towards 'integrity and continuity'*.[77] However, with the emergence of a risk society, youth 'identity' has become disembedded, less fixed and established because society is more unstable, complex and constantly shifting.[78] As a consequence young people, as we pointed out in the previous section, have now rejected the old collective identity in favour of newer values. The question we now have to ask is how and in what way does a risk society influence youth identity?

In European societies, the rise of post-modernism, which is connected to the emergence of risk societies, has had a real impact on the position of the younger generation. There is now a widespread belief that the process of coming of age is continuing despite the existence of economic and social marginalisation. In the opinion of many researchers, the level of uncertainty and fragmentation in the life start, life chances and life course of young people today is bigger than it ever was before.[79]

If societies throughout Europe and elsewhere are rapidly changing and young people can no longer achieve their ambitions, then it is possible that some young people might reject the values of the societies in which they live as well as the guidance provided by the socialisation agencies and turn instead to alternative ways of securing their life goals. According to Bob Coles, this 'alternative career' might involve criminal activity or embarking upon 'undeclared work' (i.e. working whilst receiving state benefits).[80] Coles argues that those who take this route want to find alternatives to 'hard work, long hours and low pay' but unfortunately some young people are unable to find a 'regular and legitimate job' so they simply do what they can as a means of surviving in a harsh, risk society.[81] Whilst some researchers see this drift towards crime as an extension of some young people's lifestyles (such as drug-taking), Coles points out that this 'alternative career' is *'not necessarily deliberate'* or part of a young persons *'long term development'*.[82] The key question therefore is whether or not different societies combat this activity or through 'poor legitimate employment opportunities' unintentionally encourage youth delinquency and crime.[83] Patricia Allatt adds weight to Coles' viewpoint by arguing that:

> risks and anxieties [are] multiplied for those whose transitions to adulthood are particularly difficult.[84]

Thus those sections of youth who are vulnerable and part of the underclass might feel because of their social exclusion and de-politicisation that they cannot influence their life choice or the life start of any of their offspring. Discriminated against and alienated from society, they do not possess the appropriate resources or imagery ('the good citizen') to overcome their problems or make a successful transition.[85] Unfortunately, young people in this category are living a self-fulfilling prophecy in so far as state and society expects them to act in a delinquent and deviant manner and to reject the norms and values of society. What is required to overcome this trap for all sides – young people, state and society – is a re-conceptualisation of 'vulnerability' and 'underclass' in relation to youth so that it takes into account the public/private divide and thereby enables intervention to take place early enough in order to prevent a total and irreversible rift between youth and society.[86]

Under the conditions of instability and crisis in Russia's risk society, as we saw in chapter 2, this contradiction is even more pronounced because of the lack of clarity on societal goals, on the one hand, and because of the lack of consensus on what it means to be a 'good citizen' in Russia today, on the other.

Most theoretical and empirical constructions of citizenship stem in different ways from T.H. Marshall's framework,[87] wherein Marshall emphasised that citizenship meant 'full members of the community' who shared its values.[88] According to this conceptualisation, membership of society entails the possession of certain rights (social, economic and political) and civic obligations. The latter includes a sense of duty, patriotism, being law abiding etc. All of these characteristics are crucial to any definition of citizenship. These notions are being shaped and will be consolidated in the minds of individuals providing that the conditions are right and that these rights can be realised. But if the necessary pre-conditions are absent, and the goals and means to achieve these citizenship rights and obligations are uncertain, then it is possible that young citizens might pursue other citizenship models centred around non-institutionalised and socially disapproved patterns of behaviour. These might include informal, criminal or black market activities. As a result a crisis of identity emerges. These contradictions have existed in Russia for many years but they became very pronounced during the 1990s.

So far we have seen that the shift from a modern to a risk society has a number of implications for young people. It is evident that the life-start, life-chances and life-course of youth in numerous countries is more fragmented that it was several decades ago. One of the biggest consequences of this situation is that old reference points and identities held by young people (and in the past transmitted to them by their parents) have either become distorted, transformed or disappeared altogether. This has led to uncertainties of identity and growing risks of social exclusion and marginalisation. In the past social networks and other ties helped young people determine their identity (i.e. class, ethnicity and gender) but in the 1990s and into the twenty first century these old social networks have been at least under strain and in some cases under threat. Because of the latter situation, current social networks have not proved adequate for integrating youth into society.

Evidence of an identity crisis includes changes in the historical and legal awareness and in the subjective perception of citizenship. In the case of Russia, its history has been marked by many examples of discontinuity of identity, especially among young people. At one time, youth identified with the Soviet system and all it stood for, but since the mid-1980s and 1990s, the collapse of communism and the introduction of a new reform agenda has produced an identity crisis. This stems from the breakdown of the mechanisms of social integration and the failure to indicate to youth their need to take their civil duties and responsibilities seriously. If the latter had occurred this might have provided a sense of continuity, lead to the reproduction of socio-cultural values and provided a stable environment for young people which they shared with others and which guaranteed, following Giddens, 'ontological security' on an individual basis.

Young people's confidence in society and in their social surroundings determines the sustainability of social relations on a micro level. By contrast, in situations of uncertainty and risk, youth identities tend to be contradictory and so uncertain and delinquent identities emerge in some cases. The Russian sociologist Antonina Kovaleva attributes this trend to 'deviations in the socialisation of young individuals'.[89] An 'identity moratorium' based on youth alienation from society also often occurs. Thus the number of young people who fail to identify with anything and who are largely self-centred is on the increase, this is encouraged by the liberal intelligentsia and the mass media. This is closely linked to the post-totalitarian syndrome referred to earlier in Chapter 2. After many years of having clear and certain symbols of identity thrust upon them by the communist party and state, meaning that young people had no opportunity to make their own choices, an 'individual identity' is finally emerging, in which young people want to be themselves and independent, at least on a verbal level. This means that *post-Soviet youth is starting to develop all the characteristics associated with modernity.* They are rejecting the old Soviet symbols (national heroes, heroes of Soviet Labour and so forth) and searching for new identities based on new post-Soviet symbols. However, this is far from easy.

In order to empirically measure the youth identity crisis, we asked our respondents the question 'What does being a Russian citizen mean for you?'. In replying 'Love of one's country', 'Being prepared to fight for one's country' or 'To share its history and present', our surveys indicate a strong sense of civic identity among some sections of contemporary Russian youth. However, the fact that other young people replied 'Being a Russian citizen *means nothing*' is a clear signs that an *uncertain identity* also exists in a post-Soviet world. Furthermore positive responses to another question 'Is it okay for young people to make money even if they break the law?' (see Table 6.35), namely approve rather than disapprove, was additional evidence of a *delinquent identity*. However, the latter need not necessarily mean youth identification with criminal behaviour or activities, instead it might indicate the failure to distinguish between 'right' and 'wrong' because bribes, swindling and non-payment of taxes are widespread in Russia and this is not creating an image of a 'good citizen' which youth can use as a role model.

Table 6.35 Attitude of Russian youth towards those making money at any price (answers as percent of sample), 1997

Answers to the question: Is it okay for young people to make money even if they break the law?	Age groups				
	15–17 years	18–20 years	21–23 years	24–26 years	27 years and older
Approve	13.2	13.1	11.1	13.8	9.5
Approve more than disapprove	24.0	28.7	29.2	20.6	25.4
Disapprove more than approve	38.1	37.8	35.6	37.2	33.3
Disapprove	23.9	19.2	23.3	28.4	31.8

Source: Based on Authors' 'Social Development of Youth' survey, Russian Federation, 1997.

Furthermore Table 6.36 shows what proportion of youth, by age group, would actually condemn those who break the law which ranges from a third or more among 15–17, 24–26 and 27 years and older to two-fifths among 18–20 and 21–23 year olds. *The striking thing is that nearly two-thirds of the entire sample would in fact NOT condemn those who break the law.*

Table 6.36 Attitude of Russian youth towards those breaking the law (answers as percent of sample), 1997

Answers to the question: Would you condemn those who break the law?	Age groups				
	15–17 years	18–20 years	21–23 years	24–26 years	27 years and older
Yes	37.2	41.8	40.3	34.2	34.9
No	62.8	58.2	59.7	65.8	65.1

Source: Based on Authors' 'Social Development of Youth' survey, Russian Federation, 1997.

According to data we collected in 1999, 42.2 percent of youth identified with Russia as a country, 7.5 percent had no clear identity and 12.3 percent were inclined towards a 'delinquent' identity. *In overall terms, our findings suggest that 1 in 5 (20 percent) of young Russian people have an identity crisis.* However, if we look beyond the aforementioned percentages and analyse the connection, if any, between identity models and risk, then we find, as Table 6.37 shows, that a correlation between youth identity and the level of stability of one's life situation exists. A 7 point scale was used by young respondents to estimate their life situation (stable and calm or risk and uncertainty. A relatively low mean in this instance characterises a more or less stable life situation. By contrast, a relatively high mean suggests an increasing level of risk in young people's perceptions of their life situation, which demonstrates a 'delinquent' identity. This is a contradictory finding, but an interesting one nevertheless. All in all, *this youth identity crisis is reflected in extreme forms of minimalisation and maximisation of risk.* Feelings of being a 'full citizen' is the equilibrium between these two extremes and is a sign of a high degree of self-confidence among certain categories of youth.

The crisis of identity among Russian youth emerges very clearly if we consider young people's attitudes towards reformer's desires to rapidly 're-write' history. Our findings here are shown in Table 6.38 below. It is clear that our youth sample is split into three roughly equal groups on the question of 're-writing' history. Thus 33 percent approve of it, 36.1 percent disapprove and 30.9 percent are indifferent towards the fate of their country's history. This is hardly surprising given the pace of change since the mid-1980s. Throughout the 1990s, youth values were constantly in flux, with one value quickly replaced by another. Thus such a polarisation and disorientation of youth opinion (in this case towards history) is only to be expected.

Table 6.37 Correlation between identity indicators and young people's perceptions of their own life situation (Mean on 7 point scale), Russia, 1999

Identity indicator	Young people's perceptions of their own life situation, mean on 7 point scale (in percent)							
	1	2	3	4	5	6	7	Mean
Full citizen	5.0	8.9	17.0	35.0	21.7	8.2	4.1	4.0
Uncertain identity	11.5	14.8	13.1	37.7	14.8	3.3	4.9	3.59
Delinquent identity	7.0	6.5	14.0	29.0	25.0	11.0	7.5	4.21

Source: Based on Authors' 'Social Development of Youth' survey, Russian Federation, 1999.

Table 6.38 Young people's attitudes towards the 're-writing' of history (answers in percent), Russia, 1999

Young people's attitudes towards the 're-writing' of history	Answer given
It is essential to rethink history because it is important to our present and future	33.0
It is wrong to manipulate history	36.1
I do not care about history because I am indifferent	30.9

Source: Based on Authors' 'Social Development of Youth' survey, Russian Federation, 1999.

The views indicated in Table 6.39 do not vary according to age, gender or living standards, with the exception of young members of the intelligentsia. Among the latter the proportion of youth who replied '*I do not care about history because I am indifferent*' was much lower (24 percent) with responses '*It is essential to rethink history because it is important to our present and future*' and '*It is wrong to manipulate history*' coming in at about the same (38 percent each). *Consequently there is an inconsistency between value imperatives at an institutional level and individual and mass consciousness. This manifests itself in the form of uncertainties of youth historical identities in Russia today.*

The inconsistency between youth identity models and basic value imperatives is also evident in other spheres of young people's lives such as education, work and communication, as shown by Table 6.39.

Table 6.39 Correlation between identity indicators and key values in different spheres of young people's lives, Russia, 1999

Identity indicator	Values towards (in percent)					
	Education		Work		Commun.	
	a	b	a	b	a	b
Full citizen	65.6	34.4	47.5	52.5	73.8	26.2
Uncertain identity	57.4	42.6	55.7	44.3	64.0	36.0
Delinquent identity	60.0	40.0	36.5	63.5	68.0	32.0

Key: commun. = Communication
1) a = valued in itself   b = instrumental values
Source: Based on Authors' 'Social Development of Youth' survey, Russian Federation, 1999.

The answers which young people gave on the importance of education, work and communication in their lives are all different. Table 6.39 suggests two things: firstly, uncertainty and secondly, too much flexibility in their lives. At the same time, the results of our investigation does not support the view that there has been a total breakdown in civic identity among young Russians. The emergence of a risk society has only partly affected youth identities and the degree of attachment to the past and present. Recent research shows that the younger generation still tend to 'live in the past' (*begstva vo vchera*), a term coined by Yelena Grishina.[90] *The state of uncertainty and dissatisfaction with social reality means that young people avidly search for identities not located in the present or future but in the past.* This happens partly because of the transmission of values from past to present. Thus even if young people where born in the late Soviet or post-Soviet era, they still gain knowledge of the past from their parents or other older members of their families. According to Grishina, basic elements of the past (justice, security, confidence in the future, pride, joy, lack of fear) are *all central aspects of a Russia that was stable and calm.*[91] Thus post-Soviet youth strongly desires ontological security. Hence *myths of the Soviet past are being reproduced by today's post-Soviet generation.*

The correlation between such indicators as 'Love of one's country' and 'Being prepared to fight for one's country' and risk is far more complicated than it first appears. A quarter of young people in Russia are proud of their country; the rest (three-quarters) associated present day Russia with the regime that plunged them into crisis and so their attitudes towards their country lack clarity. As a result, among those who estimated that their lives are unstable and full of risk, the proportion who were proud of their country was 1.5 times less than those young people who estimated that their lives are stable. Thus *risk does not necessarily lead to the breakdown of patriotism, it simply distorts it.* The nature and direction of such distortions is becoming more and more evident today, as shown by the growing rationalisation of civic relations and identities. Table 6.40 below shows that two civic identities have appeared in Russia's risk society, depending upon living conditions. The 'Stability' model reflects the process of rationalisation of uncertain identities whereas the 'Risk' model is more closely associated with a delinquent identity which is evident in the destruction of legal awareness, the popularity of criminal subcultures among Russian youth and their tolerance towards others involvement in criminal groups and activities. The point at which these two models diverge is in their attitudes towards the state (see Table 6.41).

Table 6.40 Comparison of youth civic relations and identity and its correlation with their life situations (Mean on 7 point scale), Russia, 1999

Citizenship is associated with:	Evaluation of life situation			
	Stability		Risk	
	a	b	a	b
Government	5.41	1	5.01	1
Constitutional rights	5.11	2	4.55	4
Obligation and duty	54.93	3/4	4.94	2
National pride and self respect	4.93	4/3	4.78	3
Security	4.87	5	4.45	5
Patriotism	4.32	6	4.37	6

Key: a Coefficient b Rank

Source: Based on Authors' 'Social Development of Youth' survey, Russian Federation, 1999.

Table 6.41 outlines different 'models of citizenship' in which the individual-state relationship varies according to the degree of stability or risk prevailing. In the stability model the 'state serves the individual' whereas in the risk model the reverse is true, namely the individual serves the state. The latter refers to the remnants of the Soviet civic model which to some extent still survives today.

At the same time, a strong one-way connection hardly exists between different models of citizenship and young people's life situations. This is evident in Table 6.42 which shows the degree of correlation between identity indicators and youth orientation towards stability and risk in Russia in 1999 emphasising in particular that every identity model involves some elements of both orientations towards reliability and risk, although in unequal proportions.

Table 6.41 Characteristics of two different models of civic identity among Russian youth, 1999

Stability model (New)	Risk model (old Soviet)
Under this model state serves the individual. Constitutional rights are prioritised and everything else follows. Citizenship therefore refers to belonging to the state, with citizens having obligations and duties to perform in exchange for the protection of their rights. All of this will be realised only if constitutional rights are observed. If this occurs a sense of security and safety will follow. The latter is the main means of strengthening the degree of patriotism among Russian youth.	Under this model the individual serves the state. In line with the old Soviet model, individual rights are secondary. Here individuals have obligations and duties to perform and then they expect the state to protect their rights in exchange for this. A sense of national pride together with a feeling of security and safety stems from this according to Russian youth. All in all, these factors generate strong patriotic feelings in young people.

Source: Derived from Authors' 'Social Development of Youth' surveys, Russian Federation, 1990–1999.

Table 6.42 Correlation between identity indicators and youth orientation towards stability and risk, Russia, 1999

Identity indicators	Prefer		
	a	b	c
Full citizen	68.4	19.9	11.7
Uncertain identity	73.5	16.7	9.8
Delinquent identity	56.5	33.5	10.0

Key: a Stability   b Risk   c No answer

Source: Based on Authors' 'Social Development of Youth' surveys, Russian Federation, 1999.

The data presented in Table 6.42 shows that some young people with an uncertain identity are obviously inclined towards stability; whereas other young people with a delinquent identity are more inclined towards risk. Having said that, though, a large proportion of young people demonstrated both orientations together. Obviously the difficulties faced by youth in their everyday lives forces some of them to estimate stability highly. This gives a strong correlation between stable living conditions and collective types of personality. Such a personality type tends to be oriented in the first instance towards the achievement of societal wealth followed by a shift towards meeting their own needs. This section of youth see their own problems in egoistic terms blaming a hostile society, full of 'grasping individuals' for their fate. In this groups view, when self-realisation is achieved at the expense of others, different risks are not simply individualised, they also become large-scale in nature. For a different section of youth, with predominantly traditional identities which barely correspond with the demands of Russia's new risk society, this situation is the main cause of instability. As a result, this particular category of youth is less adapted to individualisation and to the different patterns of life and risk prevailing. Thus the contradiction between these two extremes produces conflict in Russia's crisis ridden society. The possibility of resolving these conflicts, as we saw in chapter 4, lies with young people's total identification with contemporary values. The latter, in turn, is the pre-requisite for the successful integration of youth in a risk society.

The lack of continuity in the social world of youth, which has happened as an inevitable consequence of Russia's transformation to a risk society, has given new significance to youth ethnic identities. During the 1990s, the meaning of the 'ethnic factor' was changing and this was reflected in young people's voting patterns and in their attitude towards the 'other'. This also gave rise to growing ethnic prejudices among youth. Table 6.43 shows that a changing environment produces new risks in relation to young people's attitudes towards other ethnic groups. Our findings suggest that the character of ethnic relations among youth is closely connected with their civic identity. Thus, the aforementioned identity crisis has influenced the level of ethnic tension in contemporary Russia.[92] Furthermore, some of the aforementioned correlation also applies here. Uncertain and delinquent identities, as evident in Table 6.43, tend to produce extreme trends in attitudes towards other ethnic groups. These tensions also tend to increase as the degree of stability in young people's lives falls. If under stable conditions, ethnic hostility exists among 24 percent of our sample, then risk increases the level of tension by a further 9 percent among young Russians and Tatars, for instance. As a result, up to 33 percent of young people, possess latent inter-ethnic contradictions.

Table 6.43 Correlation between civic identity indicators and level of ethnic tension among youth (as percent of group), Russia, 1999

Civic identity indicators	Hostility towards other nationalities	
	Feel hostility	Do not Feel hostility
Full citizen	72.7	27.3
Uncertain identity	78.7	21.3
Delinquent identity	67.1	32.9

Source: Based on Authors' 'Social Development of Youth' surveys, Russian Federation, 1999.

A similar correlation was discovered in youth attitudes towards inter-ethnic marriage. Particularly noticeable here was the level of 'tolerance' prevailing, even amongst those opposed to inter-ethnic marriage (which increased from 4.9 to 7.6 percent among Russians and from 4 to 12 percent among young Tatars between 1994–1999). This risk situation influences the psychological and emotional state of those young people living in a heterogeneous environment in a negative way. Unprecedented sensitivity towards the aggressive behaviour of the 'other' is natural in such situations. Ethnic tensions, and the increased number of instances when young people experience hostility, are being grossly exaggerated by the existing feeling of insecurity and danger, meaning that young people can always pick out the 'enemy' (*braga*). This is why in many cases so-called preventive aggression is the only form of self protection under such uncontrolled conditions.

It is important to emphasise here that responsibility for all past 'Soviet' mistakes have been placed on ethnic Russian's shoulders. This has only served to heighten the Russian sense of irritation with those elements hostile towards them. Discrimination against the Russian-speaking population,[93] which is sometimes groundless, and aggression towards Russians from other ethnic groups, has provoked ethnic discord and strongly affected Russians. Our 1997 findings among young people of Russian nationality found that they believed 'ethnic biases' and 'defects' exist. Thus 24.7 percent of young people attribute good or bad personal characteristics to a person's ethnic origins. Once greater risk and uncertainty became a feature of the everyday life of half of those young people of Russian nationality we surveyed in 1999, this negativity rose by more than 10 percent.

Ethnic identity among young Tatars has been changed even more dramatically in the last decade. None of them expressed antagonism towards others in 1997, then a mere two years later, hostility based on ethnic backgrounds had increased 8– fold. Naturally, under risk conditions such hostility is double its normal intensity.

It is significant that opposed identities are based not on the conflict between two religions (Orthodox and Muslims or between Slavs and non-Slavs) as one might assume, but instead our research shows that it stems from long-term conflicts between particular groups, such as those from Caucasus (*Kavkaz*) and other ethnic groups in the territory of the Russian Federation.[94] Fostered by two wars in Chechnya, first under Yeltsin, then currently under Putin, deeply ingrained clichés about 'persons of Caucasian nationality' exist in youth consciousness and no distinction is drawn between the Chechens and other ethnic groups who have settled in the Caucasus region. These clichés reflect a real sense of danger and threat from this particular region in the minds of young people.

Whilst such politically incorrect stereotypes must be condemned, the active search for new identities under conditions of uncertainty, sooner or later, drives young people back towards their own ethnic origins and group. Thus many unstable and highly politicised identity patterns remain widespread in Russian society, so negative attitudes towards other national-ethnic traditions and cultural values will be hard to shake off. As soon as these values become more fixed in comparison to others, then they will start playing a significant role in the identity of some young Russians. However a risk society changes these identities in a very unusual way because relatively low indicators suggest a poor assimilation of ethnic culture among young Russians, which remain largely the same at times of stability or risk (see Table 6.44).

Table 6.44 Level of young people's knowledge of their ethnic traditions and ceremonies, depending upon conditions of stability and risk (in percent), Russia, 1999

Indicator	Life situation	
	Stability	Risk
Know very well	8.2	11.3
Know, but not very well	69.9	65.6
Do not know	21.9	23.0
Hard to say	6.0	0.1

Source: Based on Authors' 'Social Development of Youth' survey, Russian Federation, 1999.

Parental influence on this process is also weakening. While, as our young respondents note, their parents' aspiration to build their own lives in accordance with norms and values of their ethnic culture is on the increase (and is especially high among Tatars and Ukrainians living in the Russian Federation and is less so among Russians) there are few of them who would place the same demands on younger members of their families. *The emergence of a risk society in Russia has influenced the fundamental mechanisms of societal reproduction that are rooted in the correlation between ethnic and civic identities* (see Table 6.45).

Our findings show that there is a correlation between civic and ethnic identities in young people's consciousness. The number of young people who know their ethnic traditions (well and not very well) and whose parents observe these traditions and demand the same from their children are viewed as possessing a high ethnic identity. Their proportion in the sample with total civic identity constitutes 86.1 percent. At the same time, the proportion of young people among those with a civic identity crisis, namely uncertain and delinquent identity, is lower and they constitute 82 percent and 62.1 percent of our youth sample.

Although young people have different identity models to their parents, parental influence on the prevention and decrease in delinquent identities is still significant. This leads us to the conclusion that in cases where a positive ethno-cultural identity dominates a real opportunity for filling the vacuum left by the crisis of citizenship exists in Russia's risk society.

Table 6.45 Correlation between civic and ethnic identities among youth (in percent of different groups), Russia, 1999

Civic identity	Level of the knowledge of ethnic traditions and ceremonies			Parental attitudes towards observing ethnic traditions and ceremonies according to young people's answers			
	a	b	c	d	e	f	g
Full citizen	6.1	72.6	21.3	7.4	26.5	39.3	26.8
Uncertain identity	1.6	73.8	24.6	6.6	39.3	31.1	23.0
Delinquent identity	6.3	64.3	29.4	6.1	23.9	43.4	26.6

Key:
a Know very well
b Know but not very well
c Do not know
d Parents observe and expect same of their children
e Parents observe but do not expect same of their children
f Parents do not observe, neither do their children
g Hard to say

Source: Based on Authors' 'Social Development of Youth' survey, Russian Federation, 1999.

The contradictory processes and events taking place in Russia's crisis-ridden society demands a clear choice between 'good' and 'bad'. This difficult decision cannot be made by all of youth. Ironically any direct prompting or pressure can have the reverse effect and lead to the development of a delinquent identity. The breakdown in traditional norms and roles in Russia's risk society has led to a situation in which youth consciousness is free of all constraints and appears to be open to different patterns of identity, especially if they appear lucrative, even if this means being antisocial. This is why criminal identity among youth in Russia is on the increase and also why we are seeing a rapid growth in delinquent deviations among them.

Our analysis shows that there is a close correlation between juvenile delinquency and the degree of social transformation. By the late 1990s, a high level of crime amongst both adults and young people, especially orphans had occurred (see Table 6.46).

The number of young offenders committing different sorts of crimes known to the Russian police has increased by 36 percent from 839,000 in 1994 to 1,138,000 by 1998. One third of this group are children under 14 years of age. The latter group has also increased as a proportion of the population by 1.5 times since 1994 (i.e. from 214,000 in 1994 to 317,000 in 1998). Children remain a very active section of the Russian population in delinquency terms. Offenders under 14 constitute a third of all criminals in Russia today (see Table 6.47).

Table 6.46 Crimes committed in Russia, 1998

Type of offender	Rate per 10,000 population
Adults	92
All children and teenagers	132
Orphans and neglected children and teenagers	542

Source: Yu. V Kharmaev, 'Kriminologicheskie problemy sotsializatsii vospitannikov detskih domov i shkol-internatov', *Kand. dissertatsiya*, Moscow, 1998, p. 218.

Table 6.47 Juvenile crimes known to the police according to age group, Russia, 1994–1998

Age Group	1994		1996		1998		1998 as % of 1994
	a	b	a	b	a	b	
under age of 13 years	214,460	25.6	270,092	26.2	316,926	27.8	47.8
14–15 years	256,105	30.6	322,157	31.2	357,038	31.4	39.4

Key: a absolute numbers b in percent

Source: *Prestupnost' nesovershlennnikh v Rossii, 1994–1998gg: Statisticheskii sbornik*, Moscow, MVD Russia 1999, p. 4.

Another peculiarity relates to a transformation in the nature of juvenile crime in Russia. If in the past, juvenile crime mainly involved small-scale theft and hooliganism, nowadays young people tend to steal property and in 85 percent of cases violence is used. The number of murder cases also increased by 174 percent during the second half of the 1990s. In child and teenage crime cruelty, sadism and torture are often used on their victims (the latter has increased by 385 percent). In such cases, cruelty is not just a means to an end (the crime) it is also a goal in its own right. This is part of a general change in the 'values' of young offenders in which more are willing to accept the use of violence.[95]

In addition, new types of juvenile crimes have also appeared. Examples include kidnapping, racketeering, establishing certain 'tax regimes' for those counterparts from rich families, the production and distribution of different sorts of pornography and so on. There have also been fundamental changes in the types of juvenile crimes, with dangerous crimes (murder, robbery, rape, assault) on the increase. The number of cases of blackmail, for instance, has increased by 19.3 percent (totalling 4,000 cases), stealing of weapons by 33.7 percent (242 cases) and finally, juvenile involvement in the production and distribution of different types of drugs has risen by 114 percent, constituting 11,200 cases in 1998.[96]

All in all, we are witnessing a shift from occasional crime in the past to well organised and cruel types of juvenile crime. Thus, organised crime occupies first place among all types of juvenile delinquency and this type of crime stood at 64.3 percent in 1998. Thus, if in 1994, 76,900 members of the criminal groups were registered by police, then four years later this figure stood at 111,900. During 1998 more than 74,000 young offenders were punished for crimes committed as part of this group. Those involved in this type of crime are often as young as 10–13 years old.[97]

Pleshchakov and Kluchkova argue that the so-called informal (*neformaly*) juvenile organisations, which emerged at the end of the 1980s, have provided the basis for contemporary criminal groups.[98] If at the start of the 1990s, they represented part of a democratic opposition to Russia's establishment, then by the mid-1990s they had begun to take on a more delinquent orientation. As a result, these *neformaly* juvenile organisations became involved in different forms of crime in various regions of the Russian Federation, which have risen from 37 percent to 66 percent of all crime.[99]

Table 6.48 Category of juvenile crimes in Russia (in percent), 1994–1998

Type of crime committed by youth	Year				
	1994	1995	1996	1997	1998
Murder and attempted murder	0.6	0.6	0.6	0.6	0.5
Grievous bodily harm	1.1	0.9	1.0	0.9	0.8
Theft	60.1	61.4	60.4	59.7	59.0
Blackmail	1.5	1.8	2.1	1.9	2.1
Hooliganism	7.5	7.5	7.7	6.2	5.9
Robbery	11.6	10.7	10.4	10.4	10.6

Source: *Prestupnost' nesovershlennnikh v Rossii, 1994–1998gg: Statisticheskii sbornik*, Moscow, MVD Russia 1999, p. 4.

Whereas in the past most youth crime was associated with a youth desire for self-affirmation and establishing their own way of life this has now been gradually replaced by crime for mercenary ends, namely to make a profit. Well organised criminal activity now exists instead of occasional youth crime provoked by specific circumstances, such as hardship. Hence young people nowadays are highly organised and more professional in their approach to crime partly because of a closer association with corrupt adults.

Thus what are the factors determining the process of formation of different identity models? Besides the peculiarities of Russian modernisation, socio-demographic factors have a decisive impact on this process, as Table 6.49 shows.

Table 6.49 Correlation between youth civic identity models and socio-demographic characteristics in Russia (Contingency coefficient), 1999

Socio-demographic characteristics	Uncertain identity	Delinquent identity	Full identity
Type of activity	0.08	0.11	0.61
Gender	0.02	0.08	0.21
Age	0.16	0.17	0.77
Social origins	0.11	0.14	0.57
Region of residence	0.21	0.15	0.69

Source: Based on Authors' 'Social Development of Youth' survey, Russian Federation, 1999.

This leads us to the conclusion that each socio-demographic factor enumerated in the table influences young people's civic identity in a different way. Crisis identity (uncertain and delinquent) is predominantly determined by social factors instead of socio-demographic ones. However, the closer the links between socio-demographic characteristics and total identity, the more sustainable a civic identity will be among this group of young people. Moreover, while full identity is closely connected with all factors, delinquent identity correlates with age and social origins only. The latter proves that factors such as age and social origins largely determine deviant behaviour.

Thus, youth identity in Russian society reflects the specifics of that society's multinational character, on one hand, and the peculiarities of the process of modernisation, on the other. The correlation between ethno-national and civic identities has become the basis for the emergence of a special identity structure which is different to western models. In addition to this, the crisis in Russia as a whole affects identity structure significantly. The proportion of uncertain and delinquent identities, in particular, constantly grows under conditions of risk. This, in turn, influences the level of patriotism and increases ethnic tensions in the areas where young people live. Age, social origins and the current region of residence are the most influential factors on youth identity.

Notes

1   G.V. Osipov and V.V. Lokosov, *Sotsial'naia tsena neoliber'nogo reformirovaniia*, Moscow, 2001, p. 94.
2   Ibid, p. 58.
3   'Sotsial'no-demograficheskie tendentsii', in *Rossiya: Vyzvodyi vremeni i puti reformirovaniya*, Moscow, 1998, p. 95.
4   Ibid, p. 96.
5   Ibid, p. 97.

6 K. Evans and A. Furlong, 'Metaphors of youth transitions: niches, pathways, trajectories or navigations', in J. Bynner, L. Chisholm and A. Furlong (ed), *Youth, Citizenship and Social Change in a European Context*, Ashgate, Aldershot, 1997, p. 27. Our emphasis.
7 K. Roberts and B. Jung, *Poland's first communist generation*, Ashgate, Aldershot, 1995, p. 179. Our emphasis.
8 K. Evans and A. Furlong, 'Metaphors of youth transitions: niches, pathways, trajectories or navigations' in J. Bynner, L. Chisholm and A. Furlong (eds), *Youth, Citizenship and Social Change in a European Context*, Ashgate, Aldershot, 1997, p. 28. Our emphasis.
9 K. Roberts, 'Structure and Agency: The new research agenda', in J. Bynner, L. Chisholm and A. Furlong (eds), *Youth, Citizenship and Social Change in a European Context*, Ashgate, Aldershot 1997, p. 59. Our emphasis.
10 Roberts, 'Structure and agency', 1997, p. 59. Our emphasis.
11 Ibid, p. 60. Our emphasis.
12 On this issue see S.A. Sorokin, *Rossiiskaia sem'ya i tri zakonoproekta po ee ohkrane*, Moscow, Ekonomika, 1999, pp. 68–115.
13 See M. Heikkinen, 'Social networks in the exclusion process of young people in Finland', paper presented to the *European Network on Transitions in Youth* conference, Edinburgh 10–13 September 1998 as well as V. Puuronen, 'Marginalisation and youth sub-cultures', in H. Helve (ed.), *Unification and marginalisation of young people*, Youth Research 2000 Programme, Finnish Youth Research Society, Helsinki, 1998, pp. 162–164.
14 N. Bowers, A. Sonnet and L. Bardone, *Giving young people a good start: The experience of OECD countries* 2000, p. 17 cited at www.oecd.org/els/pdfs/Londonconf/washconf.pdf.
15 Ibid, p. 10.
16 EU, *Focus on European lifestyles* No. 5599, 24 June 1999, p. 12.
17 Bowers et al. *Giving young people a good start: The experience of OECD countries* 2000, p. 11 cited at www.oecd.org/els/pdfs/Londonconf/washconf.pdf.
18 J. Tanner, 'Reluctant rebels: A case study of Edmunton high-school dropouts', in D. Ashton and G. Lowe (eds), *Making their way: Education, training and the Labour market in Canada and Britain*, Open University Press, Milton Keynes, 1991, p. 109.
19 Ibid.
20 J. Bynner, E. Ferri and P. Shepherd, *Twenty Something in the 1990s*, Ashgate, Aldershot 1997.
21 Bowers et al. *Giving young people a good start: The experience of OECD countries* 2000, p. 12 cited at www.oecd.org/els/pdfs/Londonconf/washconf.pdf.
22 Ibid, p. 18.
23 Ibid.
24 Ibid, p. 12.
25 E. Morgan M.E.P., *European youth unemployment: A Comparative Study*, Carmarthen, Wales, 1997, p. 6.
26 *United Nations Report on the Global Situation of Youth*, cited at www.unorg/events/youth98/dackinfo/report/globl-2.htm, 1999.
27 *Young Europeans*, Eurobarometer DG XXII report, 29 July 1997.
28 Ibid.
29 EU, *Focus on European lifestyles*, No. 5599, 24 June 1999, p. 1.
30 D.R. Green, 'Taking steps: Young people and social protection in the European Union', *European Youth Forum* report 1998, p. 24 cited at www.coe.fr/youth/research.htm.
31 Ibid.
32 Ibid, p. 25.
33 B. Coles, 'Vulnerable youth and processes of social exclusion: a theoretical framework, a review of recent research and suggestions for a future research agenda', in J. Bynner, L.

Chisholm and A. Furlong (eds), *Youth, Citizenship and Social Change in a European Context*, Ashgate, Aldershot, 1997, p. 70.
34 D.R. Green, 'Taking steps: Young people and social protection in the European Union', *European Youth Forum* report 1998, p. 27, cited at www.coe.fr/youth/research.htm.
35 Ibid, p. 28.
36 Ibid.
37 Ibid.
38 L. Chisholm, 'Sensibilities and occlusions: Vulnerable youth between social change and social exclusion', in J. Bynner, L. Chisholm and A. Furlong (eds), *Youth, Citizenship and Social Change in a European Context*, Ashgate, Aldershot, 1997, pp. 109–110.
39 The Russian term is *kruzhok po interesam* which literally translated means 'interest circles' which has no direct equivalent in English, so for the sake of convenience the more commonly known 'extra-curricula' term is used here.
40 U. Nagel and C. Wallace, 'Participation and identification in risk societies: European perspectives', in J. Bynner, L. Chisholm and A. Furlong (eds), *Youth, Citizenship and Social Change in a European Context*, Ashgate, Aldershot, 1997, p. 45.
41 Evans and Furlong refer to this situation as one of 'learned helplessness' (K. Evans and A. Furlong, 'Metaphors of youth transitions: niches, pathways, trajectories or navigations', in J. Bynner, L. Chisholm and A. Furlong (eds), *Youth, Citizenship and Social Change in a European Context*, Ashgate, Aldershot, 1997, p. 36).
42 U. Nagel and C. Wallace, 'Participation and identification in risk societies: European perspectives', in J. Bynner, L. Chisholm and A. Furlong (ed.), *Youth, Citizenship and Social Change in a European Context*, Ashgate, Aldershots 1997, p. 48. Our emphasis.
43 B. Coles, *Youth and Social Policy*, University College London Press, London, 1995, p. 98.
44 See P. Buchner, M. de Bois-Reymond and H.K. Kruger, 'Growing up in three European regions', in *Growing up in Europe*, Walter de Gruyter, Berlin and New York 1995, pp. 43–70.
45 J. Wyn, and R. White, *Rethinking Youth*, Sage Publications, London, 1997, pp. 9–15.
46 K. Evans and A. Furlong, 'Metaphors of youth transitions: niches, pathways, trajectories or navigations', in J. Bynner, L. Chisholm and A. Furlong (eds), *Youth, Citizenship and Social Change in a European Context*, Ashgate, Aldershot, 1997, p. 28. Our emphasis.
47 *Young Europeans*, Eurobarometer DG XXII report, 29 July 1997.
48 On these changes see J. Bynner and K. Roberts (eds), *Youth and Work: Transition to Employment in England and Germany*, A project of the Anglo-German Foundation for the Study of Industrial Society, Rochester, c. 1991; J. Bynner, and R. Silbereisen, *Adversity and Challenge in life in the new Germany and in England*, Macmillan, Basingstoke, 1999; K. Roberts et al., *Poland's First Post-Communist Generation*, Avebury, 1995 and L. Machacek and K. Roberts, *Youth Unemployment and Self-Employment in East-Central Europe*, Institute for Sociology, Slovak Academy of Sciences, Bratislava 1997; S. Kovacheva, 'Sinking or Swimming in the waves of transformation? Young People and Social Protection in Central and Eastern Europe', *European Youth Forum*, Brussels, 2000 and L. Koklyagina Nurse, 'Patterns of Transitions into Work in Russia and Great Britain', *YOUNG*, Vol. 9 (1), pp. 41–60.
49 Bowers et al. *Giving young people a good start: The experience of OECD countries* 2000, p. 14 cited at www.oecd.org/els/pdfs/Londonconf/washconf.pdf.
50 E. Morgan M.E.P., *European youth unemployment: A Comparative Study*, Carmarthen, Wales, 1997, p. 3.
51 Bowers et al. *Giving young people a good start: The experience of OECD countries* 2000, p. 15 cited at www.oecd.org/els/pdfs/Londonconf/washconf.pdf.
52 E. Morgan M.E.P., *European youth unemployment: A Comparative Study*, Carmarthen, Wales, 1997, p. 6.

53 *Rossisskii statisticheskii ezhgodnik: Statisticheskii Sbornik*, Moscow, Goskomstat 2000, p. 122.
54 H. Williamson, 'Status Zer0 Youth and the 'Underclass': Some Considerations', in R. MacDonald (ed.), *Youth, the Underclass and Social Exclusion*, Routledge, London and New York, 1997, pp. 76–77.
55 *Young Europeans*, Eurobarometer DG XXII report, 29 July 1997.
56 *Young Europeans*, Eurobarometer DG XXII report, 29 July 1997. For more on this issue and the reasons behind it see R. Spannring, C. Wallace and C. Haerpfer, 'Civic participation among young people in Europe', *NYRIS 7 Proceedings* cited at www.alli.fi/nyri/nyris7/papers/wallace.htm.
57 *Young Europeans*, Eurobarometer DG XXII report, 29 July 1997.
58 On this see C. Williams, V. Chuprov and J. Zubok, 'The voting behaviour of Russian youth', *Journal of Communist Studies and Transition Politics*, Vol. 13 (1), March 1997, pp. 145–59.
59 Ibid.
60 For more detail here see V.I. Chuprov and J. Zubok, 'The ethnic consciousness of Russian youth', in C. Williams and T. D. Sfikas (eds), *Ethnicity and Nationalism in Russia, the CIS and the Baltic States*, Aldershot, Ashgate, 1999, pp. 103–119.
61 On this see also V.I. Chuprov and A.V. Savva, 'Etnicheskii status molodezhi', in *Rossiyskaia molodezhi: Sotsial'noe razvitie*, Moscow, Nauka, 1992, p. 37.
62 For the purposes of this study 'values' refer to certain concepts or beliefs which pertain to desirable ends, states or behaviours and which guide young people in the selection or evaluation of certain events (stability, uncertainty, risk etc.). For a detailed discussion here see S.H. Schwartz, 'Universals in the content and structure of values: Theoretical advances and empirical tests in 20 countries', in M.P. Zanna (ed.), *Experimental social psychology*, New York, Academic Press 1992, pp. 1–65; S.H. Schwartz, 'A theory of cultural values and some implications for work', *Applied Psychology*, Vol. 48, 1999, pp. 23–47 and finally, S.H. Schwartz and W. Bilsky, 'Toward a theory of the universal content and structure of values: extensions and cross-cultural replications', *Journal of Personality and social psychology*, Vol. 58, 1990, pp. 878–891.
63 P. Abramson and R. Inglehart, 'Generational replacement and value change in eight West European societies', *British Journal of Political Science*, Vol. 22, April 1992, pp. 183–228.
64 C. de Lauwe, *Pour une sociologie des aspirations*, Paris, Denoel, 1969, p. 34.
65 L. Dumont, Homo Hierarcicus, Paris Seuil, 1966 and Essai sur l'individualisme, Paris, Seuil 1991.
66 J. O'Neil, 'Religion and postmodernism: The Durkheimian Bond in Bell and Jameson', in M. Featherstone (ed.), *Postmodernism*, London, Routledge, 1991, pp. 493–508.
67 L. Guidikova, 'European youth trends', 1998, cited at www.coe.fr/youth/research.htm. For more on this issue and the reasons behind it see R. Spannring, C. Wallace and C. Haerpfer, 'Civic participation among young people in Europe', NYRIS 7 Proceedings cited at www.alli.fi/nyri/nyris7/papers/wallace.htm.
68 H. Helve, 'Values, world views and gender differences among young people' in H. Helve and J. Bynner (eds), *Youth and Life Management: Research Perspectives*, Helsinki University Press, Helsinki, 1996, pp. 171–188.
69 J.C. Lagree, 'Youth in Europe', in H. Helve and J. Bynner (eds), *Youth and Life Management: Research Perspectives*, Helsinki University Press, Helsinki, 1996, pp. 165–169.
70 H. Helve, 'Values, World views and Gender differences among young people', in H. Helve and J. Bynner (eds), *Youth and Life Management: Research Perspectives*, Helsinki University Press, Helsinki, 1996, pp. 171–188.

71 On the background to this phenomenon in Russia see I. Ilynsky, 'The spiritual and cultural values of young people in a post-Totalitarian state', in J. Riordan, C. Williams and I. Ilynsky (eds), *Young people in post-communist Russia and Eastern Europe*, Aldershot, Dartmouth, 1995, pp. 95–115.
72 These figures refer to the fact that young people think that they actually possess such qualities.
73 A.I. Kovaleva et al., *Sotsiologiia molodezhi: Teoreticheskie voprosy*, Moscow, Sotsium, 1999, pp. 150–151. See also Yu. V. Vishnevskii et al., *Praktikum po sotsiologii molodezhi*, Moscow, Sotsium, 2000.
74 A. Rattansi and A. Phoenix, 'Rethinking youth identities: Modernist and post-modernist theories', in J. Bynner, L. Chisholm and A. Furlong (eds), *Youth, Citizenship and Social Change in a European Context*, Ashgate, Aldershot, 1997, p. 143.
75 C. Griffin, 'Youth research and identities: same as it ever was?', in J. Bynner, L. Chisholm and A. Furlong (eds), *Youth, Citizenship and Social Change in a European Context*, Ashgate, Aldershot, 1997, p. 165.
76 A. Rattansi and A. Phoenix, 'Rethinking youth identities: Modernist and post-modernist theories', in J. Bynner, L. Chisholm and A. Furlong (eds), *Youth, Citizenship and Social Change in a European Context*, Ashgate, Aldershot, 1997, pp. 121, 123.
77 Erikson cited in ibid, p. 125.
78 Ibid, pp. 128–29.
79 See J. Bynner, 'Marginalisation and the new research agenda', in H. Helve (ed.), *Unification and marginalisation of young people*, Youth Research 2000 Programme, Finnish Youth Research Society, Helsinki 1998; A. Furlong, B. Stadler and A. Azzopardi, *European youth trends*, Council of Europe 2000; W.R. Heinz, 'Youth transitions and employment in Germany', *International Social Science Journal*, special issue on *Youth in Transition*, No. 164, June 2000, pp. 161–171; L. Machachek, *Youth in the process of transition and the modernisation of Slovakia*, Institute of Sociology, Slovak Academy of Sciences, 1998; C. Soares, 'Aspects of youth, transitions and the end of certainties', *International Social Science Journal*, special issue on *Youth in Transition*, No. 164, June 2000, pp. 209–219; C. Wallace and S. Kovacheva, *Youth and Society*, London, Macmillan 1995; C. Wallace and S. Kovacheva, *Youth in Society: The construction and dconstruction of youth in East and West Europe*, London, Macmillan, 1998; J. Wyn and P. Dwyer, 'New patterns of youth transition in education', *International Social Science Journal*, special issue on *Youth in Transition*, No. 164, June 2000, pp. 147–161 and J. Wyn and R. White, *Rethinking youth*, London, Sage, 1997.
80 B. Coles, 'Vulnerable youth and processes of social exclusion: a theoretical framework, a review of recent research and suggestions for a future research agenda', in J. Bynner, L. Chisholm and A. Furlong (eds), *Youth, Citizenship and Social Change in a European Context*, Ashgate, Aldershot, 1997, p. 75.
81 Ibid, pp. 75–76.
82 Ibid, p. 76.
83 Ibid.
84 B.P. Allatt, 'Conceptualising youth: Transitions, risk and the public and the private', in J. Bynner, L. Chisholm and A. Furlong (eds), *Youth, Citizenship and Social Change in a European Context*, Ashgate, Aldershot 1997, p. 90.
85 Ibid, pp. 93–97.
86 Ibid, p. 97. For more on this issue see R. MacDonald (ed.), *Youth, the 'Underclass' and Social Exclusion*, London, Routledge, 1997.
87 T.H. Marshall, *Class, citizenship and development*, Westport, Greenwood Press, 1973.
88 T.H. Marshall and T. Bottomore, *Citizenship and social class*, London, Pluto Press, 1992, p. 18.
89 A.I. Kovaleva, *Sotsializatsiia lichnosti: Norma i otklonenie*, Moscow, Sotsium, p. 109.

90 Y.A. Grishina, *Rossisskaia molodezh': problemy grazhdanskoi identichnosti*, Moscow, 1999, p. 111.
91 Ibid, pp. 111–115.
92 For more on this see Parts I and II of C. Williams and T.D. Sfikas (eds), *Ethnicity and Nationalism in Russia, the CIS and the Baltic States*, Aldershot, Ashgate, 1999.
93 For an example here see I. Saleniece and S. Kuznetsovs, 'Nationality policy, education and the Russian question in Latvia since 1918', in C. Williams and T.D. Sfikas (eds), *Ethnicity and Nationalism in Russia, the CIS and the Baltic States*, Aldershot, Ashgate, 1999, especially, pp. 245–260.
94 On the background here see G. Yemelianova, 'Ethnic nationalism, Islam and Russian politics in the North Caucasus', in C. Williams and T.D. Sfikas (eds), *Ethnicity and Nationalism in Russia, the CIS and the Baltic States*, Aldershot, Ashgate, 1999, especially, pp. 120–146.
95 Yu. V Kharmaev, 'Kriminologicheskie problemy sotsializatsii vospitannikov detskih domov i shkol-internatov', *Kand. dissertatsiya*, Moscow, 1998, p. 218 and *Prestupnost' nesovershlennnikh v Rossii, 1994–1998gg: Statisticheskii sbornik*, Moscow, MVD Russia, 1999, p. 4.
96 *Prestupnost' nesovershlennnikh v Rossii, 1994–1998gg: Statisticheskii sbornik*, Moscow, MVD Russia 1999, pp. 3–4.
97 Ibid, p. 5.
98 On this see T. Islamshina et al, *Molodezhnye subkul'tury*, Kazan, Kazan Technological University Press 1997; V.A. Pleshchakov, 'Uchastie nesovershennoletnikh v organizovannyh formakh prestupnoi deyatel'nosti', and O.V. Klochkova, 'Makrourovnevaia determiniatsiia prestupnosti vevershennoletnikh', in *Organizatsionno-pravovie problemy preduprezhdeniya prestupnosti nesoverschennoletnikh*, Moscow, Akademiia upravleniia MVD Rossii, 1999.
99 V.A. Pleschakov, 'Uchastie nesoverschennoletnikh v organizovannyh formakh prestupnoi deyatel'nosti', in *Organizatsionno-pravovie problemy preduprezhdeniya prestupnosti nesoverschennoletnikh*, Moscow, Akademiia upravleniya MVD Rossii, 1999, pp. 98–109.

Chapter 7

Conclusion: Reflections on Youth at the Start of the Twenty-first Century

Every epoch displays a particular image of the younger generation. Such images are not a statistical invention and individual young people or groups of youths will not necessarily correspond to this image. In the 1950s we talked about 'war' and 'post-war generations', then in the 1960s of the '1960s generation' or of the 'lost' or 'angry' generation'. By the 1990s it was possible to talk of youth in terms of the 'deceived' generation. All of these metaphors show the commonality of important social trends, feelings and activities of young people belonging to the same historical period, the twentieth century.

Now we are at the start of a new millennium, how might we best characterise the younger generation of the early twenty-first century? One of the aims of this book was to provide a very general overview of contemporary youth as well as the specific features of post-communist Russian youth, a decade after the collapse of communism.

The main conclusion reached by a recent UN report was that young people are more tolerant towards others, not alienated, not antagonistic and not war-like in their attitude towards their families or the older generation.[1] There is also insufficient evidence to suggest a major generational gap. Most young people are well-educated, can and want to work but prefer to shorten or reduce their working day if they receive a good wage for their job. Work is not viewed as an end in itself, but as a means to an end, namely more leisure time. Most youngsters are also optimistic in the self-estimations and in their evaluations of their own life situations.

For instance, Eurobarometer data from 1997 shows that young Europeans did not have major difficulties communicating with people from other races, nationalities and with other religions and cultures. They also failed to discriminate on the grounds of disability, sexual orientation or because people suffered from social diseases, such as alcoholism and homelessness. The fact that nearly 50 percent of young Europeans are willing to have contact with the aforementioned groups demonstrates the openness of contemporary youth.[2]

Although this Eurobarometer survey differs in many respects from the data we uncovered on Russia in the 1990s, it is still the case that Russian and European youth have more in common with each other, rather than major differences that divide them. Nevertheless, the internal strife that is tearing Russian society apart and the continuing inter-ethnic conflicts that are influencing the orientation of young Russians, has significantly influenced intolerance levels which Russians have for those from different ethnic backgrounds. However such intolerance has yet to manifest itself in actual conflict, instead Russians prefer to have as little contact as possible with other ethnic groups.

Some other typical problems facing young Europeans and Russians include the dichotomies between well-being/poverty, global subculture/counterculture, education/illiteracy, good health and leisure/sport versus drug taking, alcoholism, smoking, making something of oneself and suicide. All of these dichotomies are the consequence of the fundamental contradictions in different risk societies. Among these contradictions are those between globalisation/poverty, unemployment, different forms of social exclusion, financial crisis, increasing external debts, on the one hand, and the extension of economic ties, democratic development, the possibility of gaining an education, social growth and empowerment of youth, on the other.

Trying to overcome these contradictions might be a source of either young people's social development or the localisation of risk in various societies. The fact that contemporary risk societies do not really lead to extreme forms of youth misbehaviour on a mass scale, with a few obvious exceptions in recent years, says a great deal about the positive dynamic in this direction and that conflict can be overcome. The globalisation of risk has not assisted in the development of a new generation of risk takers in its negative, gamble sense. At the same time, there has been an increase in the number of deviations from the norm among youth. Living under conditions of risk makes young people in general more pragmatic and this situation tends to stimulate a more careful attitude towards choice of life start.

One of the common problems facing youth at the start of the new millennium is their material position. Of course living conditions and standards differ in individual risk societies but it is widely acknowledged that material and income problems exist among youth. The UN calculated recently that 12 percent of young people currently reside in countries with high incomes, set at greater than US$10,000 per annum.[3] Youth in Russia and most post-Soviet countries have experienced particularly severe declines in living conditions and standards.

The development of a risk society has been accompanied by changes in the inner structure of these societies in transition where a radical transformation in the nature and role of social class, family, gender, marriage, occupation and so forth has taken place. This is why the nature of youth transition has also changed. Youth transition has become more complex and prolonged in comparison to that of previous and/or older generations.

The class based distribution of goods and services has been replaced by predominantly individual forms of distributive relations based upon meritocratic principles. The rapid loss of class identity has led to the individualisation of social inequality. It is not social organisations but individuals who are blamed for their so-called *personal* failures (loss of job, poverty etc.) and this can be seen as the main reason for the existence of social inequality.

Family and religion have lost their former significance and meaning as agents of socialisation. Nowadays, the former are being gradually replaced by the mass media (T.V., Internet etc.). The latter are the key to the current global youth subculture and movement. As a consequence, instead of traditionalism and collectivisation, individualism is developing rapidly and so every young person is trying to shape their life start and course as far as humanly possible. Hence trajectories in the spheres of labour, education and consumption, to name but a few, are all individually determined.

This process, according to the sociologist Ulrich Beck, has a *double meaning*. It is *positive* in so far as under conditions of individualisation young people have better opportunities of gaining greater personal control over money, time, living space, education, career and work. These are desirable and attractive prospects for Russian youth under the new market conditions. In the past in Western societies all of the aforementioned possibilities were socially determined. In Russia, equal opportunities for all was a proclaimed aim but only a reality for the 'chosen' (elite). In such a traditionally modernist understanding individualisation does not have anything in common with individualism as the ideological opposite of collectivism. Instead individualism refers to the value of individuality and the desire for self-assertion or affirmation. However, the *negative* side of individualisation also exists. According to Beck's theory, a high level of competition between individuals remains, especially in the occupational sphere. Moreover, under conditions of uncertainty, individualisation of risk increases and hence individuals are forced to rely on their own ability, competence and on their capacity to make decisions that might protect them against risk. They can no longer, as in the past, rely on the state for help. In other words, the principle 'everyone for themselves' prevails everywhere not just in Russia.

Such a post modernist trend towards individualisation has been accompanied by the erosion of traditional modern values. This attitude prevails amongst youth in the USA and Northern Europe. In these countries more concrete materialistic values have been gradually replaced by abstract, humanistic ones.

Young people in successful positions in advanced countries, with post-materialist values, are nevertheless often concerned about the position of other young people less fortunate than themselves located in less developed countries (Africa) or in war zones (Chechnya and the former Yugoslavia). At the same time, young people in successful positions still blame the young unemployed in their own countries for getting themselves in such a position of risk. Participants in the youth revolts of the 1960s were frequently able to transmit their idea of humanism onto their children and at the same time, they successfully acquired the skills and character necessary in order to make a successful adaptation to uncertainty and risk in their societies.

In Southern European countries, where young people's living standards and conditions are lower, there is another trend prevailing whereby traditional and modern values co-exist. Materialistic orientations and solidarity are much more highly valued in this part of the global risk society.

Russian or post-Soviet youth finds itself at the crossroads of these two tendencies. For young Russians the co-existence of traditional values (family, friendship, love) with more modern values means that post-Soviet youth is located somewhere in-between tradition and progress. Youth has one leg in the past, and hence partly accepts the traditional values associated with Soviet cultural tradition, and another in the present, going in a new direction. Russian youth in particular, like its transition country counterparts in the former USSR and East-Central Europe, is going through a period of great risk and uncertainty.

The analysis offered in this book illustrates the usefulness of utilising the concepts of 'risk' and 'risk society' when examining the position of contemporary Russian youth. Our analysis shows that despite differences between various European societies, *convergence of risk conditions is occurring under the pressure of globalisation.* It is impossible to ignore the influence that the aforementioned factors have had on the process of coming of age (social maturity) as well as on the reproduction of risk in these societies. *Convergence has a dual impact on youth. On the one hand, it gives the process of risk reproduction an almost universal character*, as the following table shows.

Table 7.1 The reproductive basis of risk among youth

Sphere	Type of Risk
Labour market	Unemployment
Education system	Inequality of opportunities
Family	Collapse and appearance of surrogates
Business sector	Inability to compete

All of this is reflected in the typology of conflicts between youth and different societies. This typology is also maintained by three common factors for the younger generation, namely age discrimination, problems with socialization agencies and the impact of global youth subcultures. *On the one hand, convergence is also accompanied by certain unique features in these processes.* For instance, in the West, unemployment is usually the product of over-production which leads to job losses and closures; but in Russia, unemployment is primarily caused by shortages of finance, withdrawal of state support etc. Thus youth unemployment in Russia has a different nature to the same issue in other countries and produces risks in a different way.

Risks, which are typical in other countries, also impact upon Russia and its process of social reproduction. But although this changes Russian society, it does not undermine its fundamental basis. Thus at a simple level the existence of 'Rock 'n' roll' will not make Russia more like the USA. As a result, risk can become weaker if the essential conditions and mechanisms exist and if society wants this to occur. Thus Russians can resist change and pressure from outside by holding onto their national traditions, culture etc. If the reverse occurs, however, then under the pressure of uncertainty, risk will increase and have an adverse effect upon social reproduction.

All of these tendencies express themselves in the transformation of Russian youth but to see this we need to analyse youth in a broader sense and in a broader social context, namely in terms of its material and cultural production, distribution, exchange and consumption patterns and also in terms of young people's relationship to the state and key groups in society such as the political and economic elite. For instance, the expansion of the number of young people in the spheres of distribution and exchange at the expense of material production in the economically advanced West represents a normally functioning market economy, but in the case of Russia with its pre-modern and badly damaged economy, this situation is one of the main causes of risk. Thus the breakdown of the coal industry in Russia, which was sanctioned by the Russian government under pressure from the I.M.F., and led to severe hardship throughout successive winters ever since the mid-1990s, especially in Primoriye or Kamchatka, is just one example of unjustifed risk. No less a danger of the consequences of risk can be seen in the changes in young people's consumption patterns or in rising youth crime because honest work 'simply doesn't pay'. Another example is the impact that the reproduction of risk has caused as a result of the contradiction between modern patterns of identity and sufficiently sustainable traditional views, closely associated with Russian culture. The breakdown of older values and the search for new ones is always linked to uncertainty in the choice of life start and way of life. The link might occur, for instance, when self confidence has collapsed or the risk of social exclusion occurs, raising questions like 'Who am I?' and 'Where do I belong?' Overcoming risk may involve walking the tightrope between two values and identities. Thus in Russia's case this may involve the reproduction of national consciousness alongside successful integration of the younger generation into the world economy.

Analysing the problem of integration of youth in different modern risk societies, our study shows that *social integration is not just possible in a risk society but absolutely necessary for the existence of youth as a social group and for the maintenance of society as a whole*. The peculiarities of the mechanisms of social integration under conditions of uncertainty and risk have been outlined in this book. Among these peculiarities are the new, non-traditional forms of identification as well as other factors of a local and spontaneous nature. What is clear is that *risk can still act as an integrating factor*. The synergetic effect of risk leads to an increase in individual enthusiasm and energy during periods of risk. Young people's readiness to take risks, which is partly connected with age, might lead to their successful integration into society. Although, this and other peculiarities are analysed using the example of Russian youth, these are still universal in nature when taking place under risk conditions. In this way, integration, on the one hand, is an effective means of solving conflicts among young people, but on the other, integration is also a vital pre-condition for youth adaptation in a risk society.

Thus at the start of the twenty-first century, risk is a common characteristic of contemporary society. The younger generations are capable not just of overcoming their state of uncertainty, with the possibility of great success, they also *tend to reproduce risk. This can be seen as a distinctive feature of today's youth*. Along with this, the forms of risk reproduction differ according to one's life situation, in particular due to the demographic situation, different life start, prospects of self-realisation and changing values and identities held by youth today. Being *determined by national characteristics, risk situations also tend to vary in different countries. It is this fact that gives each generation it own unique features.*

Notes

1   *United Nations Report on the Global Situation of Youth*, cited at www.unorg/events/youth98/dackinfo/report/globl-2.htm, 1999.
2   *Young Europeans*, Eurobarometer DG XXII report, 29 July 1997.
3   *United Nations Report on the Global Situation of Youth*, cited at www.unorg/events/youth98/dackinfo/report/globl-2.htm, 1999.

Bibliography

Abrams, P. and McCulloch, A. (1976), *Sociology and Society*, Cambridge University Press, Cambridge.
Abramson, P. and Inglehart, R. (1992), 'Generational replacement and value change in eight West European societies', *British Journal of Political Science*, Vol. 22, April, pp. 183–228.
Adams, B. (1999), 'Industrial food for thought: Timescapes of risk', *Environmental Values*, Vol. 8 (2), pp. 219–238.
Adams, J. (1994), *Risk*, UCL Press, London.
Adelman, D. (1991), *The "Children of Perestroika": Moscow teenagers talk about their lives and future*, M.E. Sharpe, New York.
Adelman, D. (1994), *The "Children of Perestroika" Come of Age: Young people of Moscow talk about life in the New Russia*, M.E. Sharpe, New York.
Ainley, P. (1991), *Young People Leaving Home*, Cassell, London.
Al'gin, A. (1989), *Risk i ego rol' v obshchestvennoi zhizni*, Mysl', Moscow.
Allatt, P. (1997), 'Conceptualising youth: Transitions, risk and the public and the private', in Bynner J., Chisholm L. and Furlong A. (eds), *Youth, Citizenship and Social Change in a European Context*, Ashgate, Aldershot.
Allat, P. (1998), 'Young People and Families. En/Countering Social Exclusion', in Helve H. (ed.), *Unification and Marginalisation of Young People*, Youth Research 2000 Programme, The Finnish Youth Research Society, Helsinki.
Almas, R. (1999), 'Food trust, ethics and safety in risk society', *Sociological Research on line* cited at www.socresonline.org.uk/ocresonline/4/3/almas.html
Andreev, Ye. M. and Volkov, A.G. (1977), *Demograficheskie modeli*, Moscow.
Antonov, A.I. (1980), *Sotsiologiia rozhdaemosti*, Moscow.
Antonov, A.I. (1994), 'Depopulatsiia Rossii i problemy sem'i', in the collection, *Rossiia nakankune XXI veka*, Moscow.
Ashton, D.N. and Field, D. (1976), *Young Workers*, Hutchinson, London.
Averintsev, S. (2001), 'Overcoming the totalitarian past', *Russian Magazine*, 27 June.
Barr, N. (ed.) (1994), *Labor Markets and Social policy in Central and Eastern Europe: The transition and beyond*, World Bank/London School of Economics, Oxford University Press, New York.
Beck, U. (1992), *Risk Society: Towards a New Modernity*, Sage, London.
Beck, U. (1994), *Ecological enlightenment: Essays on the politics of the Risk Society*, Humanities Press, NJ.
Beck, U. (1995), *Ecological Politics in an Age of Risk*, Polity, Cambridge.
Beck, U. (1997), *The reinvention of Politics: Rethinking Modernity in the Global social order*, Polity, Cambridge.
Beck, U. (1999), *World Risk Society*, Polity, Cambridge.

Bekarev, A.A. (1997), 'Sotsiologiia nestabil'nosti', *Builleten' Akademii gumanitarnkh Nauk*, Nizhnyi Novgorod State University.
Bell, D. (1973), *The Coming of the post-industrial society*, Basic, New York.
Bellan, R. (1970), *Beyond belief: Essays on religion in a post-traditional world*, Free Press, New York.
Bennett, V. (2001), *Crying wolf: The return war to Chechnya*, Transatlantic publications, New York.
Bobo, Lo (2000), *Soviet labour ideology and the collapse of the state*, Macmillan, Houndmills Basingstoke.
Bogdanov, I. Ya. et al. (1999), *Ekonomicheskaia bezopasnost' Rossii: tsifry i fakty*, Moscow.
Bonnell, V.E. (2001), 'Russia's new entrepreneurs', in Bonnell, V.E. and Bresauler, G. (eds), *Russia in the New Century: Stability or Disorder?*, Westview, Boulder Colorado, pp. 175–200.
Bowers, N., Sonnet A. and Bardone L. (2000), *Giving young people a good start: The experience of OECD countries* 2000, p. 17 cited at www.oecd.org/els/pdfs/Londonconf/washconf.pdf.
Boxer, V. (2001), 'Who will "find" Russia? How suspicions of globalization could push Russia towards the East', *Russia Watch*, No. 5, March, pp. 25–31.
Bradbury, J. (1989), 'The policy implications of differing concepts of risk', *Science, Technology and Human Values*, Vol. 14 (4).
Braithwaite, J.D. (1997), 'The old and new poor in Russia', in Klugman, J. (ed.), *Poverty in Russia: Public policy and Private Responses*, EDI Development Studies, World Bank, Washington DC.
Buchner, P., de Bois-Reymond, M. and Kruger, H.K. (1995), 'Growing up in three European regions', in *Growing up in Europe*, Walter de Gruyter, Berlin and New York 1995, pp. 43–70.
Bynner, J. (1998), 'Marginalisation and the new research agenda', in Helve H. (ed.), *Unification and marginalisation of young people*, Youth Research 2000 Programme, Finnish Youth Research Society, Helsinki.
Bynner, J., Ferri, E. and Shepherd, P. (1997), *Twenty Something in the 1990s*, Ashgate, Aldershot.
Bynner, J. and Roberts, K. (eds) (1991), *Youth and Work: Transition to Employment in England and Germany*, A project of the Anglo-German Foundation for the Study of Industrial Society, Rochester.
Bynner, J., and Silbereisen, R. (1999), *Adversity and Challenge in life in the new Germany and in England*, Macmillan, Basingstoke.
Campbell, H. and Fitzgerald, R. (2001), 'Food scares and GM: Ambivalent technologies, fear and the politics of nostalgia', unpublished paper presented to *New natures, new cultures, new technologies* conference, Fitzwilliam, College Cambridge, July.
Campbell, H. and Fitzgerald, R. (2001), 'Bleeding/Cutting into Nature/Culture: Frankenfoods and science fictions', unpublished paper presented to *New natures, new cultures, new technologies* conference, Fitzwilliam, College Cambridge, July.
Cassells, M. (1996), *The Rise of the Network Society*, Vol. 1, Blackwell, Oxford.
Chalizde, V. (1977), *Criminal Russia*, Random House, New York.

Chisholm, L. (1994), 'Contribution des approches de la transition vers l'age adulte', in Tanguy, L. (ed.), *Les relations entre education et travail en France, Grande-Bretagne, Allemagne et Italie*, Armand Colin, Paris.

Chisholm, L. (1997), 'Sensibilities and occlusions: Vulnerable youth between social change and social exclusion', in Bynner J., Chisholm L. and Furlong A. (eds), *Youth, Citizenship and Social Change in a European Context*, Ashgate, Aldershot.

Chuprov, V.I. (1994a), *Sotsial'noe razvitie molodezhi: teoreticheskie i prikladnye problemy*, Izd. instituta molodezhi Sotsium, Moscow.

Chuprov, V.I. (1994b), '"Molodezh" Rossii: kharakteristika integratsionnykh protsessov', in Il'inskii, I.I. et al. (eds), *Tsennostnyi mir sovremennoi molodezhi: na puti k mirovoi integratsii*, Moscow.

Chuprov, V.I. (1998), 'Labour Relations and Youth Employment in the Post-Soviet Period', in Helve H. (ed.) *Unification and Marginalisation of Young People*, Youth Research 2000 Programme, The Finnish Youth Research Society, Helsinki, pp. 13–26.

Chuprov, V.I. and Chernish, M. (1993), *Motivatsionnaia sfera sozdaniia molodezhi: Sostoianie i tendentsii razvitiia*, Institut molodezhi/Institut sotsial'no-politicheskikh issledovanii, Moscow.

Chuprov, V.I. and Savva, A.V. (1992), 'Etnicheskii status molodezhi' in *Rossiiskaia molodezhi: Sotsial'noe razvitie*, Nauka, Moscow.

Chuprov, V.I. and Zubok, Yu. A. (1996), 'Sotsialisatsiya molodezhi v post-kommunisticheskoi Rossii', *Sotsial'no-Politicheskii zhirnal*, No. 12.

Chuprov, V.I. and Zubok, Yu. A. (1997), 'Obrazovaniie molodezhi: reformy i konflikty' in *Rossiia u kriticheskoi cherty: vozrozhdenie ili katastrofa*, Republika, Moscow.

Chuprov, V.I. and Zubok, Yu. A. (1998), 'Sotsial'nye konflikty v sfere obrazovaniia molodezhi', in Lisovskii V.T. (ed.), *Chelovek i Obrazovanie v sovremennoi Rossii: Sotsiologicheskie ocherki*, St. Petersburg University Press.

Chuprov, V.I. and Zubok, Yu. (1999), 'The ethnic consciousness of Russian youth', in Williams, C. and Sfikas, T.D. (eds), *Ethnicity and Nationalism in Russia, the CIS and the Baltic States*, Ashgate, Aldershot, pp. 103–119.

Chuprov, V.I. and Zubok, Yu. A. (2000), *Molodezh' v obshchestvennom vosproizvodstve: problemy i perspektivy*, RiTs, ISPR, RAN, Moscow.

Chuprov, V.I., Zubok, Yu. A. and Vil'yams, K. (2001), *Molodezh' v obshchestve Riska*, Nauka, Moscow.

Chuprov, V.I., Zubok, Yu. A. and Williams, C., 'Social Development of Youth' surveys, Russian Federation, 1990–1999.

Cockburn, A. et al. (2000), *5 days that shook the world: Seattle and beyond*, Verso, London.

Coles, B. (1995), *Youth and Social policy: Youth citizenship and youth careers*, UCL Press, London.

Coles, B. (1997), 'Vulnerable youth and processes of social exclusion: a theoretical framework, a review of recent research and suggestions for a future research agenda', in Bynner, J., Chisholm, L. and Furlong, A. (ed), *Youth, Citizenship and Social Change in a European Context*, Ashgate, Aldershot.

Connor, W. (1972), *Deviance in Soviet Society*, Columbia University Press, New York.
Coser, L. (1964), *The Functions of Social Conflict*, Free Press, New York.
Cote, J.E. and Allahar, A.L. (1996), *Generation and Hold. Coming of Age in the Late Twentieth Century*, New York University Press, New York.
Davis, N.J. (1999), *Youth crisis: Growing up in a high-risk society*, Praeger, Westport, Connecticut.
de Lauwe, C. (1969), *Pour une sociologie des aspirations*, Denoel, Paris.
Domanski, H. (2000), *On the verge of convergence: Social stratification in Eastern Europe*, CEU Press, Budapest/New York.
Douglas, M. (1986), *Risk acceptability according to the Social sciences*, Russell Sage Foundation, London.
Douglas, M. (1990), 'Risk as a forensic resource', *Daedalus*, Special Issue on *Risk*, Fall.
Douglas, M. (1992), *Risk and Blame: Essays in Cultural Theory*, Routledge, London.
Douglas, M. and Wildavsky, A. (1982), *Risk and Culture: An Essay on the selection of technological and environmental dangers*, University of California Press, Berkeley.
Dumont, L. (1966), *Homo Hierarcicus*, Seuil, Paris.
Dumont, L. (1991), *Essai sur l'individualisme*, Seuil, Paris.
Dunlop, J. (1998), *Russia confronts Chechnya: Roots of a seperatist conflict*, Cambridge University Press, Cambridge.
Durkheim, E. (reprint 1997), *Division of Labor in Society*, Simon and Schuster, New York.
Dutton, J.C. (1981), 'Causes of Soviet adult mortality increases', *Soviet Studies*, Vol. 33 (4), October, pp. 548–559.
Eisenstadt, S. (1956), *From Generation to Generation*, Free Press, New York.
Eisenstadt, S. (1999), *Revoliutsiia i preobravanie obshchestv: Sravnitel'noe izuchenie tsivilizatsii*, Aspekt Press, Moscow.
EU (1999), *Focus on European lifestyles*, No. 5599, 24 June.
European Youth Trends (1998), Council of Europe experts in youth research cited at www.ca.fr/youth/research/trends.htm.
Evans, K. and Furlong, A. (1997), 'Metaphors of youth transitions: Niches, pathways, trajectories or navigations', in Bynner, J., Chisholm, L. and Furlong, A. (eds), *Youth, Citizenship and Social Change in a European Context*, Ashgate, Aldershot.
Evans, M. et al. (2000), *Learning and work in the Risk Society: Lessons for the Labour markets of Europe from Eastern Germany*, Macmillan, London.
Feshbach, M. (1993), 'Continuing negative health trends in the former USSR', in Kaufman, R.F. and Hardt, J.P. (eds), *The former Soviet Union in Transition*, M.E. Sharpe, New York.
Field, M.G. (1995), 'The health crisis in the former Soviet Union: A report from the "Post-war" zone', *Social Science and Medicine*, Vol. 41 (11), pp. 1469–1478.
Flakierski, H. (1993), *Income inequalities in the former Soviet Union and its Republics*, M.E. Sharpe, London.
Franklin, J. (ed.) (1998), *The Politics of Risk Society*, Polity, Cambridge.

Fretwell, D. and Jackan, R. (1994), 'Labor markets: Unemployment', in Barr, N. (1994), *Labor markets and social policy in Central and Eastern Europe*, L.S.E./ World Bank, Oxford University Press, Washington D.C.

Frydman, R. et al. (eds) (1993), *The Privatisation Process in Russia, Ukraine and the Batic States*, CEU/Privatisation Report, Vol. 2, Oxford University Press/ CEU, Oxford.

Furlong, A. and Cartmel, F. (1997), *Young people and social change: Individualisation and Risk in Late Modernity*, Open University Press, Buckingham.

Furlong, A., Stadler, B. and Azzopardi, A. (2000), *European youth trends*, Council of Europe.

Furst, J. (2002), 'Prisoners of the Soviet self? – Political youth oppositionism in late Stalinism', *Europe-Asia Studies*, Vol. 54 (3), pp. 353–375.

Gall, C. and De. Waal, T. (2000), *Chechnya: Calamity in the Caucasus*, New York University Press, New York.

George, V. (1991), 'Social security in the USSR', *International Social Security Review*, Vol. 44 (4), pp. 47–65.

George, V. and Rimashevskaya, N. (1993), 'Poverty in Russia', *International social security review*, Vol. 46 (1).

Gerasimova, T.V., et al. (1995), 'Vypuskniki Moskovskikh vuzov na rynke truda', in Staroverov, V.I. et al. (eds) (1995), *Rossiia nakankune XXI veka, Vypusk II*, Moscow, pp. 495–509.

Giddens, A. (1991a), *The Consequences of Modernity*, Polity, Cambridge.

Giddens, A. (1991b), *Modernity and self-identity: Self and society in late modernity*, Polity Press, Cambridge.

Giddens, A. (1994), *Beyond Right and Left: The Future of Radical Politics*, Cambridge University Press, Cambridge.

Giddens, A. (1995), 'Elementy teorii strukturatsii' in *Sovremennia sotsil'naia teoriia: Bourdeau, Giddens, Habermas*, Novosibirsk State University Press.

Giddens, A. (1998), *The Third Way: The renewal of Social Democracy*, Polity, Cambridge.

Giddens, A. (1999), *Runaway World: How globalisation is reshaping our lives*, Profile books, London.

Gilinskii, Ia. (1995), 'Prestupnost' i bezopasnost' naseleniia: S-Peterburg na fone Rossiiskoi deistvitel'nosti', *Informatsionno-analiticheskii biulleten' MONITORING sotsial'no-ekonomicheskoi situatsii i sostoianiia rynka truda S.-Peterburga*, No.1, September.

Gilinsky, Y., Podkolzin, V. and Kochetkov, E. (1995), 'The drug problem in St. Petersburg', in Chaika, N. *HIV/AIDS, STDs, Drug use and prostitution in St. Petersburg and Russia*, St. Petersburg Pasteur Institute, St. Petersburg, pp. 13–25.

Gimpelson, E.G. and Lippoldt, D. (2001), *The Russian labour market: Between transition and turmoil*, Rowman and Littlefield, Lanham, Maryland.

Goldman, M.I. (1992), *What went wrong with perestroika*, W.W. Norton, New York.

Golenkova, Z.T. (1998), 'Teoriia modernizatsii', in Osipov, G.V. (ed.), *Rossiskaia sotsiologicheskaia entsiklopediia*, 'gruppa NORMA-IFRA', Moscow.

Golenkova, Z.T. (2000), *Transformatsiia sotsial'noi struktury i stratifikatsiia Rossisskogo Obshchestva*, Institut Sociologii, RAN, Moscow.
Golod, S.I. and Kletsin, A.A. (1994), *Sostoianie i perspektivy razvitiia sem'i: Teoretiko-tipologicheskii analiz. Emiricheskoe obosnovanie*, Institut sotsiologii, RAN, St. Petersburg.
Gorsuch, A.E. (1992), 'Soviet Youth and the Politics of Popular Culture during NEP', *Social History*, Vol. 17 (2), May, pp. 189–201.
Gorsuch, A.E. (1994), 'Flappers and Foxtrotters in Soviet Russia: soviet Youth in the Roaring Twenties', *The Carl Beck Papers in Russian and East European Studies*, No. 1102, March, pp. 1–33.
Gorsuch, A.E. (1997), 'NEP Be Damned!: Young militants in the 1920s and the culture of civil war', *The Russian Review*, Vol. 56 (4).
Gorsuch, A.E. (2000), *Youth in Revolutionary Russia: Enthusiasts, bohemians, delinquents*, Indiana University Press, Bloomington.
Gorsuch, A.E. (2001), 'Smashing Chairs at the Local Club: Discipline, Disorder and Soviet Youth', in Kuhr-Korolev, C., Plaggenborg, S. and Wellman, M. (eds), *Sowjetjugend 1917–1941. Generation zwischen Revolution und Resignation*, Essen, Klartext Verlag, 2001.
Gott, V. and Ursul, A. (1971), *Opredelennost' i neopredelennost' kak kategorii nauchnogo poznaniya*, Shtinita, Kishinev.
Green, D.R. (1998), 'Taking steps: Young people and social protection in the European Union', *European Youth Forum* report 1998, p. 24 cited at www.coe.fr/youth/research.htm.
Griffin, C. (1997), 'Youth research and identities: same as it ever was?', in Bynner, J., Chisholm, L. and Furlong, A. (eds), *Youth, Citizenship and Social Change in a European Context*, Ashgate, Aldershot.
Grishina, Y.A. (1999), *Rossisskaia molodezh': problemy grazhdanskoi identichnosti*, Moscow.
Grundarov, I.A. (2001), *Demograficheskaia katastrofa v Rossii: Prichiny, mekanizm, puti preodleniya*, URSS, Moscow.
Guidikova, L. (1998), 'European youth trends' 1998 cited at www.coe.fr/youth/research.htm.
Gurov, A. (1992), *Organizatsiia prestupnost' – Ne mif, a real'nost'*, 'Znanie', Moscow.
Gurov, A. (1995), *Krasnaia Mafiia*, 'Samotsvet', Miko 'Kommercheskii Vestnik', Moscow.
Handelman, S. (1994), *Comrade criminal: The theft of the Second Russian Revolution*, Michael Joseph, London.
Hajer, M. and Kesselring, S. (1999), 'Democracy in the Risk Society? Learning from the new politics of mobility in Munich', *Environmental Politics*, Vol. 8 (3), pp. 1–33.
Halfmann, J. (1999), 'Community and life chances: Risk movements in the US and Germany', *Environmental Politics*, Vol. 8 (3), pp. 177–197.
Heikkinen, M. (1998), 'Social networks in the exclusion process of young people in Finland', paper presented to the *European Network on Transitions in Youth* conference, Edinburgh 10–13 September.

Heinz, W.R. (2000), 'Youth transitions and employment in Germany', *International Social Science Journal*, special issue on *Youth in Transition*, No. 164, June, pp. 161-171.
Helve, H. (1996), 'Values, world views and gender differences among young people', in Helve, H. and Bynner, J. (eds), *Youth and Life Management: Research Perspectives*, Helsinki University Press, Helsinki.
Hughes, J. (2001), 'From Federalisation to Recentralisation', in White, S. et. al. (eds), *Developments in Russian Politics 5*, Palgrave, Basingstoke, pp. 128-146.
Iakovlev, A.M. (1985), *Teoriia kriminologii i sotsial'naia praktika*, "Nauka", Moscow.
Il'inskii, I.I. et al. (ed.) (1994), *Tsennostnyi mir sovremennoi molodezhi: na puti k mirovoi integratsii*, Moscow.
Ilynsky, I. (1995), 'The spiritual and cultural values of young people in a post-Totalitarian state', in Riordan, J., Williams, C. and Ilynsky, I. (eds), *Young people in post-communist Russia and Eastern Europe*, Dartmouth, Aldershot, pp. 95-115.
Illynsky, I. (1996), 'Law and Order', in Williams, C. Chuprov, V. and Staroverov, V. (eds), *Russian Society in transition*, Dartmouth, Aldershot, pp. 219-240.
Islamshina, T. et al (1997), *Molodezhnye subkul'tury*, Kazan Technological University Press, Kazan.
Iudina, Ye. (1995), 'Besplatno li bezplatnoe obrazovanie?', *Ogonëk*, No. 44, October, p. 26.
Ivanov, V.N. et al. (eds) (1994), *Etnopolicheskaia situatsiia v regionakh Rossiiskoi Federatsii (po rezul'tatam sotsiologicheskikh issledovanii v 1994g)*, Analiticheskii tsentr gosudarstvennoi dumy Federal'nogo sobraniia RF/Institut sotsial'no-politicheskikh issledovanii RAN, Moscow.
Ivanov, V.N. (1994b), *Moskvichi o gode ukhodiashchem*, Institut sotsial'no-politicheskikh issledovanii RAN, Moscow.
Ivanov, V.N. (ed.) (1995a), *Sotsial'no-politicheskaia situatsiia i mezhnatsional'nye otnosheniia v Samare v otsenkakh i predstavleniiakh massovogo sozdaniia*, Institut sotsial'no-politicheskikh issledovanii RAN, Moscow.
Ivanov, V.N. (1995b), *Sostoianie mezhnatsional'nykh otnoshenii v g. Ufa*, Institut sotsial'no-politicheskikh issledovanii RAN, Moscow.
Ivanov, V.N. (1995c), *Sostoianie mezhnatsional'nykh otnoshenii v Orenberge v otsenkakh i predstavleniiakh massovogo sozdaniia*, Institut sotsial'no-politicheskikh issledovanii RAN, Moscow.
Ivanov, V.N. (1995d), *Problemy stabil'nosti i vnutrennei bezopasnosti Rossii (Sotsiologicheskii analiz)*, Institut sotsial'no-politicheskikh issledovanii RAN, Moscow.
Jones, A. (ed.) (1994), *Education and Society in the New Russia*, M.E. Sharpe, New York.
Jones, A., Connor, W.D. and Powell, D.E. (eds) (1991), *Soviet social problems*, Westview Press, Boulder, Colorado.
Juliver, P.H. (1976), *Revolutionary law and order*, Free Press, New York.
Juliver, P.H. (1991), 'No end of a problem: *Perestroika* for the family', in: Jones, A., Connor, W.D. and Powell, D.E. (eds) (1991), *Soviet social problems*, Westview Press, Boulder, Colorado, pp. 194-212.

Kabo, V. (1990), 'Subkul'tura lagaeria i arkhetipy sozdaniia', *Sovetskaia Etnografiia*, No. 1.
Kalmykov, V.Y. (1979), *Khuliganstvo i mery bor'by s nim*, Minsk, Belarus.
Kampfner, J. (1994), *Inside Yeltsin's Russia: Corruption, Conflict, Capitalism*, Cassell, London.
Kellner, D. (n.d.), 'Globalization and the postmodern turn' cited at www.gseis.ucla.edu.
Kharmaev, Yu. V (1998), 'Kriminologicheskie problemy sotsializatsii vospitannikov detskih domov i shkol-internatov', *Kand. dissertatsiya*, Moscow.
Khorev, V. (1994), *Demograficheskaya tragedniia Rossii*, "Paleia", Moscow.
Kirillov, I. (1991), 'Potreblennie alkogolia i sotsial'nye posledstviia p'ianstva i alkogolizma', *Vestnik Statistiki*, No. 6.
Kisleyov, E. and Cassells, M. (2001), 'Russia in the information age', in Bonnell, V.E. and Bresauler, G. (ed.), *Russia in the New Century: Stability or Disorder?*, Westview, Boulder Colorado.
Kitaev, I.V. (1994), 'The labor market and education in the post-Soviet era', in Jones, A. (ed.) (1994), *Education and Society in the New Russia*, M.E. Sharpe, New York, pp. 311–332.
Klochkova, O.V. (1999), 'Makrourovnevaia determiniatsiia prestupnosti vevershennoletnikh', in *Organizatsionno-pravovie problemy preduprezhdeniya prestupnosti nesoverschennoletnikh*, Moscow, Akademiia upravleniia MVD Rossii.
Knezys, S. and Sedlickas, R. (1999), *The war in Chechnya*, Texas and A & M University Press.
Koklyagina, Nurse L. (n.d.), 'Patterns of Transitions into Work in Russia and Great Britain', *YOUNG* Vol. 9 (1), pp. 41–60.
Kolbanov, V.F. (1995), 'Vystuplenie pered predstaviteliami i mestnykh organov po trudu, obuchaiushchimisiia v IPK', unpublished Russian Federation, Ministry of Labour report, October.
Konstantinovskii, D.L. (2000), *Molodezh' 90-kh: samoopredelenie v novoi real'nosti*, Moscow.
Kostiusheva, V.V. (1999), *Molodezhnye dvizheniia i subkul'tury Sankt-Petersburga*, Norma, St. Petersburg.
Kovacheva, S. (2000), 'Sinking or Swimming in the waves of transformation? Young People and Social Protection in Central and Eastern Europe', *European Youth Forum*, Brussels.
Kovaleva, A.I. (1999), *Sotsializatsiia lichnosti: Norma i otklonenie* Sotsium, Moscow.
Kovaleva, A.I. and Lukov, L.V. (1999), *Sotsiologiia molodezhi: teoreticheskie voprosy*, Sotsium, Moscow.
Kryshtanovskaya, O. (1994), 'Rich and poor in post-communist Russia', *Journal of Communist Studies and Transition Politics*, Vol. 10 (1), March, pp. 3–24.
Lagree, J.C. (1996), 'Youth in Europe', in Helve, H. and Bynner, J. (ed.), *Youth and Life Management: Research Perspectives*, Helsinki University Press, Helsinki, pp. 165–169.
Lara-a, E. et al. (eds) (1994), *New Social Movements: From ideology to identity*, Temple University Press, Philadelphia.

Lash, S. et al. (1996), *Risk, government and modernity: Towards a new ecology*, Sage, London.
Lash, S. (1999), 'Informationcritique', unpublished paper presented to the UK-Nordic meeting, 9 April cited by *Virtual Society?* at www. Brunel.ac.uk/virtsoc/nordic/cbslash.htm.
Lash, S. and Wynne, B. (1992), 'Introduction', to Beck, U. (1992), *Risk Society: Towards a New Modernity*, Sage, London.
Lieven, A. (1998), *Chechnya: Tombstone of Russian Power*, Yale University Press, Yale.
Lisovskii, V.T. (ed.) *(1995), Sotsiologiia Molodezhi*, 3 volumes, *NII Kompleksnykh sotsial'nykh issledovanii/ St. Petersburgskogo gosugarstvennogo universiteta/ Institut molodezhi/ Komitet po delam Molodezhi RF*, Moscow.
Luhmann, N. (1993), *Risk: A sociological theory*, Aldine de Gruyer, New York.
Lukov, A., Rodionov, V.A. and Ruchkin, B.A. (ed.) (2000), *Molodezh' Rossisskoi Federatsii: polozheniye, vybor puti. Osnovye vyvod i predlozheniya Gosudarstvennogo doklada Pravitel'stvu Rossiskoi Federatsii/Gosudarstvenii komitet RF po molodezhnoi politike*, Moscow.
Lupton, D. (1999), *Risk*, Routledge, London.
MacDonald, R. (ed.) (1997), *Youth, the 'Underclass' and Social Exclusion*, Routledge, London.
Machachek, L. (1998), *Youth in the process of transition and modernisation in Slovakia*, Bratislava, Institute for Sociology, Slovak Academy of Sciences.
Machacek, L. and Roberts, K. (1997), *Youth Unemployment and Self-Employment in East-Central Europe*, Institute for Sociology, Slovak Academy of Sciences, Bratislava.
Marnie, S. (1993), 'Who and where are the Russian unemployed', RFE/RL Research Report, 20 August.
Marshall, T.H. (1973), *Class, citizenship and development*, Greenwood Press, Westport.
Marshall, T.H. and Bottomore, T. (1992), *Citizenship and social class*, Pluto Press, London.
Materialy sipoziuma 23 Marta 1994 (1994), *Institut sotsial'no-politicheskikh issledovanii Rossiiskoi Akademii Nauk*, Moscow.
Matsui, Y. (2001), 'Youth attitudes towards Stalin's revolution and the Stalinist regime, 1929–41', *Acta Slavica Iaponica*, Vol. 18, pp. 64–78.
Matthews, M. (1986), *Poverty in the Soviet Union: the lifestyles of the underprivileged in recent years*, Cambridge University Press, Cambridge.
Mau, V. (1994), *Ekonomiko-politicheskie protsessy 1994 goda i Chechenskii krizis*, unpublished Institute for the Economy in Transition report, Moscow, November.
McLuhan, M. and Powers, B.P. (1989), *The Global Village*, Oxford University Press, Oxford.
Melucci, A. (1992), 'Youth Silence and Voice. Selfhood and Commitment in the Everyday Experiences of Adolescents', in Fornas, J. and Bolin, G. (eds) *Moves in Modernity*, Almavist and Wiskell, Stockholm.
Micklethwait, J. and Woolridge, A. (2000), *A Future Project: The Challenge and Hidden Promise of Globalisation*, Heinemann, London.
Miles, S. (2001), *Social theory in the real world*, Sage, London.

Miller, J. (1993), *Mikhail Gorbachev and the End of Soviet power*, Macmillan, London.
Miller, R.F. (ed.) (1992), *The developments of civil society in communist systems*, Allen and Unwin, Sydney.
Miller, R.F. (1992), 'Civil society in communist systems: An introduction', in Miller, R.F. (ed.) (1992), *The developments of civil society in communist systems*, Allen and Unwin, Sydney, pp. 1–10.
Mitrokhina, Ye. Iu. (1999a), 'Informatsionnaia bezopasnost' lichnosti kak sotsiologicheskaai problema', *Kandidat Sotsiologicheskikh Nauk*, ISPR, RAN, Moscow.
Mitrokhina, Ye. Iu. (1999b), 'Informatsionnaia bezopasnost' kak sotsiologicheskaai problema (Nekotorye metodologicheskie podkhody)', *Bezopasnost' (informatsionnyi sbornik)*, No. 7–9 (39).
Modernizatsiia: Zarubezhnyi oypt i Rossiia (1994), Rossiiskii nezavisimyi institut sotsial'nykh i natsional'nykh problem, Agentstvo infomart, Moscow.
Molodezh' Rossii: Vospitanie zhiznesposobnykh pokolenii (Doklad komiteta Rossiiskoi Federatsii po delam molodezhi) (1995), State Committee on Youth Affairs, Moscow.
Molodezh' RSFSR. Statisticheskii sbornik (1990), Goskomstat, Moscow.
Molodezh' v usloviiakh sotsial'no-ekonomicheskikh reform: Materialy mezhdunarodnoi nauchno-prakticheskoi konferentsii (1995), Vypusk I and II, Gosudarstvennyi komitet RF po vysshemu obrazovaniiu/Komitet RF po delam molodezhi, St. Petersburg.
Morgan, E. (1997), *European youth unemployment: A Comparative Study*, Carmarthen, Wales.
MVD Russia (1999), *Prestupnost' nesovershlennnikh v Rossii, 1994–1998gg: Statisticheskii sbornik*, Moscow.
Nagel, U. and Wallace, C. (1997), 'Participation and Identification in Risk Societies: European Perspectives', in Bynner, J., Chisholm, L. and Furlong, A. (eds), *Youth, Citizenship and Social Change in a European Context*, Ashgate, Aldershot.
Nazarov, M.M. (1995), *Politicheskie tsennosti i politicheskii protest*, Institut sotsial'no-politicheskikh issledovanii RAN, Moscow.
Nikitin, S. and Feofanov, K. (1992), 'Sotsiologicheskaia teoriia riska: v poiskakh predmeta', *Sotsiologicheskie Issledovaniia*, No. 10.
Nikolaev, Yu. K. (2002), *Chechnya Revisited*, Nova Science Publishers.
Nikolov, K. (1999), *Russia: The 1998 Crisis and beyond*, Social Market Foundation, Centre for Collectivist Studies, London.
Novik, B. (1988), 'Informatsionne aspekty riska', in *Sistemnaia kontsepsiia informatsionnykh protsessov: Sbornik trudov*, VNIISI, Moscow.
O'Donnell, G. et al. (1986), *Transitions from authoritarian rule: Comparative perspectives*, John Hopkins University Press.
OECD Economic Surveys (1995), *The Russian Federation*, OECD, Paris, September.
OECD, *Public expenditure on Income programmes* (1976), OECD, Paris.
OECD (2001), *The Social crisis in the Russian Federation*, OECD, Paris.
Oigezikhm, V. (1972), *Problema riska v grazhdanskoi prave*, Dushambe.

O'Neil, J. (1991), 'Religion and postmodernism: The Durkheimian Bond in Bell and Jameson', in Featherstone M. (ed.), *Postmodernism*, Routledge, London, pp. 493-508.
Orlova, I. (1994a), 'Migratory processes in ex-USSR under conditions of social catalysm', paper presented to the XIII World Congress of Sociology, Bielefeld, Germany 18-23 July.
Orlova, I. (1994b), *Demograficheskaia i migratsionnaia situatsiia v Rossii (Sravnitel'nyi analiz)*, Institut sotsial'no-politicheskikh issledovanii RAN, Moscow.
Osipov, G.V. (1994), 'Reformirovanie Rossii: Itogi i perspectivy', in *Rossiia nakankune XXI veka*, Moscow.
Osipov, G.V. et al. (eds) (1994a), *Reformirovanie Rossii: Mify i real'nost' (1989-1994)*, 'Academia', Moscow.
Osipov, G.V. et al. (eds) (1994b), *Sovremennaia sotsial'no-demograficheskaia situatsiia i zaniatost' naseleniia Rossii*, Institut sotsial'no-politicheskikh issledovanii RAN, Moscow.
Osipov, G.V. et al. (eds) (1995), *Sotsial'naia i sotsial'no-politicheskaia situatsiia v Rossii: Analiz i prognoz (Pervoe polugodie 1995 goda)*, 'Academia', Moscow.
Osipov, G.V. et al. (eds) (1999), *Rossiia v poiskakh strategi: Obshchestvo i vlast'. Sotsial'naia i sotsial'no-politicheskaia situatsiia v Rossii v 1999 godu*, PiTS, ISPR, RAN, Moscow.
Osipov, G.V. and Lokosov, V.V. (2001), *Sotsial'naia tsena neoliber'nogo reformirovaniia*, Moscow.
Oxenstierna, S. (1992), 'Trends in Employment and Unemployment', in Åslund, A. (ed.), *The post-Soviet Economy: Soviet and Western Perspectives*, Pinter Publishers, London.
Pahl, R. (1988), 'Friendship: the social glue of contemporary society', in Franklin J. (ed.), *The Politics of Risk Society*, Polity Press, Cambridge.
Parsons, T. (1965), *The Social System*, Simon and Schuster, New York.
Perspektivy razvitiia molodoi sem'i (dannye edinovremennogo obsledovaniia) (1993), Goskomstat, Rossiisskoi Federatsii, Moscow.
Pilkington, H. (1994), *Russian youth and its culture: A Nation's constructors and constructed*, Routledge, London.
Pilkington, H. et al (eds) (2002), *Looking West? Cultural globalisation and Russian youth cultures*, Penn State University Press, Pennsylvannia.
Pleshchakov, V.A. (1999), 'Uchastie nesoverschennoletnikh v organizovannyh formakh prestupnoi deyatel'nosti', in *Organizatsionno-pravovie problemy preduprezhdeniya prestupnosti nesoverschennoletnikh*, Moscow, Akademiia upravleniia MVD Rossii.
Politovskaya, A. (2001), *A Dirty War: A Russian reporter in Chechnya*, Harvell Press.
Polozhenie detei v Rossii 1992 god (sotsial'nyi portret) (1993), Moscow.
Porket, J.L. (1989), *Work, Employment and Unemployment in the Soviet Union*, St. Antony's/Macmillan, London.
Prestupnost' v Rossii v devianostykh godakh i nekotorye aspekty zakonnosti bor'by s nei (1995), Kriminologicheskaia Assotsiatsiia, Moscow.

Puuronen, V. (1998), 'Marginalisation and youth sub-cultures', in Helve H. (ed.), *Unification and marginalisation of young people*, Youth Research 2000 Programme, Finnish Youth Research Society, Helsinki.
Rattansi, A. and Phoenix, A. (1997), 'Rethinking youth identities: Modernist and post-modernist theories', in Bynner, J., Chisholm, L. and Furlong, A. (eds), *Youth, Citizenship and Social Change in a European Context*, Ashgate, Aldershot.
Rawlinson, P. (1995), 'Organised crime in Russia', paper presented to the BASEES Annual conference, Fitzwilliam College, Cambridge, March.
Rigby, T.H. (1992), 'The USSR: End of a long, dark night?', in Miller, R.F. (ed.) (1992), *The developments of civil society in communist systems*, Allen and Unwin, Sydney, pp. 19–23.
Riordan, J. (ed.) (1989), *Soviet youth culture*, Macmillan, London.
Riordan, J. (ed.) (1992), *Soviet social reality in the mirror of glasnost*, Macmillan/ St. Martin's Press: London/New York.
Riordan, J. (1995), 'The Rise and Fall of a Youth Elite in Russia', in Riordan, J., Williams, C. and Ilynsky, I. (eds), *Young people in post-communist Russia and Eastern Europe*, Dartmouth, Aldershot 1995, pp. 81–95.
Riordan, J., Williams, C. and Ilynsky, I. (1995), *Young people in post-communist Russia and Eastern Europe*, Dartmouth, Aldershot.
Roberts, K. (1995), *Youth and employment in Modern Britain*, Oxford University Press.
Roberts, K. (1997), 'Structure and Agency: The new research agenda' in Bynner, J., Chisholm, L. and Furlong, A. (eds), *Youth, Citizenship and Social Change in a European Context*, Ashgate, Aldershot.
Roberts, K. et al. (2000), *Surviving post-communism: Young people in the former Soviet Union*, Edward Elgar, Cheltenham.
Roberts, K. and Jung, B. (1995), *Poland's first communist generation*, Ashgate, Aldershot.
Romashov, O.V. (1993), 'Sotsial'naia zashchita trudiashchikhsia: problemy puti resheniia', *Sotsiologicheskie issledovaniia*, No. 1.
Rossiia v tsifrakh (1990), Goskomstat, Moscow.
Rossiia v tsifrakh (1991), Goskomstat, Moscow.
Rossiia v tsifrakh (1992), Goskomstat, Moscow.
Rossiia v tsifrakh (1993), Goskomstat, Moscow.
Rossiia v tsifrakh (1994), Goskomstat, Moscow.
Rossiia v tsifrakh (1995), Goskomstat, Moscow.
Rossiia v tsifrakh (1996), Goskomstat, Moscow.
Rossiia v tsifrakh (1997), Goskomstat, Moscow.
Rossiia v tsifrakh (1998), Goskomstat, Moscow.
Rossiia v tsifrakh (1999), Goskomstat, Moscow.
Rossiia v tsifrakh (2000), Goskomstat, Moscow.
Rossisskii statisticheskii ezhgodnik: Statisticheskii Sbornik (1990), Goskomstat Moscow.
Rossisskii statisticheskii ezhgodnik: Statisticheskii Sbornik (1991), Goskomstat Moscow.

Rossisskii statisticheskii ezhgodnik: Statisticheskii Sbornik (1992), Goskomstat Moscow.
Rossisskii statisticheskii ezhgodnik: Statisticheskii Sbornik (1993), Goskomstat Moscow.
Rossisskii statisticheskii ezhgodnik: Statisticheskii Sbornik (1994), Goskomstat Moscow.
Rossisskii statisticheskii ezhgodnik: Statisticheskii Sbornik (1995), Goskomstat Moscow.
Rossisskii statisticheskii ezhgodnik: Statisticheskii Sbornik (1996), Goskomstat Moscow.
Rossisskii statisticheskii ezhgodnik: Statisticheskii Sbornik (1997), Goskomstat Moscow.
Rossisskii statisticheskii ezhgodnik: Statisticheskii Sbornik (1998), Goskomstat Moscow.
Rossisskii statisticheskii ezhgodnik: Statisticheskii Sbornik (1999), Goskomstat Moscow.
Rossisskii statisticheskii ezhgodnik: Statisticheskii Sbornik (2000) Goskomstat Moscow.
Rudkin, C. (1995), 'Is there really a link between Russian business and organised crime? Problems of methodology', unpublished paper presented to the BASEES Annual conference, Fitzwilliam College, Cambridge, March.
Rukavishnikov, V. et al. (1994), 'The dynamics of civil and political society in Russia', paper presented to the XIII World Congress of Sociology, Bielefeld, Germany 18–23 July.
Rutkevich, M. (1992), 'Sotsial'naia polarizatsiia', *Sotsiologicheskie issledovaniia*, No. 9.
Rutkevich, M.N. and Pomanov, V.P. (1995), *Posle shkoly. Opyt sotsiologicheskogo issledovaniia*, Moscow.
Ryan, M. (1990), *Contemporary Soviet society: A handbook*, Edward Elgar, Aldershot.
Ryvkina, R. (1988), 'Reactionary traditions and revolutionary needs', *Vek XX* and *Mir 3*.
Sakwa, R. (1990), *Gorbachev and His reforms, 1985–1990*, Phillip Allan, London.
Sakwa, R. (1993), *Russian Politics and Society*, Routledge, London.
Saleniece, I. and Kuznetsovs, S. (1999), 'Nationality policy, education and the Russian question in Latvia since 1918', in Williams, C. and Sfikas, T.D. (eds), *Ethnicity and Nationalism in Russia, the CIS and the Baltic States*, Ashgate, Aldershot.
Schlesinger, A. (1992), *Etnicheskaia obosoblennost'*, Moscow.
Schwartz, S.H. (1992), 'Universals in the content and structure of values: Theoretical advances and empirical tests in 20 countries', in Zanna, M.P. (ed.), *Experimental social psychology*, Academic Press, New York, pp. 1–65.
Schwartz, S.H. (1999), 'A theory of cultural values and some implications for work', *Applied Psychology*, Vol. 48, pp. 23–47.
Schwartz, S.H. and Bilsky, W. (1990), 'Toward a theory of the universal content and structure of values: extensions and cross-cultural replications', *Journal of Personality and social psychology*, Vol. 58, pp. 878–891.

Shchendrik, A.I. (1990), *Dukhovnaya kultura sovetskoi molodezhi: sushchnost, sostoianie, puti razvitiya*, Molodaya Gvardiya, Moscow.
Shegortsov, A.A. (1997), *Molodezh' i obshchestvo: oypt sotsiologicheskii analiza*, Moscow.
Shelley, L.I. (1980), 'Crime and Delinquency in the Soviet Union', in Pankhurst, J.G. and Sacks, M.P. (eds), *Contemporary Soviet Society: Sociological perspectives*, Praeger, New York.
Shelley, L. (1991), 'Crime in the Soviet Union', in Jones, A., Connor, W.D. and Powell, D.E. (eds), *Soviet social problems*, Westview Press, Boulder Colorado.
Shephard, B. and Hayduk, R. (eds) (2003), *Urban protest and community building in an era of globalisation*, Verso. London.
Shlapentokh, V. (1987), *The politics of sociology in the Soviet Union*, Westview Press, Boulder, Colorado.
Smakotina, N. (1999), *Osnovyi sotsiologii nestabil'nosti i riska*, Moscow.
Smeeding, T.M. et al. (1990), *Poverty, inequality and income distribution in Comparative perspective*, Harvester Wheatsheaf, New York.
Smith, S. (2001), *Allah's Mountains: The Battle for Chechnya*, St. Martin's Press, New York.
Soares, C. (2000), 'Aspects of youth, transitions and the end of certainties', *International Social Science Journal*, special issue on *Youth in Transition*, No. 164, June, pp. 209–219.
Sorokin, S.A. (1999), *Rossiiskaia sem'ya I tri zakonoproekta po ee ohkrane*, Ekonomika, Moscow.
Sosnova, I.A. (1996), 'Informatsionnaia ustroichivost' i informatsionnaia bezopasnost' sotsil'nykh sistem', in *Analiz sistem na poroge XXI veka: teoriia i praktika, t. 2*, Intellekt, Moscow.
'Sotsial'no-demograficheskie tendentsii' (1998), in *Rossiya: Vyzvodyi vremeni i puti reformirovaniya*, Moscow.
Spannring, R., Wallace, C. and Haerpfer, C. (n.d.), 'Civic participation among young people in Europe', *New YorkRIS 7 Proceedings* cited at www.alli.fi/nyri/nyris7/papers/wallace.htm.
Spirkin, A. (1988), *Osnovy filosofii*, Politizdat, Moscow.
Standing, G. (1992), 'Recruitment, training and human resource management in Russian industry', paper presented to a conference on *Employment Restructuring in Russia*, Moscow and St. Petersburg, 21–29 October.
Staroverov, V.I. et al. (eds) (1995), *Rossiia nakankune XXI veka, Vypusk II, Institut sotsial'no-politicheskikh issledovanii Rossiiskoi Akademii Nauk*, 'Nauka', Moscow.
Sting, S. and Wulf, C. (eds) (1994), *Education in a period of social upheaval*, Waxman Munster/New York.
Sutherland, J. (1999), , *Schooling in the New Russia: Innovation and Change, 1984–1995*, London, SSEES/Macmillan 1999.
Tanner, J. (1991), 'Reluctant rebels: A case study of Edmonton high-school dropouts', in Ashton, D. and Lowe, G. (eds), *Making their way: Education, training and the Labour market in Canada and Britain*, Open University Press, Milton Keynes.
Tekyshchii arkhiv NiTS pri Institut Molodezhi (1994), Moscow, April.

Touraine, A. (1998), *Vozrashchenie cheloveka deistviushchego: Ocherk Sotsiologii*, Nauchnyi Mir, Moscow.
Turner, B.S. (1994), *Orientalism, Postmodernism and Gloablism*, Routledge, London.
United Nations Report on the Global Situation of Youth (1999) cited at www.unorg/events/youth98/dackinfo/report/globl-2.htm, 1999.
Vail', P. and Genis, A. (1998), *60–e mir sovetskogo cheloveka*, Novoe literaturnoe obozrenie, second edition, Moscow.
Vaksberg, A. (1991), *The Soviet Mafia*, Weidenfeld and Nicolson, London.
Vishnevskii, Yu. V. et al. (2000), *Praktikum po sotsiologii molodezhi*, Sotsium, Moscow.
Voronina, T.P. (1995), *Informatsionnia obshchestvo: sushchost', cherty, problemy*, IO TsAGI, Moscow.
Vorotnikov, V.P. et al. (eds) (1995), *Sotsial'naia politika i predprinimatel'stvo*, Vypusk I, Institut sotsial'no-politicheskikh issledovanii RAN, Analiticheskii tsentr gruppy MOST, Moscow.
Vososel'skii, V. (1995), *Sostoianie rynka truda Rossii v 1992–1994 goda i pervoi polovine 1995 goda*, Russian Ministry of Labour Report, dated 15 June.
Vybory Prezidenta Rossisskoi Federatsii (1996), *Elektoral'naia staistika*, Ves'mir, Moscow.
Walicki, A. (1975), *The Slavophile controversy: History of a Conservative Utopia in Nineteenth Century Russian Thought*, Oxford University Press, Oxford.
Walicki, A. (1980), *A History of Russian thought: From the enlightenment to Marxism*, Clarendon Press, Oxford.
Wallace, C. and Kovatcheva, S. (1995), *Youth and Society*, Macmillan, London.
Wallace, C. and Kovatcheva, S. (1998), *Youth in Society: The construction and deconstruction of youth in East and West Europe*, Macmillan, London.
Wallerstein, I. (n.d.), 'Uncertainty and creativity' cited at http://fbc.binghampton.edu/iwuncer.htm
Ward Kingkade, W. (1993), 'Demographic prospects in the republics of the former Soviet Union', in Kaufman, R.F. and Hardt, J.P. (eds) (1993), *The former Soviet Union in Transition*, M.E. Sharpe, New York.
Webber, S.L. (2000), *School, reform and society in the New Russia*, London, CREES/Macmillan.
Webster, F. (1995), *Theories of the information society*, Routledge, London.
Weigle, M.A. (1994), 'Political participation and party formation in Russia, 1985–1992: Institutionalising democracy', *Russian Review*, April.
Wildavsky, A. and Dake, K. (1990), 'Theories of risk perception: Who fears what and why?', *Daedalus*, Special Issue on *Risk*, Fall.
Williams, C. (1995a), *AIDS in post-communist Russia and its successor states*, Avebury, Aldershot.
Williams, C. (1995b), '"Respectable fears" versus "Moral panics": Youth as a social problem in Russia and Britain', in Riordan, J., Williams, C. and Ilynsky, I. (eds) (1995), *Young people in post-communist Russia and Eastern Europe*, Dartmouth, Aldershot, pp. 29–50.

Williams, C. (1996) 'Health care in transition', in Williams, C., Chuprov, V. and Staroverov, V. (eds), *Russian Society in transition*, Dartmouth, Aldershot, pp. 183–202.

Williams, C. (2000) 'The New Russia: From Cold War strength to post-communist weakness and beyond', in Anderson, P.J., Wiessala, G. and Williams, C. (eds), *New Europe in Transition*, Continuum, London, pp. 248–266

Williams, C. (2001), 'Kosovo: A fuse for the lighting', in A. Weymouth and S. Henig (eds), *The Kosovo Crisis: America's last war in Europe?*, Pearson Education, London, 2001, pp. 15–38, 288–290.

Williams, C., Chuprov, V. and Zubok, J. (1997), 'The voting behaviour of Russian youth', *Journal of Communist Studies and Transition Politics*, Vol. 13 (1), March, pp. 145–59.

Williams, C. with Golenkova, Z.T. (2001), 'Russia: Walking the tightrope', in A. Weymouth and S. Henig (eds), *The Kosovo Crisis: America's last war in Europe?*, Pearson Education, London, 2001, pp. 204–225, 298–300.

Williams, C. and Sfikas, T.D. (eds) (1999), *Ethnicity and Nationalism in Russia, the CIS and the Baltic States*, Ashgate, Aldershot.

Williamson, H. (1997), 'Status Zer0 Youth and the "Underclass": Some Considerations', in MacDonald, R. (eds), *Youth, the Underclass and Social Exclusion*, Routledge, London and New York.

Wyn, J. and Dwyer, P. (2000), 'New patterns of youth transition in education', *International Social Science Journal*, special issue on *Youth in Transition*, No. 164, June, pp. 147–161.

Wyn, J. and White, R. (1997), *Rethinking Youth*, Sage Publications London.

Yanitskii, O.N. (1998), 'Sotsiologiia i riskologiia', in *Rossiya: Riska i opasnosti "perekhodnogo obshchestva"*, Instituta Sotsiologii, Moscow.

Yanitskii, O.N. (2000), 'Rossiya vseobshchego riska' in *Sotsiologiia i Obshchestvo. Tezisy dokladov Pervogo Vserossiiskogo Sotsiologicheskogo Kongressa*, St. Petersburg.

Yanovskii, R.G. (1995), 'Dukhovno-nravstvennai bezopastnost' Rossii', *Sotsiologicheskii Issledovaniia*, No. 12.

Yanovskii, R.G. (1999), *Global'nye izmeniia i sotsial'naia bezopasnost*, Akademiia, Moscow.

Yanowitch, M. (1978), *Social and economic inequality in the USSR*, Martin Robertson, London.

Yardley, S. (1991), *The Green case: A Sociology of environmental issues*, Routledge, London.

Yardley, S. (1996), *Sociology, environmentalism, globalization: Reinventing the Globe*, Sage, London.

Yemelianova, G. (1999), 'Ethnic nationalism, Islam and Russian politics in the North Caucasus (with special reference to the Republic of Dagestan', in Williams, C. and Sfikas, T.D. (eds) (1999), *Ethnicity and Nationalism in Russia, the CIS and the Baltic States*, Ashgate, Aldershot, pp. 120–147.

Young, C.M. (1987), *Young People Leaving Home in Australia; The Trend Towards Independence*, Australian Family Formation Project Monograph, No.9, Canberra.

Young Europeans (1997), Eurobarometer DG XXII report, 29 July.

Young, M. and Shuller, T. (1991), *Life after work: The arrival of the age-less society*, HarperCollins, London.
Zhuravleva, I.V. (2002), *Zdorov'e podrostkov: Sotiologicheskii analiz*, Nauka, Moscow.
Zdravookhranenie v Rossiiskoi Federatsii: Statisticheskii sbornik (1995), Goskomstat, Moscow.
Zouev, A. (ed.) (1999), *Generation in jeopardy: Children in Central and Eastern Europe and the Former Soviet Union*, UNICEF/M E Sharpe, Armonk, New York.
Zubok, J. (1999), 'Social Integration and the Exclusion of the Youth in an Unstable Society', in Puuronen V. (ed.) *Youth in Everyday Life Contexts*, Joensuu, University of Joensuu, pp. 297–304.
Zubok, J. (2000), 'Integration versus exclusion: youth and the labour market', *International Social Science Journal*, June, Vol. LII, No. 2, June, pp. 171–183.
Zubok, J. (2001), 'Social Integration of Russian Youth – Trends in the Risk Society', in Puuronen V. (ed.), *Youth on the Threshold of 3rd Millennium*, University of Joensuu, Joensuu, pp. 103–117.
Zubok, Y. and Williams, C. (1999), 'Youth and crime in Russia', unpublished paper delivered at the German Youth Studies Institute, Leipzig, 25 August.
Zubok, Yu. A. (1998a), *Sotsial'naia integratsiia molodezhi v usloviyakh nestabil'nogo obshchestva*, Moscow Sotsium.
Zubok, Yu. A. (1998b), 'Iskliuchenie v issledovanii problem molodezhi', *Sotsiologicheskie Issledovaniiia*, No. 8.
Zubok, Yu. A. (1999), 'Exclusion in the study of the problems of young people', *Russian Education and Society*, September, pp. 39–53.
Zubok, Yu. A. (2000a), 'Molodezh' mezhdu integratsieu i isluicheniem: sotsial'no-ekonomicheskii aspekt', *Sotsial'no-gumanitarnoe Znanie*, No. 2.
Zubok, Yu. A. (2000b), 'Subkul'turnoe povedenie molodezhi', in Lisovskii V.T. (ed.), *Molodezh': Tendentsii sotsial'nykh izmenenii*, Izd. St. Petersburgskogo universiteta, pp. 166–177.

Index

Abrams, P. 118
Abramson, P. 172
abuse 145
acceptable risk 18
accidents 11, 12, 53
achievement, attitudes to 177–8
Adams, John 19
adolescents *see* young people/youth
age discrimination 94, 153–4
agriculture 153, 162
Akhmadulina, Bella 103
alcoholism 75, 104, 201
Al'gin, Anatoly 9, 33, 34
alienation of young people 73, 96, 103, 159
Allatt, Patricia 75, 117, 181
America *see* United States of America
Americanisation 45, 46
anomie 73, 172
apathy 79, 105, 172
apprenticeship 74, 136, 137
attitudes and opinion 12, 46, 59
    attitudes to 'West' 123–4
    on youth/young people 75
    towards politicians 60
Australia, education in 136
Austria 139
    unemployment in 154
autonomy 178–9

Babosov, Y. 21
banking system 55
Beck, Ulrich 7, 12, 13, 14, 21, 22–7, 28, 29, 31, 32, 34–6, 43, 76, 111, 122, 134, 203
Bekarev, A.A. 20, 21
Belgium 154
Bhopal accident 11
birth rate 127, 128–9, 132–3
Boxer, Vladimir 46
budget deficit 48
Bynner, John 137

Canada, education in 136
capitalism 24
    ascendancy of 13–14, 35
Cassell, Manuel 14
Chechnya 56, 60, 190, 203
Chernobyl' accident 11, 24
Chernomyrdin, Viktor 56
children
    crime and 192
    ill-health of 130, 132
Chisholm, Lynne 97, 145
Chuprov, Professor 80
church 88, 101, 167, 173, 190, 202
cinema 88
class 28, 29, 76, 95, 97, 152, 202
    middle class 47, 51, 85–6, 134
    New Russians 51, 123, 134, 159–60
classical and reflexive modernisation 25, 34
coal industry 204–5
Coles, Bob 151, 181
collectivism 45
command-administrative system 44
Communist Party of the Russian Federation (CPRF) 56, 57, 168
Communist Party of the Soviet Union (CPSU) 55
communitarianism 32
competition 29
conflict 93–106
    arising from inequality of social status 94–5
    resolution of 109–25
    sub-cultural basis of youth conflicts 101–104, 120
    with socialisation agencies 95–101
conformity 109, 115
construction 163
consumer goods 47
consumerism 11
consumption 49
corruption 51, 55
crime 60–61

young people and 1, 75, 83, 100, 120,
    181, 183, 192–4
crises
    economic 48–53, 61–2, 80, 121
    in values 100, 101–104
    of trust 117
    of youth identity 180–95
culture
    cultural values 101–104
    life start situation and 148–9
    moral and social reference points 172–80
    socio-cultural basis of risk 16–20
    sub-cultural basis of youth conflicts 94,
        101–104, 120
Czech Republic, education in 136

Dake, Karl 18, 19
death *see* mortality trends
debt problems 48
democracy, risk and 31–2, 33, 123–4
demographic trends 127–33
Denmark
    employment in 154
    housing in 144
    political involvement of young people
        166, 167
    toleration in 173
    unemployment in 154
dependency 45–6, 75, 145
differentiation 111
disability 201
discrimination 5, 94, 153–4
divorce 129
Domanski, Henryk 86
Douglas, Mary 8, 9, 16–18, 27, 28, 34
drinking and alcoholism 75, 104, 201
drug problems 1, 75, 104, 131
Duma (parliament) 56, 62
elections 56, 57, 167–8
Durkheim, Emile 114

East-Central Europe 3, 53
ecological risk 12, 31
economic participation 1
    see also employment
economic reform
    collapse and social crisis in Russia and
        48–53, 61–2, 80, 121
    perestroika 2, 46, 78, 103, 140
    values and 147
    see also private sector
education 74, 86, 122, 123

inequality in 98
life start situation and 134, 135–42,
    147–8
proportion giving up school 138
risk assessment and 18
self-realisation and 159–60
youth conflict and 97–9
    see also vocational training
egalitarianism 172
Eisenstadt, S. 10, 102
elections
    Duma (parliament) 56, 57, 167–8
    Russian Presidential 56–7, 58, 59, 79,
        167, 168–9
employment
    labour right 45, 94
    young people and
        denial of labour rights 94
        employment trends and realisation of
            occupational goals 80–82
        future employment 82–4
        learning to work in OECD countries
            136
        occupational mobility 153, 160
        self-realisation and 160, 161–6
        state sector 113–14
entertainment industry 14
environmental issues 52, 172
    pollution 13, 31, 52
environmental risk 12, 31
ethnic conflict 56, 60, 190, 201
ethnic identity 171, 190
Eurobarometer surveys 73, 76, 201
European Union
    environmental risk in 12
    young people in 73–4, 76, 77, 153, 167,
        201
Evans, Karen 116, 125, 133–4, 152
exclusion 5, 29, 74, 75, 100, 104, 114, 135,
    137
    self-exclusion 159

family 2, 28, 74, 128, 202
    creation of 128, 132
    dependency on 75
    identity formation and 118
    intention to start 132
    life start situation and 134, 135
    youth conflict and 96–7
    youth identity crisis and 191
Fatherland All-Russia party 167–8, 168

Index

fatherland/motherland (patriotism) 89–90, 186
Feofanov, K. 21
Former Soviet Union *see* Soviet Union
France
  employment in 154
  housing in 144
  unemployment in 154
freedom
  choice and 47
  comparative measures of 53, 54
  lack in Soviet system 45
Freedom House 53
friendship 118
Furlong, Andy 116, 125, 133–4, 152

gender 28, 29
  education and 137, 142
  employment and 137
  individualism and 29
  life start situation and 145, 150
  moral and social reference points and 173
geographical mobility 153
Germany
  class in 76, 152
  housing in 144
  toleration in 173
  unemployment in 154
Giddens, Anthony 7, 14, 15, 21, 22–7, 28, 32, 36, 37, 50, 63, 69, 73, 75–6, 117, 122
Gimpelson, Vladimir 80–81
glasnost 2
globalisation 204
  information society and 14, 15
  risk and 13–14, 15, 16, 24, 122–4
  Russia and 16, 46
Golenkova, Z.D. 51, 113
Gorbachev, Mikhail 2, 4, 46, 47, 55
Gott, V. 10
Greece, unemployment in 154, 156
Green, D.R. 143, 144–5
Grishina, Yelena 186

health 51–3, 77, 104–105, 127, 130–131, 132
Hegel, Georg 10
Heikkinen, M. 135
Helve, Helena 173
history
  historical consciousness in Russia 45, 123, 185

  rewriting of 184, 185
homelessness 144–5, 201
housing 143–5
human factor, technological risk and 12–13
human rights issues in Russia 53–5
Hungary, education in 136

identity
  formation 116–18
  crisis in young people 180–95
  uncertainty of 106
incomes 49–50, 51, 55
  non-payment of 53–4, 55
  young people and 81, 84–6, 139
individualism 28–9, 116–18, 120, 134, 172–3, 203
industrial accidents 53
industry, decline of 74
inequality 29, 93, 97
  conflict and 94–5
  in education 98
  rich-poor gap 50, 51
inflation 47, 55
information society
  risk and 14–16, 43
  work and 30
Inglehart, R. 172
innovation 109, 111
instability 44, 78, 181
  political 55–61
  sociology of 20, 21
insurance 8, 9
interest rates 48
inter-generational mobility 86, 87
international division of labour 24
international trade 48
Internet 14, 15
investment 47
Ireland, housing in 144
Islam 190
Italy, unemployment in 154, 156

Japan
  education in 136
  unemployment in 154
jobs *see* employment
Jung, B. 133
justice 45, 47
juvenile crime 1, 75, 83, 100, 120, 181, 183, 192–4
juvenile delinquency 75, 115, 117, 183, 184

Kiriyenko, Sergei 56
Kluchkova, O.V. 194
Komsomol 1
Korea, employment in 154
Kovaleva, Antonina 182
Kovatcheva, S. 2

labour
    international division of 24
    labour market *see* employment, young
        people and
labour right 45, 94
Lagree, Jean Charles 173
language skills 143
Lash, Scott 14
law, lack of respect for 62, 83
learning to work *see* vocational training
Lebed, Alexandr 56
leisure activities 88, 145–7, 166, 167, 175
liberal democracy 47
Liberal Democratic party 56, 168
life expectancy 77, 127, 131
Lippoldt, Douglas 80–81
living standards 29, 81
localisation of risk 119–22
Luhmann, Niklas 8
Lupton, Deborah 7, 16, 17

McCulloch, A. 118
Machachek, Ladislav 95
McLuhan, M. 14
Mafia 60–61
malnutrition 52
market transition *see* economic reform
marriage 129, 132
    inter-ethnic 190
Marshall, T.H. 181
Marxism-Leninism 1, 101
maturity 69, 93
Mead, Margaret 134
media 56–7, 59, 101, 202
mental illness 75, 130
middle class 47, 51, 85–6, 134
migration 153
military 24
militsia (police) 60–61
Mitev, Petar-Emil 134
Mitrokhina, Ye. Iu. 16
mobility
    geographical 153
    inter-generational 86, 87
    occupational 153, 160

social 69–70
modernity
    definition of 7
    information society and 14
    peculiarities of modernisation in Russia
        44–6
    reflexive modernisation and 23–5, 31, 34,
        63
    risk and 7, 10
    risk society and 22–7
    work and 30
morbidity levels 130–31
Morgan, E. 156
mortality trends 52, 127, 129, 131, 132
Moscow 170
motherland/fatherland (patriotism) 89–90,
    186
motivated risk 9
music 175

Nagel, Ulrich 99, 111, 151
national mentality 15
Netherlands
    education in 137
    toleration in 173
    unemployment in 156
networking 2, 135
New Russians 51, 123, 134, 159–60
Nikitin, S. 21
non-motivated risk 9

occupational mobility 153, 160
Okudzgava, Bulat 103
older people 77, 132
ontological security 23, 63, 75, 186
Organisation for Economic Cooperation and
    Development (OECD) 135, 137, 139
Our Home is Russia party 56, 168

Pahl, R. 118
parliament *see* Duma (parliament)
Parsons, T. 113
participation 1, 32, 100
    economic participation 1
        see also employment
    political participation 1, 79, 166, 167–9,
        172
    social participation 1, 166
part-time employment 30, 137
patriotism 89–90, 183, 186
perestroika 2, 46, 78, 103, 140
personal characteristics 178–9

Phoenix, Ann 180
planning 44
Pleshchakov, V.A. 194
Poland, unemployment in 154
police (militsia) 60–61
politics
    political instability in Russia 55–61
    political participation 1, 79, 166, 167–9, 172
    politicisation of risk 17, 33
    young people and 79, 166–9, 172
pollution 13, 31, 52
population (demographic trends) 127–33
Portugal 76
    unemployment in 156
post-modernism 172, 180, 203
post-structuralism 69
post-totalitarian syndrome 45–6, 182
poverty 29, 48, 49–50, 51, 55, 121, 170
    young people and 77, 84–6, 202
Powers, B.P. 14
presidency of Russia 55–6, 62, 111
    elections for president 56–7, 58, 59, 79, 167, 168–9
Primakov, Yevgenii 56, 58
private sector
    perception of risk in 31
    in Russia 46, 47
        young people and 82, 83–4, 114, 142, 153, 164–5
probability, risk and 8–10
production, fall in 48–9
professionalism 95, 162
propaganda 115
property rights 55
protests 13–14, 103
public opinion *see* attitudes and opinion
public sector
    decline in 82
    young people in 113–14, 153
Putin, Vladimir 48, 56, 58, 59, 168
Puuronen, V. 135

qualifications
    chances of improving 81
    numbers of qualified young people 80–81
    self-realisation and 161

Rattansi, Ali 180
reflexive modernisation 23–5, 31, 34, 63
refugees 55
regionalism 59, 98

religion 88, 101, 167, 173, 190, 202
    Islam 190
reproduction of risk 73–80
rich-poor gap 50, 51
rights
    human rights issues 53–5
    in Soviet system 45
    political rights 58, 59
    youth conflict and 94
risk
    avoidance 8, 18
    contemporary sociology and risk 20–22
    globalisation and 13–14, 15, 16, 24, 122–4
    information society and risk 14–16
    localisation of 119–22
    management of 31
    origins of risk 8–10
    probability approaches 8–10
    pros and cons of risk theory 27–8
    reproduction of 73–80
    risk production in Russia 46–8
    risk-taking 8, 18
    Russian youth and 34–5
    society in transition and 43–4
    socio-cultural basis of risk 16–20
    technological risk 11–14
    theories and concepts of 7, 8–37
    typologies of 19, 104–106
    uncertainty and risk 10–11, 20, 21, 105–106
    young people and 34–5, 70, 78
        coping strategies 151
        typology of 104–6
    see also risk society
risk society
    concept of 20, 22–7
    definition 28–34
    differential politics and 33
    globalisation of risk and 13–14
    re-industrialisation and 32–3
    Russian transition to 1, 2–4, 36, 43–63
        common and specific trends 61
        risk factors 61–2
        risk production factors 48–61
        risk production in reform period 46–8
    scientific and technological development and 12
    young people and 1, 2–4, 67–91
        changes in position of young people in Russia 80–90

contradictions and conflict in social
    integration 112–19
reproduction of risk 73–80
risk trends in life situation 127–95
young people in different risk
    societies 68
Roberts, Ken 2, 116, 117, 133, 134
Rome Club 11
Rozgdestvenskii, Robert 103
rule systems 32
Russia
    economic collapse and social crisis
        48–53, 61–2, 80
    economic wealth 46
    globalisation and 16, 46
    historical consciousness in 45, 123, 185
    human rights issues 53–5
    identity as citizen of 183
    information society and 16
    peculiarities of modernisation in 44–6
    political instability 55–61
    risk theory and 34–6
    Soviet system 1–2, 45, 70–71
    transition to risk society 1, 2–4, 35,
        43–63
        common and specific trends 61
        risk factors 61–2
        risk production factors 48–61
        risk production in reform period 46–8
    young people in *see* young people/youth
Russian National Republican Party 168

safety issues 53, 104–105
science, risk and 12, 31
security, risk and 9
self-determination 123
self-exclusion 159
self-realisation 89–90, 105–106, 115
    possibilities for 150–71
sexual minorities 201
sexuality 130
sexually transmitted diseases 130, 131
Shuller, T. 94
single-parent families 129
Smakotina, Natalya 17, 21, 34
social change 2
social class *see* class
social inequality *see* inequality
social information 15–16
social innovation 109, 111
social justice 47
social maturity 69, 93

social mobility 69–70
social participation 1, 166
social reproduction 67, 70–73
social status, youth conflict and 94–5
social welfare systems 76
    unemployment income coverage 156,
        157
socio-cultural basis of risk 16–20
socio-demographic situation 127–33
sociology, risk and 20–22
Soviet Union
    collapse of 2
    as industrial society 47
    Russian attitudes and 45
    social reproduction in 70–71
    young people in 1–2, 70–71, 182
Spain 76
    housing in 144
    unemployment in 154
speculation 55, 78
sports facilities 131
state sector *see* public sector
Stepashin, Sergei 56
sub-politicisation 32
suicide 75
survival model of behaviour 50, 85
Sweden 139
    education in 136, 137
    housing in 144
    political involvement of young people
        166, 167
    unemployment in 156
Switzerland, education in 136

Tanner, Julian 137
teachers 97
technological risk 11–14
technology transfer 33
terrorism 58, 60
Three Mile Island accident 11
Toffler, Ye. A. 14
toleration 173, 190, 201
totalitarianism, dependency and 45–6
Touraine, Alain 20–21
trade 48
trade unions 30, 166, 167
training 80–81, 82, 98–9
transport sector 164
trust 23, 62–3, 75
    crisis of 117
Turner, Bryan S. 12, 24–5, 27–8, 37
typologies of risk 19, 104–106

uncertainty
    of identity 106
    of life-course 72
    of values and norms 73, 106
    risk and 10–11, 20, 21, 105–106, 174, 175
underemployment 30, 50
unemployment 29, 48, 50
    young people and 69, 74, 77, 134, 142–3, 154–8
        unemployment income coverage 156, 157
Union of Right Forces party 168
United Kingdom
    class in 76, 152
    education in 137, 139
    environmental risk in 12
    housing in 144
United Nations 13, 74–5, 201
United States of America 139
    education in 136
    young people in 74, 76, 77
    see also 'West'
Unity party 58, 168
urban areas
    advantages of 98, 170
    demographic trends in 129
Ursul, A. 10, 21
USSR see Soviet Union

values and norms 106
    crisis in 100, 101–104
    moral and social reference points 172–80
    risk assessment and 17
    sub-cultural basis of youth conflicts 101–104, 120
    transition to market and 147
    uncertainty of 73, 106
violence 193
    terrorism 58, 60
Vizir, P. 10
vocational training 98, 99, 136–7, 160
    apprenticeships 74, 136, 137
Vysotsky, Vladimir 103

wages see incomes
Wallace, Clare 2, 99, 111, 151
Wallerstein, Immanuel 11
war
    Chechnya 56, 60, 190, 203
    Yugoslavia 123, 203
water supply 52

Weber, Max 25
Webster, Frank 14
welfare system see social welfare systems
'West' 2
    anti-Westernism 45, 46
    jealousy of 45
    risk society and 2–3
    Westernisation 13, 45, 63
    young people's attitudes to 123–4
    youth integration in 113
White, Rob 97
Wildavsky, Aaron 18, 19
Williams, Christopher 80
Williamson, Howard 158
work
    risk society and 30
    see also employment, young people and
World Trade Organisation 13–14
Wyn, Johanna 97

Yabloko party 56, 168
Yanitskii, Oleg 21, 44
Yavlinskii, Grigory 56, 58
Yeltsin, Boris 4, 46, 48, 56, 57, 59, 71, 111
Yevtushchenko, Evgenii 103
Young, M. 94
young people/youth 77–90, 201–205
    chances of improving qualifications and incomes 81
    conflict and 93–106
        arising from inequality of social status 94–5
        resolution of 109–25
        with socialisation agencies 95–101
        sub-cultural basis of youth conflicts 94, 101–104, 120
    crime and 1, 75, 83, 100, 120, 181, 183, 192–4
    definition of youth 7
    education 74, 86, 123
        life start situation and 134, 135–42, 147–8
        proportion giving up school 138
        self-realisation and 159–60
        youth conflict and 97–9
    employment
        employment trends and realisation of occupational goals 80–82
        future employment 82–4
        in state sector 113–14
        occupational mobility 153, 160

self-realisation and 160, 161–6
identity crisis 180–95
incomes 81, 84–6, 139
juvenile delinquency 75, 115, 117, 183, 184
leisure activities 88, 145–7, 166, 167, 175
life start situation 133–50
   education and 134, 135–42, 147
   models of 147–8
living alone 143, 144
moral and social reference points 172–80
numbers of 67
politics and 79, 166–9, 172
poverty 77, 84–6, 202
rewriting of Russian history and 184, 185
risk and 34–5, 70, 78, 93–106
   coping strategies 151
   typology of 104–106
risk society and 1, 2–4, 67–91
   changes in position of young people in Russia 80–90
   contradictions and conflict in social integration 112–19
   reproduction of risk 73–80
   risk trends in life situation 127–95
   young people in different risk societies 68
   self-realisation 89–90, 105–106, 115
   possibilities for 150–71
social development of 67–8
social mobility 69–70
social policy and 75
socio-demographic situation 127–33
Soviet system and 1–2, 70–71
stability and 1, 174
training 80–1, 82
transition to adulthood 69, 73–4, 75, 90, 99
unemployment 50, 69, 74, 77, 134, 142–3, 154–8
   unemployment income coverage 156, 157
youth organisations 1, 79, 166, 167
Yugoslavia 123, 203

Zhirinovsky, Vladimir 56, 58
Zubok, Julia 80
Zyuganov, Gennady 56, 57, 58